GOOD WIVES?

GOOD WIVES?

Mary, Fanny, Jennie & Me
1845–2001

Margaret Forster

Chatto & Windus
LONDON

Published by Chatto & Windus 2001

2 4 6 8 10 9 7 5 3 1

Copyright © Margaret Forster 2001

Margaret Forster has asserted her right under the
Copyright, Designs and Patents Act 1988 to be identified
as the author of this work

First published in Great Britain in 2001 by
Chatto & Windus
Random House, 20 Vauxhall Bridge Road,
London SW1V 2SA

Random House Australia (Pty) Limited
20 Alfred Street, Milsons Point, Sydney,
New South Wales 2061, Australia

Random House New Zealand Limited
18 Poland Road, Glenfield,
Auckland 10, New Zealand

Random House (Pty) Limited
Endulini, 5A Jubilee Road, Parktown 2193, South Africa

The Random House Group Limited Reg. No. 954009
www.randomhouse.co.uk

A CIP catalogue record for this book
is available from the British Library

ISBN 0 7011 6914 1

Papers used by Random House are natural,
recyclable products made from wood grown in sustainable forests;
the manufacturing processes conform to the environmental
regulations of the country of origin

Typeset by Deltatype Ltd, Birkenhead, Merseyside
Printed and bound in Great Britain by
Clays Ltd, St Ives PLC

Contents

List of Illustrations

Margaret, seated front right

Prologue

In July 1949, when I was eleven years old, I was a bridesmaid. I was just young enough still to be thrilled with the rose-pink satin dress and with the coronet of tiny rosebuds, which sat so perfectly on my long, wavy fair hair. At last I was that creature I'd always yearned to be, a princess. I could hardly wait for the wedding, when I would have the honour of carrying the bride's white chiffon train all the way down the aisle. But my deeply religious mother disapproved of my wild excitement. Weddings were serious. A man and a woman were to be married in the sight of God – this was not a party, not an excuse for the sort of preening in which I gloried. She didn't want me being 'silly'. There were to be no giggles, no tossing of my hair, no calling of attention to myself. Instead, in church I was to *listen*. I was to listen very carefully indeed to the words.

So I listened, as my mother undoubtedly knew I would. For a child, I was a good listener (too good, it was often said, because my listening inevitably resulted in irritating questions of the sort difficult to answer). I stood behind the bride, glad to have the posy of white and pink roses back in my eager hands once I'd relinquished the train, and I listened intently to what the vicar said. It was simple enough when it came to the vows, merely a question-and-answer routine. But I spotted the difference in the questions easily. 'Wilt thou have this woman to thy wedded wife?' the bridegroom was asked, and then, a little later on, 'Wilt thou love her, comfort her, honour, and keep her in sickness and in health? . . .' But to the bride, the vicar said, 'Wilt thou have this man to thy wedded husband . . . wilt thou *obey* him, and serve him, love, honour, and keep him, in sickness and in health? . . .' I remember looking around to see if anyone else had noticed something odd, and catching the eye of my mother, who frowned and gestured that I should pay attention. But I *was* paying attention. And I'd heard that word *obey* only when the bride was being questioned. Why did she have to promise to obey and he did not?

It was only 1949. It was only an ordinary parish church in Caldewgate, a poor area of Carlisle. It was only a marriage service which had been used for hundreds of years without anyone apparently finding one word in it unfair. I doubt if there was a single woman, never mind a man, in that congregation who objected to the bride's making that promise. But I objected. The moment the photographs had been taken, I was pulling at my mother's sleeve. 'Why did Jean have to say she'd obey Ian, and Ian didn't say he'd obey her? Why?' 'Because that's the order of service in the prayer-book,' my mother said. 'Who said it had to say that? Who? Why?' My mother sighed. She knew it was no good just telling me to be quiet, or saying I should just accept that this was how things were, because that, in her experience, would only result in exhaustion – her exhaustion – as she valiantly tried to satisfy my curiosity. So she said what she was quite often obliged to say – 'Later, we'll go into it later, not now.'

She wasn't hoping I'd forget. Alas, she knew I wouldn't, and I didn't. Wedding over, the inquisition began. She didn't know who had designed the marriage service, how those words had got into the prayer-book, but she thought the 'obey' word must have been put into the bride's vow because men earned the money, they were the bosses in that respect, and so the woman had to be prepared to acknowledge this. Before I could ask why, or attempt to tear holes in this flimsy explanation, she said it was useless to pester her any more, and if I was going to want to know more I would have to ask the vicar, but not *that* vicar, our own vicar. 'I will, then,' I said, but I guessed that I wouldn't – it was quite daunting, even for cheeky girls such as myself, to go up to our vicar and put such questions to him. But I had one question I knew my mother herself could answer. 'Did you do it?' I said. 'Did you promise to obey Dad?' 'Yes,' she said. 'Well, I won't,' I said, 'I wouldn't promise to obey the man if he won't promise to obey me.' 'Then you won't be able to get married,' my mother, my dutiful church-going mother said. 'You won't ever be a wife.' She said it smiling, not trying to dismay me, and if pressed I'm sure she would have mentioned register office marriages where there was no need to promise to obey, but for once I didn't press her. In a way I felt quite satisfied. Something had been decided.

I never wanted to be a wife, that feeble creature who obeyed.

It was a conviction that only hardened during adolescence. I spent those years watching as well as listening and I hated what I saw. The lot of a wife seemed terrible to me. Wives, in 1950s Carlisle, on our council estate anyway, cooked and cleaned and shopped and looked after children, and never went anywhere or did anything else. They had no money of their own. Every Friday, my father came home from the Metal Box factory, where he worked as a fitter, a maintenance engineer, and opened his wage packet. Out of it he extracted an undisclosed amount (precious little) and gave my mother the rest (precious little) for housekeeping. It was always a struggle for her to make it last the week, no matter how carefully she budgeted, and that was very carefully indeed – she was a genius at managing. There was nothing to spare for herself. The money was my father's, the reward for his labours. Her labours got no monetary reward (and not much of any other kind either). This was the bargain she accepted when she got married, and I thought it a poor one. More than ever, I knew it was one to which I would never, never agree.

The puzzle to me was not only that my mother had entered into this one-sided contract in the first place, but that she still, in spite of everything, seemed to think it inevitable. When she was referred to as 'a good wife' she was gratified – she didn't seem to appreciate that it was like being called 'a good beast of burden'. There was one Christmas when, at the end of the traditional dinner, my father's elderly aunt, who was with us for the day, suddenly said, 'Arthur, you're a lucky man, you've got such a good wife in Lily. Such a good wife.' My father, mellowed by the vast amounts of turkey he'd consumed and the two port wines he'd had before it (only allowed, together with sweet sherry, at Christmas, and otherwise no alcohol in the house), said, 'And I'll tell you something, Jessie, I've never regretted making her my wife either.' *What?* I was beside myself with fury. I don't think I'd yet made the acquaintance of the term 'patronising', but I understood the concept, that he was patronising my mother, implying that by marrying her he'd been conferring an honour and that she ought to be pleased *he had never regretted it*. To my astonishment, my mother appeared flattered – that was quite the worst and most inexplicable part of this little scene. She blushed. She even smiled. She got up to clear the dishes self-consciously, as though she had just won a prize and the spotlight was on her. She had been paid what was for my father the most extravagant of compliments, and in public too. She was a good wife. What more could she want than such a tribute?

A very great deal, in my youthful opinion.

Some years later, aged nineteen, I stood on a doorstep in Manchester and said no, I was not his wife. That's what the woman who had opened the door had asked – 'Are you his wife, then?' We, Hunter and I, had come in answer to an advertisement, for a bed-sitting-room to be rented. He had just started working as a journalist on the *Manchester Evening Chronicle* and I was in my first year at Oxford. We wanted to live together in my vacations, so we'd both gone looking for a suitable bed-sit for him to rent full time and for me to join him there. It was 1958.

The landlady gave a little smirk. 'Thought not,' she said, and then, 'you'll have to look elsewhere. I don't take unmarrieds.' She looked so proud of herself as she closed the door, as though her own virtue had been put to some sort of test and proved incontestable. Her attitude was ridiculous, but also common – this was the fourth advert we'd replied to; the fourth time we'd been turned down, though never in such a straightforward fashion. No pets, no children, no coloureds, no unmarrieds, and no one in the least worried about saying so. What were we to do? The obvious thing. Let him rent the room, then smuggle me in when I came. Either that, or pretend to be married. But I wouldn't pretend to be his wife. Why should I? (Answer easy, of course: so that nobody would mind renting a room to us.)

The bed-sitting-room we ended up in was in Cheetham, next to a raincoat factory. It was horrible. One not very large room on the ground floor of a dark and neglected house. The furniture was battered and ugly – a settee which opened up into a bed, a gate-legged table with four heavy chairs round it, and a large mahogany wardrobe. I got to know the wardrobe rather well, because I stepped into it every time the landlord paid an unexpectedly late visit to collect the rent. Sometimes we'd be eating and there'd be two plates, two unfinished meals, on the table when I leapt into the wardrobe, but the landlord never seemed to think this strange. This was during the Easter vacation, a matter of a few weeks, but the thought of months in the summer, popping in and out of my hiding place like a figure on a weather-house was too much. For the long vacation we would have to find somewhere better.

Reader, I compromised my principles. No, I didn't marry him, not then, but I did pretend to be his wife. We bought a ring in Woolworths – where else? – and I jammed it on to my protesting finger (it was a curtain ring and too small, one of those tiny little things which get attached to bigger ones, sold then in packets of twenty). Immediately, we were respectable. We rented a two-room flat in Daisy Bank Road in a much nicer area of Manchester. I was the wife who 'worked away'. Either that, or I paid regular visits to sick relatives – such a caring soul, I was. The other people in the house were only mildly inquisitive and the landlady was seen only once, when we paid the rent three months in advance. I was known as Mrs Davies but I managed to bear it. Wearing the wretched ring was the most maddening part of this trivial deception, even after I bought a cheap but proper one. I felt I was branded and made a fuss about it, pulling it off as soon as we were in the flat and there was no one to see.

I was a mistress, I supposed, though I didn't like that label either. For three years, while I was at Oxford, I pretended, when necessary, to be a wife, and grew quite used to it. We went on holiday once or twice and stayed in pubs or small hotels where we were signed in as Mr and Mrs Davies. It felt quite daring as well as a good joke. But my finals at Oxford loomed and a much more momentous decision would have to be made. Was I going to go on pretending? For ever? By then, we were in London, in a flat in Kilburn, and nobody gave a damn about whether we were really married – that was no longer a difficulty. The difficulty was our parents. They hadn't known about our living together – I was always going off on long, adventurous trips with girlfriends, so far as my parents were concerned, and since these friends obligingly helped me make this convincing I'd never been 'found out'. They'd have to find out, though, if this state of affairs became permanent, if I was going to live in sin – as it was quaintly called – for ever. And I couldn't do it to them, simply couldn't cause my mother in particular such distress. I wasn't brave (or cruel?) enough to tell her the truth. It was easier to give in and get married, wasn't it?

It was. Marriage I decided was only a piece of paper (because I certainly wouldn't marry in a church and say the 'O' word). On 11 June 1960, I got married, the words of the register office service perfectly acceptable. I can't actually remember what they were, but I'd inspected them in advance and they were simple, obvious and harmless. It was surprising how little had to be promised, how little was asked. I'd done it. I'd betrayed my principles and become a wife. I became Mrs Davies. I even wore a ring (silver, prettily engraved with ivy leaves, bought at an antique shop in Hampstead's Heath Street). But I squirmed every time I was referred to as 'Mrs'. In retrospect, I cannot believe how easily I accepted the trappings, the 'Mrs' bit and the ring – surely I could have got married for the same reasons, but without accepting that title and the badge of office? Looking back at my twenty-two-year-old self it occurs to me now that I was not being entirely honest: maybe there was a tiny bit of me that liked the title, was proud of the ring? Such a strong-minded young woman, did she really condescend to wear a ring when she didn't have to? Surely not.

I still wear it, forty years later. It's a broad ring. If I take it off, the skin underneath is startlingly white and soft, and my finger looks somehow sad and pathetic. Once, about twenty-five years ago, I lost it. It turned up some months later, down the back of a sofa. But the interesting thing is not just how upset and sentimental I'd been while it was missing, but that I had actually bought a substitute to wear, another silver ring as near to the lost one as I could find. So perhaps the ring does mean something. I must want people to know I am married, that I am a wife. But what I also want them to know is that the word *'wife'* does not mean what it meant while I was growing up. A wife today is not, or need not be, the same creature as a wife in 1949, or even 1960, and she is a million miles away from the wife of 1845 or 1860. In fact, the understanding of what a wife *is* has changed so much in the last hundred and fifty years that it calls into question whether the referring to a woman as 'a good wife' is still, as it once was, a compliment today. Does it not imply rather that she is nothing more than that? Is it still a title to be borne with pride? Or is it an admission of defeat?

I don't know the answers, but I'd like to. The question widens into another one, of course: is marriage still valid if you have no religious faith? The statistics for the number of marriages that fail are startling – there were 145,000 divorces in England and Wales in 1999 – but so are those for the number of marriages, which still took place – 131,757 women still became wives. Why, in the twenty-first century, in a social climate where it is acceptable to live in a partnership, and even to have children within one without any stigma, why, I wanted to discover, does any woman still want to be a wife? Is the trade-off worth it? I thought I'd like to look at what a 'good wife' once was, what she became, and what (if anything) she now is, and set it within the framework of my own marriage and my own times. To do this, I chose to examine the marriages of three women who, in my opinion (though not always in the opinion of their contemporaries), were 'good' wives in very different ways. Their lives cover the best part of one and a half centuries during which the common understanding of 'a good wife' changed beyond recognition. What I myself have made of being a wife is part of that change.

The three women to whom I was drawn did not lead ordinary lives and yet each of them reflected in what she made of the role of 'wife' the standards of her own time. They faced the same problems in their domestic and emotional lives as all women faced, and had to struggle with the same challenges to their independence. Once the façade of the marriages is ripped away and the personal details of each woman's day-to-day existence are revealed, the astonishing thing is how *similar* their difficulties were to my own during forty years of being a wife. Echoes vibrate down the years in spite of the enormous changes that have taken place both in life in general for women and in the laws and customs affecting marriage. It is the sense of identification which shocks, not that of alienation.

And yet it was the feeling of being utterly remote from the life of Mary Livingstone, with whose story I begin, which first made me curious to understand what a 'good' wife was. I was visiting my daughter, who lives in Botswana, and had taken with me Tim Jeal's biography of David Livingstone. In it, I came across a passage in which Livingstone writes to a friend with news of his impending marriage, describing his wife-to-be in such insulting terms that I was immediately defensive on her behalf. Even more insulting was the way in which the biographer accepted that the sole reason Livingstone married Mary was because he needed someone to look after him and give him the necessary status in the eyes of the Africans he was trying to convert. It didn't matter if she was plain and fat so long as she could run his house properly and make him comfortable. This Mary did, in the most difficult of circumstances; the sufferings she endured during the exhausting journeys she was obliged to make with her husband were such that I could hardly bear to read about them. Few women had to endure what she did in her marriage but on the other hand her spirit of submission to her husband was shared by millions. Marriage in the mid-nineteenth century, when Mary became a wife, was about servitude of one sort or another. Nothing had changed since Francis Bacon's pertinent observation:

> Wives are young men's mistresses,
> Companions for middle age,
> And old men's nurses.

But nevertheless, women still wanted above all else to marry, such was the ignominy, and the insecurity, of remaining a spinster. It made me shudder to think of being a wife like Mary Livingstone and yet, once I'd become intimately acquainted with her marriage, I was embarrassed to see that in some respects I had had something of her attitude in my own interpretation of 'good wife'. I might have thought myself entirely liberated from any kind of submission but however outrageous the thought, perhaps I, too, sometimes had accepted a secondary role without realising it.

It was a relief to move on to Fanny Stevenson, the wife of Robert Louis Stevenson. Fanny had guts. She wasn't going to be like Mary, bowing her head meekly and doing whatever her husband wanted. She was an American, and within her lifetime great changes were taking place in women's lives, with the early feminists fighting to win the vote together with all kinds of other previously withheld privileges and rights. Fanny thought herself the equal of her husband (in all except genius). And yet, following her life, with all its romance and excitement, moving from America to France and back, and finally to the South Seas, it was chastening to discover that Fanny was not after all, in essence, so different from Mary as a married woman. She was humiliated to have to accept that she was constrained simply through being a wife. Louis, her husband, held all the ace cards – his welfare, his ambitions, his concerns were always the more important. The lot of the wife still had not changed enough between the marriage of Mary (in 1845) and Fanny's marriage to Louis (in 1880), even though the early feminists were doing all they could in those intervening years to reinvent the role (that is, when they were not trying to abolish marriage as an institution). Nevertheless, women went on becoming wives, however unsatisfactory the condition of marriage, and the status of spinster went on having few attractions. By the end of the nineteenth century, 82 per cent of women in England were married or widowed.

Then, at last, came a real revolution in thinking. Jennie Lee, daughter of a Scottish miner, born in 1904, was one of those women who decided as a girl that she would never become a wife. She fascinated the House of Commons in 1929 when she arrived there, and she fascinated me. Beautiful, sexy and daring,

Jennie gave her whole heart to socialism and was determined to devote her life to a political career. Marriage would never be allowed to get in the way of her ambition. She would have affairs, but never at the expense of her career. But it was for the sake of her career, and that of her lover Aneurin Bevan, that eventually she capitulated and married him in 1934. He was destined for a prominent role in government (he was to become Minister of Housing and Health in the 1945 Labour government and go on to be instrumental in founding the National Health Service) and it would have been disastrous for his political future to live with a woman to whom he was not married, as well as utterly disastrous for Jennie's own ambitions to be identified as that woman.

So Jennie, most reluctantly, became a wife, though determined to redefine the role to suit herself. In doing so, she was way ahead of her times and yet, in turn, her attitude was a sign of those times. Women, in the inter-war period, had begun to want careers *and* marriage, and the two could not run in tandem without some change in the understanding of what being a wife meant. Two Acts were of great importance in opening gates for women, the Parliament (Qualification of Women) Act 1918, and the Sex Disqualification (Removal) Act 1919. Slowly, women were entering the professions and relishing a different kind of self-fulfilment from that bestowed within marriage. They were on their way to what has become known as 'having it all', and Jennie Lee was one of those who tried to make that work. She was not always sure she had passed the test. She became as puzzled as I have often been about her role as wife, fearing that in spite of her efforts the onus was on her, as the woman, to give way during times of stress in marriage in order to support the man. It was all so much more complicated than she had ever thought, trying to make a 'good' wife mean something other than what it had meant for centuries before.

The question still is: what *is* a wife? Who is 'good'?

PART ONE

Mary Livingstone
1821–62

I

In March 1839, a battered-looking troopship struggled into Table Bay, Cape Town, and finally anchored at the quayside. It had already been many weeks at sea, on its way to England from China, and conditions on board were bad, with the smell from the animals it carried (to provide provisions) unbearably foul. But eagerly waiting to board was the Moffat family – Robert Moffat, a missionary with the London Mission Society, his heavily pregnant wife, his six children and his African servant. Robert desperately wanted to get to London where his translation of the New Testament into Setswana, over which he had laboured for years, could be printed. He knew perfectly well that there would be no sort of comfort on this ship but no other was scheduled to arrive and he could not wait any longer. His wife, though she was within three weeks of giving birth to her ninth child (two had died), did not try to hold him back, seeing it as her duty to put his work first. He had, she wrote home, 'poured his whole soul' into his translation and nothing must stand in the way of seeing it printed.

So the entire Moffat family embarked, with Mrs Moffat helped on board by her eldest daughter, Mary, eighteen the following month. Mary was afraid of the sea. Born and brought up at Kuruman, the mission station her parents had established 600 miles (965 km) north of Cape Town, to the south of the Kalahari desert, the sea had existed for her only in the stories she'd heard of the voyages out from England (stories full of storms and shipwrecks and drownings) until, when she was fourteen, she had her own experience of it in sailing from Port Elizabeth to Cape Town. It had been a terrifying voyage and she had never forgotten it. She dreaded this much longer voyage ahead and there was nothing to reassure her about either the ship or the weather. A gale was forecast and there was a great hurry to get everyone on board and beat the storm. Mary was kept busy attending to her six-year-old brother James, who was feverish and suspected by his mother of sickening with measles. Mrs Moffat was anxious about him and it may well have been this anxiety, together with the strain of embarking, which contributed to the onset of her labour. Hardly had the heavy, squat ship managed to lumber its way against the huge waves out into the bay than she gave birth to a girl, quickly named Elizabeth and baptised by her father.

Meanwhile, James's condition worsened. His sister Mary could not pacify him and hearing his cries his exhausted mother called for him to be brought to her. She held the new-born baby in the crook of one arm and cuddled James with the other, barely able to raise her head from the pillow. The ship plunged violently as it held its course, in rapidly worsening weather, with the rain and wind driving against it strongly. But James, secure in his mother's arms, was now peaceful. His fever mounting, he was deluded and spoke of angels all around him. Two days later, he died. His tiny body was wrapped in sailcloth and lowered over the side after the most brief of services. A birth, a death, a storm – it was traumatic for the whole family. For the young Mary, it served as the most devastating of warnings: this was what a good wife such as her mother had to endure. She had to be strong and unselfish and never try to thwart a husband's wishes. The blueprint could not have been more clearly drawn for her. If she had not realised that marriage was primarily for the procreation of children, and that it involved submission to a husband's needs of one sort or another, then she learned it on board that terrible ship. Her mother, returning to her home country after twenty years of being a missionary's wife, had suffered more than her family could possibly know. But she had suffered gladly.

The wife of a missionary had a harder time than most wives of that era but nevertheless serving and supporting a husband was the common experience of all wives in the mid-nineteenth century. Mrs Moffat was proud to be the wife of a man so dedicated to the work of converting the heathen and was triumphant that she had overcome her parents' objections to a match that would take her so far away from them. Arriving in Cape Town in December 1819 and marrying Robert immediately, she was sure she'd made the best decision of her life, writing home that her cup of happiness was almost full – she loved her husband passionately and could think of nothing more thrilling than being his wife. Small, slight and delicate though she was, nothing dismayed her. She and Robert set off from Cape Town in an ox-wagon hundreds of miles into the interior where he was to establish a mission station, and there was not a murmur from her about the discomforts of the journey or the endurance called for in the boiling heat. This pretty young woman, aged twenty-five, showed herself at once to be far tougher than she looked and far more able and willing to adapt to her new circumstances than her parents had thought possible. She never complained, never wept, but instead was determined to find everything exciting.

Once settled at Kuruman, where Robert was to build his mission, the young Mrs Moffat quickly realised how different her life was to be from the lives of those married women of her class she had known in England. There was no lying on sofas directing servants in how to run the household. On the contrary, she hardly ever sat down (and there were no sofas). Her role as wife entailed constant physical activity – in order to look after Robert she had to do everything herself, and this included a good deal of manual labour. Kuruman was a desolate place when the Moffats arrived, the river a mere channel and the country surrounding its low banks, barren and stony. The dry, sandy plain they settled in was covered for much of the year in long, straw-like grass with scattered bushes and a few dark green camel-thorn trees. Beyond it was the true desert, except towards the north-east where, some 200 miles (320 km) away, there were woods. In this inhospitable landscape, in temperatures of searing heat, young Mary Moffat from Manchester had to set up house in a hut. She had to learn how to cook, how to wash her clothes, how to cope with insects, and all this without any of the help she would have had as a middle-class wife in England. Her leisurely, privileged life at home was soon a dream. She became little better than a skivvy and, since she would not drop the standards she had been used to, she made things even harder for herself (like many wives before and since). Refusing to adopt African ways she insisted on imposing her own, and so, instead of using the river to wash clothes, she had to have a wash-tub made.

But more important than the domestic work was her support of her husband in his missionary endeavours. She discovered that a missionary's wife had to be a very special being. In her opinion, and she was full of strongly expressed opinions, she belonged to a peculiar category of wives. Looking after her husband's material welfare was only one part of being a missionary's wife. Back in England, the wives of her acquaintance knew little about their husbands' work, and certainly most of them were not involved in it, but here in Africa, Robert's work was, to a very real extent, also *her* work. Before she had arrived to marry him, Robert had written to his father that 'a missionary in this country without a wife is like a boat without an oar'. She had to row with him or the boat would not move forwards. When he went off, as he frequently did, in search of more converts, it was his wife who had to hold things together at the mission station. No one else would. The Africans would simply drift away and revert (with some relief) to their old non-Christian habits unless Mary kept up his Christian standards. She found it hard, writing to him once when he was away that 'It requires the exercise of some fortitude to be calm and serene . . . you know I dread your departure exceedingly . . . [I] suffer a good deal myself from low spirits in my great solitude.' Hers was not the solitude of an English wife, sighing with boredom in an empty house, but of a missionary's wife, living in a hut among people whose language she did not at first (and for some considerable time) speak, afraid of wild animals, not to mention marauding tribesmen, and having to do every single thing herself. But she coped, always.

This is what her daughter Mary witnessed throughout her childhood. *A wife coped.* It was the first rule of being a wife. Mary Moffat's children were never afraid when their father was absent. When he was at home, they saw, as many children still do, that their mother's load was increased rather than lightened. As his wife, she thought it her job to safeguard his health and that meant arranging for him to have peace and quiet to get on with his work. By the time she had had four children – Mary (1821), Ann (1823), Robert (1827) and Helen (1829) – this was a struggle, but somehow she saw to it that her husband was given the seclusion he needed. It was she who, in effect, ran the Kuruman mission station.

Yet her daughter Mary saw that her mother was clearly a happy wife, who loved her husband. Coupled with this love was a shared religious faith hardly less passionate – it justified everything they had to go through together. All this the young Mary, Ann and Helen absorbed as they grew up, it was part of their training to be wives in their turn. The standard set was the highest, but their mother had achieved it.

Mrs Moffat ran a disciplined household. Visitors to Kuruman were impressed by how immaculate everything was, how ordered and comfortable. The Moffat daughters were brought up to be capable of performing every household task themselves without depending, as their counterparts in England depended, on others. They knew not only how to sew (though that was part of every girl's upbringing in England too) but how to cook, how to garden, and how to nurse. From the earliest age they had to be *useful* – it was physically exhausting merely to exist at Kuruman and no one could be allowed to shirk hard work. A missionary wife was a maid-of-all-work and so were her daughters. They were not ornaments, pretty things there to delight the eyes of men. Their mother herself had known what it was to be admired in society, but they were completely unaware of this kind of behaviour. At Kuruman there were none of the usual Victorian functions at which Mary, Ann and Helen could witness the social side of a middle-class wife's role – how to entertain a husband's colleagues, how to pour tea in the drawing-room, how to leave calling-cards, how to preside over a formal dinner-party. They did not see their mother entering public rooms on her husband's arm or making polite conversation. People did visit Kuruman but they were either missionaries themselves or big-game hunters and, though the hospitality was generous, it involved no ceremony. The girls learned to be polite but the mysteries of social intercourse in the Victorian style remained unknown.

This, to their mother, seemed no bad thing, but their education was another matter. A wife should be educated to a sufficient standard to be of use to her husband; she must not disappoint and shame him with her ignorance. But such an education was not available at Kuruman or within hundreds of miles of it. Mrs Moffat tried to teach the children herself, but by the time young Mary was seven, her mother felt she was failing. She wrote to a friend that soon she would have to find a proper school for Mary and Ann, because 'keeping them at home is beyond doubt highly improper'. She wanted her daughters to be educated enough not only to support their future husbands, but so that they in turn could teach the African children. Mary in particular seemed to have the ability and temperament to be a good teacher. She was patient, conscientious, hard-working, intelligent and eminently biddable – show, or tell, young Mary what to do and she obeyed without argument. But what would be especially valuable in a teacher was her ability to speak Setswana fluently (she was bilingual) and also the difficult language of the Bushmen (because her nurse had belonged to their tribe).

So young Mary was groomed from childhood to be something more than a good wife. She was to have a vocation, unusual for a girl of her class had she lived in England. But first she would have to go to a good school. The London Missionary Society, unlike the Methodists, had not yet established schools for the children of their missionaries in southern Africa so the Moffats had no choice except to send their daughters to the only school they knew of, Salem, in the Cape Province, near Grahamstown, and so far away that it would mean not being able to see them for years. The arduous, even perilous, journey would take a minimum of six weeks.

The whole family set off on 15 June 1830 to take Mary and Ann to Salem, arriving at Grahamstown in the first week of August and leaving them at the school in September. Salem was the largest school in the province, catering for sixty boys and fifty girls as boarders. The headmaster was William Henry Matthews, who had taught in Hackney, London, for a while, before coming out to Africa. Mr Matthews was actually self-taught and had no qualification for his post (not that many schoolmasters did then) but he had very decided ideas as to what should be taught to his pupils. He had no time for Mathematics, Latin, Drawing or Music or Art. All that was on offer was a plain education where nothing but the sound teaching of English was attempted. There was only one textbook: the Bible. The pupils learned how to write by copying out verses and to read by reciting them. Mrs Moffat, though she found leaving her girls agony, left feeling that they were in good hands. Some friends at nearby Grahamstown agreed to have Mary and Ann in the holidays (because the journey was too long for them to return home even for the longest vacation).

Mary was the older of the two and felt responsible for her sister, something of a burden for a girl of only nine, who was of a quiet, even timid, disposition and used to a mother who had always dominated her life. She found it easy, as ever, to be 'good', but perhaps not so easy to be the leader. The two years which passed before a visit from her mother were very long, requiring stoicism to endure, and the holiday arrangements were not ideal. Mary and Ann were not welcomed with much enthusiasm by their host families. They were tolerated, fed and looked after, but that was it.

In 1833, Mrs Moffat (who in the meantime had had two more children) arrived to see them bringing their brother Robert, then nearly seven, to join the school. She wrote to a friend that both girls seemed well and that their academic progress was satisfactory, but two more years later she decided to move all three children to a school in Cape Town and travelled to Salem to oversee the move herself, taking the three younger children with her. By the time she reached Salem she was exhausted. The help of Mary and Ann, reunited with their family, was sorely needed. They all travelled from Salem to Port Elizabeth to look for a ship that would take the three older children on the eleven-day, by no means easy, journey round the coast to Cape Town. The moment the sailing date was fixed, Mary, the calm, sensible, docile fourteen-year-old Mary, fell ill. What precisely was wrong with her was never stated. No

symptoms were listed. There was no mention of fever, coughing, vomiting, aches or pains, all of which in letters at other
times during different illnesses were minutely detailed. It looks
suspiciously as though Mary, used to being absolutely obedient,
was, in the only way open to her, registering some kind of
protest against being moved.

Her mother was distraught, all her plans wrecked, but the
more her agitation increased, the worse her daughter's unspeci-
fied symptoms became. She decided Ann and Robert would
have to go alone, in the charge of a chaperone found from
among the other passengers, and they were duly taken aboard.
But the wind was not in the right direction for sailing, and
while the ship still stood in the bay Mrs Moffat observed that as
soon as her siblings had departed Mary began to show signs of
recovering. She promptly had her carried on board and
reported 'she bore it well'. The three children had 'rather a
dangerous passage' but arrived safely and their greatly relieved
mother returned slowly to Kuruman. How Mary adapted to her
new school was never mentioned in the Moffat letters that have
survived and she appears to have written none of her own. Two
years went by and then came the voyage to England.

By the time the family arrived there, in June 1839, Mrs
Moffat had recovered. She had many relatives to visit (though
the dearest of these, her own mother, was dead) and only hoped
she could fit them all in before Robert's New Testament was
printed, and they were all on their way back to Africa. In the
event, instead of staying in England the planned few months,
the Moffats were there four years. It was a curious period in the
children's lives. They saw their father being lionised, such was
the Victorian reverence for missionary endeavours, and their
mother, as his wife, called upon to play quite a different role.
While Robert Moffat toured the length and breadth of the
country, speaking to rapt audiences and rousing them to
contribute financially to the great work of converting the
heathen in Africa, their mother was obliged to stay at home
with them. 'Home' was not even one place but a succession of
different addresses before relative permanence was achieved in
Walworth. It had to be, because Mrs Moffat had yet another
baby, Jane, in August 1840. She was unable to travel with her

husband and had the, for her, unusual experience of being very nearly frustrated and bored with her lot. Instead of making all the decisions, instead of labouring from dawn to dusk to look after her family, she was, she wrote, 'everywhere taken care of as a hot-house plant'. It was a reminder that in Victorian England this was the lot of wives of her class. But, interestingly, she did not relish the luxury and longed to get home. 'We are seldom together as a family', she wrote, and said: 'Since my baby was born Robert has never been with us except for a few hours.'

Her children were not always with her either, except for the baby and the toddler Elizabeth. The older ones went to stay with various friends and relatives, fitting uneasily into an entirely different social pattern from the one they were used to. For Mary and Ann these visits were particularly difficult, since they had neither the right clothes nor much awareness of correct society manners. They were colonial girls, unsophisticated, with strange accents and an ignorance of how the world worked. And for young Mary at least, the British way of life does not seem to have been preferable to life at Kuruman. She hated the cold, quite different from the sharp, clear cold of an African winter's morning when in a couple of hours the sun would gloriously burn the chill away. She missed the vast African landscapes, feeling cramped and claustrophobic in the overfurnished houses and in the streets of crowded buildings. The cultural opportunities seem to have passed her by and there is no record of her making friends of her own age, of either sex.

The only real excitement, in fact, was watching the effect her father had on his audiences. She and Ann and Robert dutifully supported him when his wife could not, though keeping well in the background. It was easy for Mary to be unobtrusive – she was unprepossessing in looks, a small, rather thick-set young woman with an unattractive hair-style and a swarthy complexion. She looked like her father, but whereas on a man his features were handsome, on a young woman the pronounced nose, strong bone structure and thick, black eyebrows were not thought pretty. Nor did Mary's personality draw attention – she was quiet, her eyes were habitually cast down, and her most common expression was one of a misleading blankness. She rarely talked in company, and when that company included her voluble mother, not at all. All Mary's assets were hidden and it would need determination to uncover them.

David Livingstone certainly had plenty of determination but professed to have no romantic interest in women during this period. He was residing in a lodging-house for trainee missionaries, in Aldersgate, preparing to go out to Africa. His landlady, Mrs Sewell, had tried to persuade him that a missionary needed a wife, as did Mrs Moffat when she visited, on one occasion, with her husband. But Livingstone had told the directors of the London Missionary Society that he was convinced he would work better on his own – a wife, in his confident opinion, would only get in the way. But he was not quite as impervious to female charms as he liked to assert. There was Catherine Ridley, and her sister, whom he'd met while studying in Essex, and there was some mysterious episode in his youthful past: in a letter to Mrs Sewell he once wrote that he knew she thought him 'foolish and obstinate' on the subject of marrying, but said: 'You don't know my history and the knowledge of it is absolutely necessary before you could understand my apparent obstinacy. If I had the time or inclination to be egotistical you would see neither mother's nor sisters' conduct influenced my mind but, on the contrary, certain conundrums.' What 'history', what 'conundrums'? Whatever experience it was, and however vital to understand his resistance to the idea of looking for a wife, it had made him suspicious of all women. Only with his landlady, Mrs Sewell, did he seem to have any kind of rapport, and she was married with three grown-up children, a woman whom he said he regarded as a mother and to whom his own mother desired him to express her gratitude 'for the happiness and comfort I have enjoyed under your roof'.

If Livingstone met the Moffat daughters, he never commented on them, though he had plenty to say about their mother and was greatly influenced by their father. Like Mary, he lacked social graces and, though his background was very different from hers, he shared her sense of not belonging to the fashionable world. He was a working-class Scot, and just as Mary had been brought up in an atmosphere of unremitting toil at Kuruman, so had he in Blantyre were he had worked in a cotton-mill from a young age.

Livingstone went ahead of the Moffats to Africa, arriving there in March 1841. From the moment he began the long trek from the Cape to Kuruman he loved the country, feeling a sense of freedom in the landscape which he had never felt before. Once at Kuruman, and engaged on the missionary work he had come to do, he was more sure than ever that a wife would be a distraction. The missionary he had travelled out with, William Ross, seemed to him to be burdened rather than supported by his wife, who had moaned and groaned so much throughout the voyage that her husband was fully occupied in looking after her.

But by the time the Moffats returned to Kuruman two years later, in the spring of 1843, Livingstone's attitude towards finding a wife had begun to change. He was now thirty years old, and though the change was barely perceptible at first in his correspondence it was there, beginning with a confession that, though he had 'a good stock of spirits' and could 'bear up against loneliness' it sometimes 'requires all my philosophy'. He had left the Kuruman station to join a Mr Edwards and his wife further north and, though he had little respect for Mrs Edwards (whom he thought a bad housewife) being with them nevertheless emphasised his own solitary state. He still stoutly defended his contention that he did not *need* a wife, but he gradually admitted that there were practical advantages to having one. It was not that he thought a wife would be useful to protect his reputation – 'with respect to scandal ... *married* men have been charged with incontinency ... I conclude that marriage, like vaccination for smallpox is not specially preventative to scandal in Africa' – but that a man with a wife was thought by the African tribes to come in peace. He also had to admit, now that he had visited several mission stations, that the wives there 'are an invaluable part of the machinery of missions in this country'. Nevertheless, he was annoyed by attempts to find a wife for him. 'My friends at Griquatown', he wrote, 'imagined I must be dying for want of a wife and kindly sent their daughter ... by way of experiment.' Mrs Ross apparently explained this away by spreading the rumour that he was in love with a young widow in London called Mrs Sewell. This amused him, but also made him think gloomily that a widow might be his only hope, because he found that the daughters of missionaries had 'miserably contracted minds' and that 'colonial ladies' at the Cape were worse. He once risked making a joke about the impossibility of his ever marrying and having children, when he mentioned that some baby clothes included in a box of clothing sent out for the Africans were 'not the thing for me', but then rather regretted it because it might have been interpreted as 'saucy'.

Saucy was something Livingstone definitely was not. There could never have been a more serious young man when it came to considering whether he should marry and he obviously had met no available woman who appealed to him by the time he was wounded by a lion in February 1844, three years after he had arrived in Africa. Since by that time he had spent several weeks at Kuruman after the Moffats' return, Mary and Ann, and even Helen, have to be included in his general condemnation of missionaries' daughters. None of the Moffat girls was ever mentioned in his letters, not even to dismiss them as possibilities. They were invisible, unlike their mother. Livingstone had noted what a brilliant housekeeper Mrs Moffat was, and how superbly the Kuruman station ran, thanks to her, but he also noted how bossy and domineering she was. She ruled the roost and in spite of her efficiency was exactly what he would not wish for in a wife. He wrote to Mrs Sewell that Mrs Moffat never stopped boasting of her own 'excellencies' and he found this insufferable.

His opinion of her obviously put him off the thought of considering one of the Moffat girls as a wife but it cannot be the whole reason why he never mentions them. It is more likely that at first he simply was not physically attacted to them and therefore not interested in getting to know them. But sexual frustration perhaps had more to do with his eventual decision to find a wife than he was ever prepared to admit. He was young, healthy, and so far as is known had had no sexual experience. The 'history' he referred to in his letter to Mrs Sewell is unlikely to have involved a serious sexual encounter – he was deeply religious, immensely self-controlled, and on his own admission a puritan. But he noticed women and was compassionate towards them. He is on record later as swearing he could see no beauty in African women, and that he couldn't imagine anyone wanting 'criminal sexual congress' with them, but he observed them with great interest and frankness, disliking the dismissive way they were treated. There are many instances of his kindness and even tenderness towards women and girls, and all of this side of his personality needed more fulfilment.

He also had a highly developed sense of family, believing that the family unit worked best for any society. His devotion to his mother and his two sisters, and to his landlady Mrs Sewell, was openly exhibited, and he was a man who loved children. When he was a student, he had asked the directors of the London Missionary Society if they would pay for him to take extra tuition at St Bartholomew's Hospital, not just in midwifery but in the treatment of children's diseases. In Africa he treated the children with compassion and wished always that he could do more for them. He also delivered babies, though he always waited to be asked to help, not wishing to usurp the position of the midwives. Inevitably, he would be called on only during a difficult labour, and his skill in safely delivering the baby and preserving the mother's life made him something of a local hero.

This, then, was not the sort of man who seemed fated to be a bachelor, but there was still the problem of finding a wife congenial to him. The lion did him a favour. After three months trying to recover under the far from tender care of Mrs Edwards at Mabotsa, during which time the wound suppurated and he was gravely ill with fever, Livingstone was moved to Kuruman to convalesce. Mrs Moffat was in her element supervising his needs, but it was Mary and her sister who did much of the actual nursing. The invalid had plenty of time to study a young woman he had never appeared to notice before and the more he studied Mary the more he liked her. His biographers, with wonderful male arrogance, have always considered Mary lucky to have 'caught' him, apparently considering that because she was not pretty and was rather plump and didn't sparkle, Livingstone cannot possibly have actually fallen in love with her. It was, they allege, a marriage of convenience. They have not for one moment taken into consideration their hero's own intelligence and sensitivity, quite sufficient to make him discover in Mary qualities with which he could indeed fall in love. But no, it seems that men cannot love fat, plain women.

But Livingstone obviously did. Why his love for Mary should ever have been doubted is partly his own fault. He famously wrote to a friend that his wife-to-be was 'a matter-of-fact lady, a little thick, black-haired girl, sturdy and all I want'. Not flattering, it's true, but very much in Livingstone's self-deprecating style. The phrase 'all I want' has been taken to mean 'not up to much but she'll have to do', whereas if the emphasis is put on the '*all*' it can just as well be read as 'everything I want' (which is how I read it). Later, he wrote to Mary that he had loved her when he married her and went on to love her even more. He grew physically more attracted to her, too, writing to her in October before they were married, 'I wish I could embrace you' – which, for a puritanical Scot, counted as fulsome. Curiously, pity is all Mary rates from his biographers, yet a man of Livingstone's uncompromising principles would never have married out of pity or desperation – it simply was not in his character. Throughout his life, he had to believe passionately in every action he took before he could proceed, and marriage was no different.

There was, after all, plenty in Mary for him to love. She was calm and quiet, kind and caring, and skilled in many of the ways Livingstone valued. She was far from being empty-headed (like the colonial ladies he despised) or from having a miserably contracted mind. On the contrary, she had a serious mind and had been trained to teach. She taught competently in the school at Kuruman and he saw how popular she was with the children. He was impressed, too, because she was bilingual, something he could never hope to become (though he found Setswana easy to learn). Mary's response to his overtures is not known, but since pride was all to him, some kind of rapport must have existed, or he would never have risked a proposal. He had to be sure she would accept. Here again, accepted wisdom dictates that *of course* a fat, plain, dull girl like Mary would accept, desperate not to be left on the shelf. But before her, Mary had the example of her mother and father's love-match and she knew the difference between a passionate commitment and a purely practical arrangement. It is insulting to them both to doubt that their marriage lacked genuine mutual attraction, or that Mary could never have refused Livingstone.

The Moffat parents expressed themselves astonished – 'Mr Livingstone's marriage was to us a most unexpected event' – but delighted. Their daughter would stay within the mission fold and near to them. Mrs Moffat did have a few doubts about her son-in-law (as he had more than a few about her) whom she saw as headstrong and reckless, and whom she suspected would dominate her daughter perhaps to her detriment. But there was general rejoicing on the Kuruman station when on 9 January 1845 the marriage took place. No one had any doubts that, whatever else, Mary would make '*a good wife*' – capable, biddable, supportive. And absolutely no challenge to her husband's authority.

II

The speed with which David Livingstone decided how happy he was to be married was remarkable. If the idea of having a wife had filled him with foreboding, the reality filled him with a delight he did not attempt to conceal, and, as with all converts, his desire to persuade others to do what he had once argued against was strong. He now encouraged his bachelor friends to find wives for themselves. 'The woman', he wrote to his friend D. G. Watt, 'is the glory of the man. I am very contented and very happy in my connection.' And to Mrs Sewell, later, he was even more forthcoming, hoping that a mutual friend who was about to marry would be 'abundantly compensated by the amount of conjugal bliss he will enjoy [unlike] the misery he endured while compelled to live the glorious life of a bachelor'.

Bliss apart, he also relished the material comforts which having a good wife brought. He told his mother and sisters of his pleasure at having clean linen on his bed and his every domestic want catered for. His suddenly well-run household reminded him of his mother's and made him appreciate her more in retrospect. He was glad to have his own house at last, modest though it was and built by himself during his engagement to Mary, though it was two months after his marriage before he was able to take his bride there, to Mabotsa, some 125 miles (200 km) north-east of Kuruman. The journey was in effect their honeymoon and when Mary arrived at her new home she was pleased by the sight of the lush green countryside through which streams and rivers flowed. It looked the perfect place to set up a mission station (at least in March it did). All around, it was true, was forest, home to lions and leopards, but the situation of their house itself was attractive, sitting as it did in a kind of amphitheatre of hills. The house was built of stone to waist height and then continued in mud, in the local fashion, which involved layering wet earth in stages, and the roof was thatched.

Here Mary went about the same kind of arduous daily duties that her mother had performed and trained her in, but she also taught the African children and started classes in reading and sewing for the women. She soon realised that teaching the children at Kuruman had been far easier because the Kgatta tribe were more co-operative than the Tlhaping tribe who inhabited Mabotsa. At Mabotsa, the chief sometimes let the children come to be taught by her but often the demands of planting and herding required their presence elsewhere – learning to read and write had a very low priority. It was the same for the women. The younger women were too valuable to spare. They did the labouring, the carrying and collecting of firewood and water, the hoeing and weeding, often carrying their babies on their backs while pregnant again. There was not much demand for Mary's services, but she persevered and her husband admired her, writing to his family with pride of how she worked even though she was soon pregnant and feeling ill. His concern for her health was real, but it was not real enough for him to give her the stability and security she needed at such a time. On the contrary, he was disillusioned with Edwards, his fellow missionary at Mabotsa, and determined to move and find another mission station on his own.

It was the last thing Mary wanted. She had seen Mabotsa becoming another Kuruman, growing and flourishing as her parents' station had done. She had a house there, and, more important, a garden which had taken a great deal of work, her work, to establish and was now producing cabbages, lettuce, turnips and onions. All this would be lost. She had no apparent influence on her husband – his work and his vision proved to be more important than her wishes, and he had convinced himself his work could only be done to best effect somewhere else. Leaving Mary behind, he went to scout for a new location, and when he had found one at Chonwane, north of Mabotsa, he left her frequently, to start preparing a home for them to move to once the baby was born. Almost at once Mary's first hint of failure as a perfect wife was exposed: she hated being without her husband. She not only hated it, she could hardly endure being alone. Being solitary unnerved her. From being calm and dependable when her husband was there, she became tearful and uncertain, quite unlike her mother who, though she had dreaded her husband's absences, had seemed to radiate confidence and never once thought of begging him to stay. But then, she had been a wife without parallel, never burdening her husband with her own fragility, never worrying him with her dependence. But Mary Livingstone *was* dependent, and in her dependency similar to so many wives before and since. Her husband recognised this but would not give in to her need. Instead he bought a horse, so that he could travel more quickly between Mabotsa and Chonwane. When he received a message that his wife had terrible headaches, or that she was terrified because lions had come out of the woods and surrounded the house, he galloped back to be with her, but he would not give up his new project. Mary must learn to manage. Wives had to.

Her sister Ann's visit helped, and might have been repeated, but Ann had a terrifying experience on her way home to Kuruman and couldn't be expected to risk the journey again. She travelled with only a maid and two African boys to look after the oxen who pulled her wagon. When a lion attacked, at night, as they were all sitting round the campfire, there was no one to protect them. Ann, her maid and the boys leapt safely into the wagon, but all night long they heard the horrible sounds of the lion crunching the bones of an ox and knew it could have been their own bones. Mary just had to hope that her husband would be with her for the birth, and not only for the psychological support; he would be needed to deliver his own child.

In the event, he did deliver his son. Mary's pregnancy lasted ten months (as all her pregnancies did), not nine, and her husband was with her to deliver Robert on their wedding anniversary. It made the bond between them stronger but also increased Mary's dependency by adding the relationship of doctor/patient to that of husband/wife. In Victorian England, a husband was never in the bedroom while his wife went through labour and childbirth, and even husbands who were doctors would rarely deliver their own children. This was only one respect in which missionary couples differed from couples back home but it was perhaps the most significant and made missionary husbands unique in their own time. There were none of the mysteries of womanhood for them, and this in turn affected how their wives saw them. Far more than any 'new' man of our own day, proud to be present at his wife's delivery, Livingstone shared in the experience. It drew them even closer.

Once Robert was born, the rival demands of being a mother and a wife were difficult to meet. Robert was from the first a fretful child, and it did not help that almost as soon as he was born his parents moved to Chonwane. Mary arrived there to find an unfinished house in an area that looked barren. There was virtually no water – the streams had dried up, since there had been no rain since November (it was February) – and the wind swept sand and dust across the plain. There was little food available, and Livingstone had been allocated no new funds to buy supplies from the Cape. She didn't feel well, and neither did her husband, who had excruciating toothache. There was, of course, not the faintest possibility of finding a dentist – he had to be his own dentist just as he was his own doctor. But he was unable to pull out his own tooth. He had a pair of 'shoemaker's nippers' which he used for all manner of tasks, but he couldn't get them round his own tooth and pull at the same time. Someone else would have to do it, someone who could position him to the best advantage and see what they were doing. This 'someone' must be his wife. He instructed her carefully: he would lie on the floor, mouth wide open, and she would kneel over him, place the 'nippers' securely round the offending tooth, and then haul it out. Obedient as ever, Mary did what she was told, but as soon as she started pulling her husband began to writhe in agony, roaring and knocking her hand away. But it had to be done, and so Mary set to again. When the tooth finally yielded, they were both exhausted. Childbirth, dental extractions – there was little mystery in this marriage.

The move to Chonwane was disastrous and, to make matters worse, Mary became pregnant again in August. Her mother, arriving for a visit in September, was shocked by what she found. This was no Kuruman, but an inhospitable place where no amount of hard work could compensate for the lack of water. Her daughter was thin for the first time in her life, and worn out, looking after a constantly crying baby while trying to keep her pathetic household together. The Livingstones were grateful for the supplies she brought (though they had dreaded her visit, since she was sure to be critical). Mrs Moffat left feeling that she had made some difference even if her opinion of her son-in-law was unchanged – her admiration for his obvious commitment to missionary work was offset by her suspicion that her daughter's health was being endangered by his recklessness and that she had neither the will nor the strength of character to challenge him.

Indeed, Mary accepted, at that stage, everything that happened to her, and the hardest thing to accept was the knowledge that however much her husband loved their child he was putting Robert at risk. From being merely fretful, her baby, only ten months old, became ill in October, with a form of pneumonia. He survived it, but a few weeks later his father took him and the pregnant Mary off on an exploratory trip to the east of Chonwane and on their return Robert suffered a relapse, developing a fever just as the party was fording a river. Mary finally broke down and wept, sure that either her son would die from his fever or else they would all be drowned. Looking at his wife who, in spite of her pregnancy, was thin and worn, Livingstone was glad of the face-saving excuse he had to take her to Kuruman, to attend the meeting of the District Committee of the London Missionary Society. The truth was, he was almost destitute; the supplies brought by his mother-in-law had been long since used up. To be at Kuruman for a while, especially with another baby due, would be a blessing.

It was Mary's first visit home. She had left a mere two years before, a plump and healthy young bride, and now apart from her swollen belly, she was haggard, her face stripped of flesh, her arms and legs stick-thin: a bad advertisement for marriage. There was general shock at her appearance, and Livingstone himself ruefully reported that the African women who had known Mary since she was a child and crowded round to meet her wondered aloud if he had been feeding her at all, because she looked starved as well as ill. He had to admit he could see why they were concerned, but he resented implications that *he* might be the cause of her ill-health – as if he were responsible for the drought at Chonwane from which in his view all their troubles stemmed. He and Mary had been unlucky, that was all. Everything had been against them, but God was in charge and somehow all that had happened had been meant.

At any rate, they were now at Kuruman, in safe hands and with plenty to eat. Mary benefited enormously. Writing to Mrs Sewell, Livingstone acknowledged this – 'Our visit proved very beneficial to Mrs Livingstone. We got a daughter there too.' Agnes, named after his mother, was born in May and to his relief proved a much more contented baby than Robert had been. Doctor though he was, he seemed to make no connection between the nursing mother's circumstances – her mother and sisters being able to look after her – and the baby's contentment. As soon as he could, he left Kuruman with Mary and the two children and travelled slowly back to Chonwane, a journey of nearly 700 miles (1,125 km), reaching there at the beginning of July, only to decide to move on again. 'Chonwane was a bad spot for a European to live in,' he told Mrs Sewell. 'Water very scanty and bad.' The chief of the tribe agreed and had already found a place to which everyone could move, at Kolobeng. 'We have of course,' Livingstone wrote, 'to begin again at the beginning.'

Of course. And a good wife had to accept this inevitability, which meant that yet again she would be condemned to live in a makeshift hut while a more substantial dwelling was built. She had had only a year of stability at Mabotsa, then another year and a half at Chonwane, and now, with a baby and a small child (often ill), she had to face moving again. Not once does her husband record her protesting, or accusing him of thinking only of himself – but then, she wouldn't. She was obedient not so much to his wishes as to the driving force which made him want to go into parts of Africa unseen by any missionary or explorer and to bring God's word to the inhabitants. He himself never saw any selfishness in this – he did nothing on a whim, but acted on reasons he saw as perfectly logical, dictated by conditions beyond his control. Mary, as his wife, had to share both his sense of mission and his way of seeing things, or their marriage could not flourish. For her to be a 'good wife' his belief had to be hers, his total commitment to what he saw as right hers too. Otherwise nothing made sense, none of the hardships she suffered could be justified. A wife had to have trust above all, and that Mary had. But perhaps she had too much. Her faith in her husband was, if not blind, then inclined to ignore what was merely stubborn about him. He reacted badly to criticism, so it would not have done much good for her to argue against his decisions – he was, as he once wrote to his parents, like a Shetland pony, obstinate and immovable at any attempt to force him to do what he did not want to do. But a different wife, one who had the insight to point out the error of his ways on occasion, and who did it calmly and with love, was what he needed. Giving credit to Mary for obedience was to give her no credit at all.

Yet Livingstone did not dominate his wife in the unpleasant way this might suggest. Mary had been dominated by her mother all her life, and if her mother's correspondence is anything to go by she had never once rebelled (it was Helen who finally did so). There was something in her nature that made her accede to the demands of others without argument and, in fact, she found much more pleasure in being led by her husband than she had ever found in bowing to her mother's wishes. She admired his strength of will and even seems to have felt that it was an honour to support him. She was far from a cipher, a woman without a mind of her own, or of limited intelligence, but unlike her own mother she found self-abnegation acceptable. She was a stoic, seeing it as her place to interpret her marriage vows literally. The price her husband paid for this 'heroism' (as he more than once described it) was that he had, in turn, to accept her emotional dependence. He had learned that, excellent wife though she was, Mary disintegrated emotionally if left on her own. Her devotion to him was absolute but was not always in her own, or her children's, best interest.

In August 1847, he left her at Chonwane and set off to Kolobeng to start work on establishing a new mission.

'Itinerancy is good, if you have a permanent sphere, a focus', he commented. Good for him, but not of course for his wife, left behind. He liked what he saw at Kolobeng immediately, especially the sight of the river, which reassuringly was 18 feet (5.5 m) wide. Not only was there abundant water, but also plenty of wood to build with, since the area was thick with trees, and among the trees and in the meadowland near the river were animals that could be hunted and killed for meat. He worked ferociously hard with his African helpers, digging a canal to provide irrigation and planting every variety of seed. Meanwhile, 25 miles (40 km) away, Mary struggled to keep calm, counting the weeks, fearful of what might have happened to her husband, fearful as ever that the lions she could hear roaring were coming nearer. Almost an entire lifetime in Africa had not lessened her fear of lions – on the contrary, she knew what they were capable of and how they could sense vulnerable targets. She heard them prowling round the mission, half-deserted because most of the men were with Livingstone at Kolobeng, and could hardly bear the long nights of worrying about her safety and that of her children. In the end, she sent a message to Kolobeng, describing the activity of the lions, hoping it would bring her husband racing back, as it had done once before.

But he failed to come immediately. It was another two weeks until Livingstone came to take her and the children to their new home. Before they set out she had to watch the home they were leaving be burned to the ground. Her husband didn't want the Boers taking up residence there. Settlers of Dutch and German extraction, the Boers had refused to bow to British rule in the Cape Province, especially after the abolition of slavery, and had been trekking further and further inland taking land from the Africans as they went. They were hostile to the missionaries, whom they believed were supplying the Africans with guns to attack them. In previous weeks, parties of Boers had come nearer and nearer to Chonwane, intent on destroying all before them in order to expand their own farms. Livingstone wanted not just to build a new mission but to move further away from this threat.

When he'd collected the nails (needed for building work at

Kolobeng) from the ruins of a house that had meant little to him (itinerant as he proclaimed himself) but a great deal to his wife, they were off, in an ox-wagon. At least Mary had the pleasure of finding Kolobeng attractive and infinitely preferable to Chonwane – the river, the trees, the new houses already built made a good first impression. But it was misleading. The temporary house they were living in was only a hut, made of mud and reeds, and the wind blew through it constantly, a hot wind during the day and a cold one at night, bringing with it dust and flies. The dust irritated the children's eyes and then the flies settled on the sores; and altogether the hut barely provided any shelter. Mary had mysterious pains in her chest; then her own eyes became infected and she could hardly see. There was grit everywhere – no matter how scrupulously she cleaned, dust settled on every object and her hands felt always dirty. But worst of all was seeing the plentiful water dry up. Yet again, drought had followed them and though the irrigation canal kept some few vegetables growing, most perished.

Her husband went off again, on a trek to reach the huge lake rumoured to exist to the north, where he was hopeful of finding an enormous population ready for conversion. He got nowhere near the lake, returning home fairly quickly after discovering the Boers had been there, looting and burning, and likely to return. Once back, he set himself to complete a new house for his family. He chose a site on a rocky outcrop and began building an impressively large house, based on the design of the best houses at Kuruman, with a sitting-room, a study, two bedrooms, a verandah and even a stone fireplace. There were windows with glass in them, and a lean-to kitchen. On 4 July 1848, the family moved into their new home, the most comfortable building they had ever inhabited. It was a significant moment, symbolising as it did an end to makeshift arrangements. Livingstone solemnly recognised this by making a metal plate and attaching it to one of the walls. At last, Mary was content. She had a solid and (for that area and those times) splendid home, which she set about beautifying as best she could. Although he pretended to grumble that it was luxury gone mad, her husband did not oppose the order for a sofa, and he was willing to put up shelves for books and to make an oven so that Mary did not have to bake bread in a lidded pot set straight on to coals. There was even time to think of that most frivolous of concerns, clothes. Mary, her husband reported, wanted him to order, from his sisters, a decent jacket to be sent out, something that could be regarded as 'respectable . . . not fustian . . . a thin dark coloured [jacket], something green, will do'. He professed to be amused at her dissatisfaction with his normal tattered apparel, but all the same was prepared to indulge her – a wife had rights. If she wanted him to look smart occasionally then he would oblige. A wife, even a wife with no clothes sense whatsoever, knew about such things. Indeed, it was perhaps one of her many duties to see her husband looked 'respectable'. So his measurements were sent: 'collar to waist $16\frac{1}{2}$ inches, elbow to end of sleeve 12 inches, round chest 2 feet 11 inches, waist $29\frac{1}{4}$ inches'. The family was settled, and Mary could establish a routine, following the pattern of domestic order instituted by her mother.

In the light of what had gone before, this was domestic bliss, but it was still a hard life. Mary rose at dawn, as most people living in Africa do, to light the fire for the breakfast of maize porridge; then came family worship and after that the day's routine began. Before she baked the daily loaves of bread, she had first to supervise the cleaning and milling of the grain; before she washed clothes, in cold water and always short of soap (a very valuable commodity), they had to be soaked overnight because they were so ingrained with dust in the dry season and mud in the wet; before she made coffee, a luxury she and Livingstone allowed themselves, she had to go and collect water to boil, then skim the cream from the milk to add to it. As she and other missionaries' wives commented, they were maids-of-all-work, more like farmers' wives than anything. There was no afternoon rest to follow the gruelling morning's essential work. Then, she left the two children with a girl and trudged in the ferocious heat to the mission meeting-house where she taught the African children. She made them wear some kind of clothing, much against their will (but following her mother's ruling on what was 'decency') and tried to discipline them to learn how to count, read and write. Afterwards, when the day had begun fractionally to cool, she taught the girls sewing and then walked further into the town – Kolobeng was a kind of town in African terms by then – to talk to the women and help those most in need. She was mother, housewife, teacher and social worker all in one and, not surprisingly, exhausted by nightfall. She knew just as much about juggling roles as any wife today. There was not much time or energy for reading, but when she did read it was religious tracts or magazines or books such as George Cheever's lectures on *Pilgrim's Progress*. Her husband, meanwhile, turned to *Punch* – Mrs Sewell sent out copies and he told her how much they made him laugh.

At least her husband appreciated her. His letters home are full of praise for her hard work and very ready with acknowledgement of how much she did at great cost to her own health. He was proud of her success and popularity with the children – 'the native children are fond of her' – and aware that she lacked female friendship. He had to be her friend, she his, and this bred an intimacy different from the existing marital relationship. She was his 'rib', she was 'the main spoke in the wheel', she was 'a heroine'. And she seemed content to be all of these things in a way that touched him. All she dreaded was that their new-found stability should be disrupted, especially when in the summer of their first full year in Kolobeng she became pregnant again.

It was her third pregnancy in three years, but then there was nothing remarkable about that – she had seen her mother give birth with the same kind of regularity. Livingstone, like all the missionaries, saw children as a blessing and would have been unlikely to try any form of contraception to give his wife some respite at such an early stage in their marriage. Total abstinence was the only alternative and clearly not practised.

Pregnancy was never easy for Mary and this time she was very sick and had more pains in her chest which her doctor husband could not account for. She had to give up teaching, and languished at home, barely able to attend to the hyperactive Robert and the lively, but much more easy-going, Agnes. By November, when she was five months pregnant, the weather was 'excessively warm', touching nearly 100° Fahrenheit in the coolest part of the house, and Mary felt worse than she had ever done. Her husband dreaded the coming birth for her, and wished he had some of the newly invented chloroform he'd read about.

But, to his relief, a son, Thomas, was born in March with comparative ease, after a labour of three hours. Mary, however, was not allowed to recover slowly – there was a threat of attack again from the Boers and she had to force herself to get ready to flee with her children. Fortunately, the attack did not materialise on this occasion, but her husband was anxious about leaving her while he went off on another expedition. He had been more or less fixed at Kolobeng for longer than he wanted, feeling the same urge to press on and bring God's Word to other tribes – and to explore deeper into the continent. When Mary's parents invited her to Kuruman he was relieved – once his family was there, he would be free to travel again. Mary had little choice. She couldn't survive on her own with a new baby and the ever-present rumours of a Boer attack, and she couldn't go with her husband. Livingstone took her to Kuruman in April, on the first leg of what was a two-week journey. When he said goodbye she broke down and sobbed – 'My poor lady is away out crying all the road in the full belief that I shall not be seen by her again.'

But his wife's tears had other causes too. She had not wanted to leave her home and be sent off to her mother's house where she never seems to have been happy after her marriage. Even seeing the children thrive on a diet infinitely better than any she could provide at Kolobeng, didn't compensate for the absence of her husband. Nor could the company of her sister Ann. The children were happy though, in the company of their grandparents and in no hurry to return home. It was Mary who was desperate to go back, against all advice and even common sense, and after four months she packed up and left with the children, though her husband was not yet back from his travels. He'd gone far north, as she knew, in May, with his two big-game-hunting friends, William Cotton Oswell and Mungo Murray, to find Lake Ngami. She knew and liked Oswell, the perfect English gentleman, 6 feet tall (1.8 m) in his stockings and so well developed as a schoolboy at Rugby that he'd been called the Muscleman. He'd come from India to Cape Town to convalesce after an attack of fever. Once recovered, he felt restless and wanted to spend some time exploring and hunting, so he travelled first to Kuruman, where he was charmed by the Moffats, and was sent on by them to see Livingstone. Surprisingly, the two men liked each other immediately and Oswell was only too willing to accompany Livingstone on his travels. They were supposed to be home by August, though Mary knew perfectly well how unlikely such accurate timing would be. But she seems not to have cared. It was almost as though she felt that if she were there, waiting for them, her husband would come – her need for him would summon him.

It was a dismal arrival for her and the children. It was August (winter there) and drought had once more dried everything up and made the cattle lean. The east wind she hated blew across the whole mission station, filling every nook and cranny in her house with sand. It was so cold at night that there was frost on the ground in the early morning, and the Africans coughed and wheezed with the respiratory infections the season always brought. The children picked up these infections and lost the bloom they had had acquired under their grandmother's care at Kuruman. She felt ill, drained from nursing Thomas and from hard manual labour, and the Africans depended on her, coming to her for medicines and food which she needed to conserve for herself. She could have admitted defeat and gone back to Kuruman, but she refused to consider this. Instead, showing the first faint spark of rebellion against the circumstances inflicted on her by her husband, she sent a message north, hoping the messenger would find him or at least someone who knew where he was. He had to come back to her – she could not endure being on her own any longer, and it was wrong of him to expect her to do so. Past caring about how her own mother had coped (for once), Mary let her feelings be known.

Livingstone got the message and made all haste to return home, leaving the main party and riding on ahead. He got back on 9 October and found his family if not well, at least in less desperate straits than Mary's message had led him to fear. She had been two months on her own and the isolation had shattered her emotional health, just as bronchitis and other infections had wrecked her children's. His sympathy was tempered by a stout justification for his absence. His work required it. Mary does not appear to have pointed out to him that there was plenty of work to be done at Kolobeng, plenty of souls to save there without going off looking for other tribes. Nor does she seem to have pointed out what his absences were doing to his children, especially Robert. The three-year-old boy, always highly strung, had suffered not just the upheaval of moving between Kolobeng and Kuruman but also the full weight of his mother's distress. What he needed, more than did Agnes and the baby, was a settled environment and the confidence his father's presence gave him.

Livingstone's nature was such that he could not provide both. For Robert, to be with his father meant being unsettled, going off with him on his travels, in an ox-wagon. It was the last thing Mary wanted to do, but in May of the following year, she found that if she wanted to be with her husband, she must travel with him. To add to her misery, she was pregnant again, nearly six months pregnant when they set off in a cavalcade without anything like adequate provisions, and accompanied by twenty African helpers. Mary, unlike her mother, hated ox-wagon travel, though she was an exerienced packer, knowing exactly how to arrange the contents. In the smaller chest at the front she put the daily supplies of tea, coffee, rice and sugar, all packed in small metal canisters, and in the bigger chest at the back larger quantities of the same goods from which the fore-chest was filled weekly. In the side-chests went plates and cups and clothes. A mattress formed a seat, with a movable wooden back put up during the day. Under the wagon she suspended a basket with meal in it and she hung six carriage bags made of sailcloth round the inside with cooking utensils in them. Within this confined space she and the children lived, and Robert and Agnes either played there or else trotted alongside the wagon. Since the wagon train moved so slowly, never more than 3 miles (4.8 m) an hour, it was easy enough for them to keep up, and it gave them vitally needed escape and exercise.

In spite of her temperament, phlegmatic and stoical most of the time, this way of living didn't appeal to Mary. Other missionary wives enjoyed sitting high up on the bench at the front in enforced idleness – the jolting, rolling motion over the uneven ground made even sewing impossible. But she preferred to be at home, solid ground beneath her feet and plenty of space around her. For a woman who had been born to the life, she showed an especial fear of the wagon's overturning (though when it did, on this very journey, she was brave) and of lions attacking. She never felt safe in an ox-wagon and it held no compensatory romance for her. The spirit of adventure was something she did not share with her husband, the excitement of exploration never appealed. She worried about the children, who were bitten all over by mosquitoes and other insects, and who had little choice of food. Water was a constant worry too – sometimes the wagon travelled all night as well as all day in an attempt to find drinking water before it ran out – and so was malaria. It was a relief to reach Lake Ngami (which Livingstone had reached previously and now wanted to go beyond) where the children could play in the water and pick up shells. Mary was to be left there while her husband moved on. The prospect that she might go into labour before his return and have no one to deliver her baby, terrified her. All she could do was trust her husband to return within the short time he had said he would.

But before he could leave, one of the drivers of the oxen came down with fever, thought to be an unusual type of malaria; then Agnes and Thomas both caught it. Even Livingstone realised that, faced with this calamity, there was only one option – they must all flee the fever-ridden area and make for home as rapidly as possible. By a piece of good fortune to match the bad, Oswell was waiting for them at the ford across the Botei river where he had supplies of potatoes and fruit to sustain the sick children. Agnes was soon better, though pale and drawn, but eighteen-month-old Thomas was so ill that Mary had to hold him all the time and carry him everywhere when they were not in the wagon – exhausting for an almost full-term pregnant woman. But at least they were all going home together and her husband's ambitious scheme to go further than the lake was for the moment shelved. This expedition in itself had been costly and it would be some time before another could be mounted. They returned to Kolobeng having lost eight of the oxen, with one of the wagons hardly fit for travel and another needing attention to make it safe. But the human cost was higher still.

Quite how high became apparent only three weeks later when Mary gave birth to a daughter, Elizabeth. The baby was very small, and though her father joked about this in a letter, saying she was about the size of her grandmother's finger, her likely low birth weight (though not recorded and probably not even known) contributed to her lack of resistance to disease. Even before Elizabeth became ill, Mary herself suffered fits of violent trembling on the third and fourth days after giving birth. She had earache too, and her husband deduced that this pain came from a bad tooth which, when she was well enough, he would extract. Meanwhile, she stayed in bed, exhausted and immobile, unable to do anything but feed her baby. Livingstone assumed that rest would see to his wife's recovery, but he was wrong. He noticed that when she tried to smile, one half of her face did not move. She couldn't speak clearly, and when he checked her limbs he found she couldn't move her right leg. She had, in fact, had a mild stroke, a cerebral haemorrhage due either to a malarial infection caught when Agnes and Thomas contracted fever at the lake, or, more likely, to pre-eclampsia brought on by stress, heat and high blood pressure in late pregnancy.

Mary's mother refers to a letter her daughter wrote to her after the birth, but the letter itself has not survived. It was written to tell her of a far greater tragedy than her own health – on 18 September, the baby Elizabeth died. She'd been ill two weeks, with what was referred to as inflammation of the lungs, and in spite of her father's best efforts was not strong enough to survive. Livingstone's anguish was genuine – the baby's last cry haunted him for years – but nevertheless he had as usual to excuse himself of responsibility for what had happened. He recorded no remorse, no confession that he had been partly to blame for subjecting his pregnant wife to the ordeal of travelling in an ox-wagon into a malarial region. It was all God's will. The baby would have died wherever they were. Mary would have had a stroke even if she had stayed at home. It was the only way he could deal with what had happened.

This was not how his indomitable mother-in-law saw the situation. Even before her daughter's letter reached her, she had set out from Kuruman with supplies, not knowing the new baby was dead. When she reached Kolobeng, she was horrified not just at the news of the death and the state of her daughter's health, but at the conditions she found. The Livingstones appeared to her practically destitute, and the house, once proudly spoken of, had so many broken windows that the wind blew from one end to the other over her sick daughter. To her fury, her son-in-law would not mend them, saying ventilation was a good thing. He himself was exhausted, as she could see, so she managed to restrain her anger. Instead, she busied herself getting Mary well enough to stand the journey to Kuruman, and then she took her daughter and the children off with her, determined to restore them once more to health. The only silver lining of the whole calamitous episode, in her opinion, was that Mary would obviously never again go off on one of her husband's mad treks while she was pregnant. In fact, she made her daughter promise that she never would – it would be taking obedience and loyalty as a wife to absurd and dangerous extremes. Sometimes a wife had to rebel. When her son-in-law came to collect his family she made it clear what she thought about any future expeditions.

But as a promise, it proved worthless. Within eight months of giving birth to a baby who died aged six weeks, Mary was once more committing herself to accompanying her husband on another expedition, while pregnant. It was insane, but she wrote to her mother that 'I must again wend my weary way to the far interior, perhaps to be confined in the field.' This was the most provocative way of expressing herself that she could possibly have chosen – the pathetic use of the word 'weary', the suggestion of the distance to be travelled in the 'far interior', and above all the image conjured up by 'confined in a field'. It sounded like a woman being forced against her will, and it had what can only have been the desired effect, a blast of rage and disgust from her mother towards her husband.

Mary, like many women, was certainly aware of the latent hostility between her husband and her mother. Though not wishing to cause trouble between them, she was not above using her mother as an indirect means of challenging her husband. She needed a champion, and like many a wife turned to the only person with the authority to tackle her husband and try to shame him.

'My dear Livingstone', her mother wrote:

> Before you left the Kuruman I did all I dared do to broach the subject of your intended journey, and thus bring on a candid discussion, more especially with regard to Mary's accompanying you with those dear children. But seeing how averse both you and Father were to speak about it, and the hope that you would never be guilty of such temerity (after the dangers they escaped last year), I too timidly shrank from what I ought to have had the courage to do. Mary had all along told me that should she be pregnant you would not take her, but let her come here after you were fairly off. Though I suspected at the end that she began to falter in this resolution, still I hoped it would never take place, i.e. *her going with you*, and looked and longed for things transpiring to prevent it. But to my dismay I now get a letter, in which she writes, 'I must again wend my weary way to the far interior, perhaps to be confined in the field.' O Livingstone, what do you mean? Was it not enough that you lost one lovely babe, and scarcely saved the others, while the mother came home threatened with paralysis? And will you again expose her and them in those sickly regions on an *exploring* expedition? All the world will condemn the cruelty of the thing to say nothing of the indecorousness of it. A pregnant woman with three little children trailing about in the company of the other sex, through the wilds of Africa, among savage men and beasts! Had you *found a place* to which you wished to go and commence missionary operations, the case would be altered. Not one word would I *say*, were it to the mountains of the moon. But to go with an exploring party, the thing is preposterous. I remain yours in great perturbation. M. Moffat.

It was a splendid letter, but it had no effect whatsoever. As far as her son-in-law was concerned, he was not going off 'exploring' but to establish a new mission, and in his eyes the end justified the means. His wife's fate, and the fate of his children, were in God's hands, not his, or his mother-in-law's. Mary herself appears to have had no influence on his decision. The only comfort for her this time, on this journey, was that her husband intended to settle his family permanently when they reached the end of it. And also she had the reassuring presence of Oswell from the beginning. This ensured that the party was properly provisioned – Oswell's wealth and experience were invaluable. Mary liked him and he liked her, noting her 'courage, her devoted attention to her husband and her unvarying kindness to myself'. She was like no wife he had ever known and he marvelled at her stamina, and at her faith in her husband. It was a faith tested many times over on that trip when once again drought proved the worst enemy and the children nearly died of thirst. The heat, as usual, was terrible, the insects vicious, and still Livingstone pressed on towards Linyanti. Thirty miles (48 km) short of it, he decided that the only way to continue, because the undergrowth of the River Chobe's banks was so thick, was by canoe. Mary and children, with suitable protectors, would have to be left behind. It was, wrote Oswell, the only time he saw Mary 'fail'.

It was the end of June and she was eight months pregnant. But she recovered her composure, and her husband and Oswell set off down the Chobe. They were back mercifully quickly, after reaching the Upper Zambesi accompanied by the great chief of the region Sebetwane. The chief had been taken ill and had died, and while they were delayed Livingstone had scouted around the area – and had to face up to the realisation that there was nowhere suitable to build a new mission, even if the new chief gave him permission. Mary's prophecy, that she would give birth in a field, looked like being fulfilled and he had no alternative but to turn round and make for home. There was no chance of getting to Kolobeng in time. Travelling in the dark, to keep the lethal tetse-fly off the oxen, they lumbered homewards, following another river, spotting leopards by the light of the moon, and on 23 August reached the Zouga river. They went 18 miles (29 km) along its banks, then crossed over, travelling over heavy sand to a hollow where they camped. The oxen were weak, but after a rest they continued slowly, reaching some rapids on 11 September. There, they met two travellers who gave them two bottles of port wine as thanks for help with mending a wheel. 'It was', wrote Livingstone in his journal, 'providential.'

Indeed. Providential because it helped Mary through the labour of giving birth to a son on 15 September. 'She never', wrote her husband, 'had a better or easier time of it.' And the baby was strong and healthy. They named him after Oswell, who had not even been aware of what was happening the previous night. He thought they seemed to be camping a long time in a not particularly suitable place; it was only when he suggested they should move on that Livingstone casually mentioned that his wife had given birth. Oswell was astounded, his admiration for Mary increasing even more – she appeared to him to have given birth without making a sound. He was only too willing to stay in the camp to give Mary time to recover, but then Thomas came down with fever and the need to get away from the river with its malarial water became urgent. Mary, Thomas and the tiny baby, plus the other two children, were hustled into the best of the wagons and the whole cavalcade set off again. It had become obvious by then that far from having 'an easy time' of it, Mary was once more in the grip of some kind of paralysis. She couldn't feel anything down her right side apart from some pain – the muscles refused to work. But they reached home relatively quickly, in late November, and she had recovered a little. 'Mary', her husband wrote, 'is much better than she was . . . but she has had a severe illness.'

Severe enough for him at last to realise that if he intended to go on another expedition she and their children could not accompany him. Separation, and a lengthy one, was inevitable. The very thing his wife dreaded most would have to be endured. It didn't matter how 'good' she was, she and the children were now a handicap to him and the fulfilment of his greater purpose.

III

Livingstone wrote to his father-in-law at the end of September 1851: 'the children must go to England for their education . . . we have concluded to send them, with their mother, home.' But 'home' was a foreign country to his wife. The place she called 'home' was Kuruman. It would have made far more sense for her to stay there while he went off on his travels and for the children to go to Salem or some other school in the Cape. But instead she was to go first to his parents' house, in Scotland, and then to rent a furnished cottage nearby. Though it was presented as a joint decision, that 'we' sounds unconvincing.

For Mary to *choose* to leave her husband, upon whom she was so obviously dependent, and travel with four young children to another continent, to a country where she had never felt comfortable, seems unlikely. But she was a wife who *obeyed*, and perhaps her husband had given her an attractive image of how his family would receive her. His mother, she had learned, was gentle and kind, and unlike her own, never sought to impose her own authority. Mary was a trusting soul, not especially imaginative, and she had absorbed only what was reassuring about her husband's family. His mother and sisters emerged from their letters as preoccupied with clothes and hats and health, and didn't seem in the least formidable. They sent things for the children and affectionate messages enquiring after her own health and she could be forgiven for thinking they would be her true friends, taking the place of Ann and Helen (both of whom had by then married and left Kuruman). Janet and Annie Livingstone were near her own age, and unmarried, and would be likely to take Robert, Agnes, Thomas and Oswell to their hearts. Never emotionally close to her own mother, Mary may also have entertained fantasies of becoming close to her mother-in-law.

But there was Neil Livingstone to consider. Her husband cannot have deluded her about his father, of whom he always spoke with respect but without attempting to deny his severity and rigidly moral conduct. Mary knew this was a father whose word had to be obeyed to the letter, a man who was capable of locking his young son David out of the house because he was not back at the agreed time, a man who could sleep knowing his child was shivering on the doorstep. Her own father was not such a martinet. He had never punished his children, and though a towering figure of a man he never terrified them. If the prospect of life with Neil Livingstone came into Mary's reckoning it can only have caused her hesitation.

At any rate, whether she was persuaded or simply allowed her husband to decide, she and the children left Kolobeng in December 1851, Livingstone taking them himself to the Cape to embark. Mary expected, of course, to return, and so left her house full of her husband's books, and of the furniture brought there with such difficulty, and even of his phials and bottles of valuable medicines; all helped reassure her that this was only a temporary separation. But it also emphasised how little time she had been given to spend there – she was a wife no sooner settled and organised than constantly expected to disrupt her domestic routine. Oswell, and other visitors, had described how she delighted, in her quiet way, in being hospitable and how she busied herself at Kolobeng seeing to everyone's needs. She was a woman who preferred to be in her own home, and not in other people's.

But she enjoyed Cape Town. After the long, hard journey there, it was such pleasure to be settled in what to her seemed to be luxurious lodgings between Table Mountain and Lion's Head. The family arrived looking like tramps in their worn-out shabby clothes, but Oswell had foreseen the possible embarrassment this would cause Mary (her husband hadn't, since he was never embarrassed by anything as trivial as appearances) and arranged for them all to have new outfits. Cape Town was a smart place and Oswell would not have the woman he admired so much looked down upon. Wearing the first new dress she'd had for years, Mary took the excited children round the town, eager herself to see how it had flourished since she had last been there. It had fine buildings now, and a Botanical Garden, well kept and pretty, and a few hotels which seemed impossibly grand. The streets were still sandy, though, and too many carts and traps thundered up and down them, making them dangerous thoroughfares, especially for people used to the bush. 'Mary', wrote her husband to her father, 'never was better than at present. The sea air agrees well with her . . .'

So did the easy life, the kind of life she could have enjoyed as the wife of one of the many Cape Town missionaries – all of whom Livingstone despised for not going into the interior where the real challenge was waiting. But enforced contact with these people, every one of them eager to meet him since his and Oswell's 'discovery' of the Zambesi (news of which had reached Cape Town and was already on its way to England), made him value his wife more than he already did. He was proud that Mary was, as he put it, 'impervious' to any attempt to get her to gossip. She was the soul of discretion, exactly as a good wife should be. On the way to the Cape, they had stayed in Griquatown and there he had been impressed with one woman in particular, describing her as 'a very good wife, I think, but I thought my own wife better than either of the Griquatown ladies'. But it was none the less her place to do as she was told and free him to carry on his great work.

No sooner had Mary and the children embarked on the *Trafalgar* (on 23 April 1852) than Livingstone missed them and yet again paid tribute to his wife: 'How I miss you now . . .', he wrote, 'my heart yearns incessantly over you . . . You have been a great blessing to me . . . I loved you when I married you and the longer I lived with you, I loved you better.' He worried about her health, and had already written to Arthur Tidman (Foreign Secretary of the London Missionary Society) saying:

> I should feel obliged if you [will] procure the advice of Mr Bennett or some other eminent medical man (Mr Solly perhaps) in reference to a return of the paralysis. The whole right side of the face was perfectly motionless and

drawn to the opposite side, and pains along the whole side and extremities ever since may indicate deep-seated disease.

The anxiety confessed here ran contrary to the casual way he wrote about his wife's stroke to others. If she really did have a 'deep-seated disease' then Africa was no place for her to be, and sending her to England for a medical consultation was an additional justification for the decision to separate.

Whether Mary did ever see a doctor in London is not recorded, but Tidman at least met her and organised her ongoing journey, first to Manchester, then to Scotland by train. The train in itself was a shock, as much for her as for her children, but then so was everything about arriving in England with four children and having to make every decision on her own. Her husband had always been the disciplinarian in the family, and even he had found their children hard to silence – they had been born and reared in the bush, where they were used to having plenty of space and no need to consider others. They were not well-brought-up middle-class Victorian children, used to sitting up straight and still. Obedience was so natural to Mary's own character that it puzzled her when her own children seemed to find it difficult, especially Robert. He was like his father, wilful and obstinate, and she found it exhausting to persuade him to do even the simplest things. On Livingstone's own admission, his children did a lot of 'roaring and ranting', and he complained that whereas other children slept in the burning heat of the day his did not – they were ever energetic.

Trying to control this energy became Mary's hardest task, and arriving at her in-laws' home in Hamilton (near Glasgow) was not the blessed relief she had hoped. Instead, it proved an ordeal of an unexpected, but not exactly unpredictable, kind. She never described what happened (or if she did, the letters have not survived) but it is clear that she soon left the Livingstones' house and moved into a rented cottage which she could scarcely afford. Neil Livingstone wrote Tidman a stilted and angry letter in which he enquired after our grandchildren, having no other way of getting news about them, as their mother Mrs Livingstone was pleased to forbid all communication with us no less than three different times. We received a note from her this morning which I enclose, but owing to her remarkably strange conduct ever since we became acquainted with her, we have resolved to have no more intercourse with her until their (*sic*) is evidence that she is a changed person.

If Neil Livingstone is to be believed (and the enclosed note from Mary has not survived) then this showed more strength of character in his daughter-in-law than she had ever exhibited before, or else was a sign of her desperation. In another letter to Tidman, Neil Livingstone writes:

we feel anxious about David Livingstone's children . . . please be so kind as to inform us . . . if they are at school and any other particulars you may happen to know regarding them. Mrs L. does not write to us, nor are we anxious that she should, neither do we wish her to know that we are enquiring about them, yet we do love the children much . . .

A fairly desperate situation, then, but not uncommon. The grandparents loved the children but not their son's wife. They offered, in one of the letters to Tidman, to 'receive Robert and Thomas, and put them to school' but they wanted nothing to do with Mary. She had somehow become repugnant to them and the implication was that this was entirely her own doing – she had committed some heinous crime in Neil Livingstone's eyes, making her unworthy of being his daughter-in-law. Mary, for her part, breathes not a word of criticism of her father-in-law in her own letters to Tidman. She does not even mention him. The fifteen letters she writes during this period are all to do with money and offer no explanation as to what had taken place in Ingraham Cottage, Burnbank Road, Hamilton, in the winter of 1852. But perhaps it needs no explanation: a daughter-in-law arrives tense and nervous, worn out after a long sea-voyage, in charge of four boisterous children she can barely control; she is plain, lacks charm, speaks in an unfamiliar accent (and can barely understand her in-laws) and is, in short, not what was expected; she shivers all the time and complains of the cold, though it is only autumn; she appears to have no money at all and contributes nothing to the household; and – worst of all – she *drinks*. Only a little brandy to steady her nerves, such as she has been used to since her mother recommended it, and partook of herself on sea-voyages to settle the stomach, but none the less this counted as drinking.

It may well have been only the alcohol which caused trouble so spectacular that it resulted in Mary's having to leave the Livingstones' teetotal house. 'A little brandy' was as shocking as a bottle to a Scotsman who had signed the pledge. Alcohol relaxed Mary, as it does most people, and when 'relaxed', possibly very relaxed, her nature changed – she became uncharacteristically boisterous and voluble. But there is no way of estimating how much she drank at this stage and there is no record of anyone commenting in 1852 on her drinking (though there is much unfortunate comment later). Every description of Mary which has survived up to this time stresses her calm demeanour, her patience, her kindness, her eagerness to please. Whether she drank or not, she was no drunken harpy, but on the contrary, a young unhappy wife in a strange environment struggling to look after four confused children and missing her husband desperately. From her point of view, the scenario is equally easy to imagine: forbidding father-in-law, who rarely smiles and expects total obedience, imposing a routine to which it is hard to adjust; mother-in-law and sisters-in-law very much under his thumb and afraid to side with her; a house so cold she is never warm and so cramped the children whine constantly to go out but can't, because outside it is freezing and raining, and they haven't adequate clothing; all her attempts to be pleasant misunderstood and disappointment evident on every face; no husband to negotiate on her behalf and stand up for her. No wonder she turned to drink.

At any rate, within six fraught weeks Mary had vacated the cottage she'd rented and was in lodgings in Almada Street, Hamilton. She rented one room only, for the five of them – one room in a dark, stone house in a street of similar houses.

Humbly, she wrote to Tidman: 'as you so kindly gave me permission to write to you, I now sit down . . . to tell you of my difficulties. My health has been very poor since we arrived in Scotland, but I am a little better now. We are in lodgings at £15 a quarter, independent of food and other expenses.' She tells him she cannot go on paying that but that she knows of an unfurnished cottage she can have for £7 a year. She can furnish it with help from her parents' friends and sell everything when she goes back to Africa, but she needs a contribution from the London Missionary Society. Scrupulously, she accounts for the £30 they have already given her on her arrival – £5 customs duties, £12 train journeys, £5 rent so far, £2 other expenses, stating (inaccurately) that this leaves only £5, which has to cover food. She asks for another £20 (which is granted). But then she decides to leave Scotland entirely and spends 1853 going from one set of her parents' friends to another, moving between Manchester, London and Kendal. The travelling costs money, and so does buying warm clothes for the growing children, and in spite of the generosity of these hospitable people she is soon begging Tidman for another contribution. 'I trust you will not refuse,' she writes, in February 1853, 'as I have no one else to look to.' By October of that year she is

> not able to go on for want of money . . . I would beg of you to be lenient with me, I don't attempt to justify myself, I may not have been so discreet in the use of my money . . . if you do not think it proper to give any allowance, will you kindly let me have £5 of Mr Livingstone's salary, I shall acquaint him of it.

By then, eighteen months after arriving with such high hopes in England, she had had enough. Never mind the children's education – they were getting very little education anyway in the circumstances – she wanted to go home. She hated the itinerant life and wanted to be in her own house among her own things. But even that, supposing she could have arranged her return to Africa, was denied her – her home at Kolobeng had been attacked and gutted in a Boer raid, all the furniture wrecked, the books torn up and scattered. She had no home to return to, only a tantalising image of what it had been, to which to cling. But in any case, the London Missionary Society would not send her home and her husband wanted her to stay where she was. Whatever she was suffering, he wrote to her, she couldn't suffer worse than he did, trekking from west to east across Africa on his latest expedition, or worse than the enslaved women he described to her in his letters – 'each has an iron ring round her wrist, and that is attached to a chain, which she carries in her hand.' If this, and the account of his own hardships, was meant to cheer her up, it failed.

But she was trapped in England, without the power to direct her own fate. The person to whom she might naturally have turned, her sister Helen, who had married and now lived with her family in Surrey, seems not to have extended a prolonged welcome. Helen, to whom Mary had never been as close as she was to Ann, had two children of her own and was also housing Bessie and Jane, the two youngest Moffat sisters who had been sent to England for their education. To take in her eldest sister plus the four Livingstone children may simply have been too much to contemplate. So there were no close relatives to take charge of Mary and she had to fall back on kind friends of her parents, like the Braithwaites in Kendal. She stayed with them a long time, obviously finding some solace in their uncritical company and even in Kendal itself – a small town in the middle of beautiful hills, much more congenial to her than the cities of Glasgow or London, or Manchester. The children had some freedom there, and it was healthier for them. Not for her, though. She was ill in January 1854 – 'my illness has been long and severe', she told Tidman. But at least medical attention had cost her nothing, so she wasn't begging for money to cover bills (the doctor 'kindly refused any remuneration for his services'). She was writing to tell him it was her duty 'to acquaint you that it is neither just to myself nor to you for me to remain any longer in England than the ensuing quarter'. The doctor has said she will be fit to travel in May and that the sea-voyage would in fact be beneficial. Her husband, she maintains, will meet her at the Cape in August and she will wait there for him. Revealingly, she adds: 'I have asked him to come to England, but he sternly refuses to do so, on account of this throat, which would be aggravated by the damp weather in this country.' That 'sternly' was significant and pointed – clearly, her pleas had been rejected because she was thinking of herself and not of him. But she still needed the London Missionary Society's money to get to the Cape and her request for it becomes increasingly passionate – 'I beg and entreat you . . . I have had much to try me in every respect . . . I ask . . . you not to deny my request . . . a longer residence in England will not improve me. Let me go before I do get ill again.'

May came and went and still she was stuck in England, by then at Epsom with another Moffat friend. By July 1854, she is writing in a panic to Tidman: 'I have no money whatever.' Some was sent, and she staggered on, still wretchedly unhappy, but at least not ill. Robert and Agnes were at the Quaker school in Kendal, living with the Braithwaites, and she could manage the five-year-old Thomas and three-year-old Oswell better. But mentally she was very low, ever anxious for news of her husband. Livingstone seemed to have disappeared: he certainly had not turned up at the Cape, where he was supposed to be going to meet her, and she had to wonder if she would ever see him again. Soon, she might be a widow, rather than a wife, and a widow with no means of support and no family nearby, willing or able to help her. To the London Missionary Society, she was becoming a nuisance, the wife not of a highly admired missionary but of a man whom they suspected of being more explorer than missionary (though he denied it) and whose explorations they were less and less inclined to finance. Wife or widow, Mary knew she would get little help from them. But Tidman was kind, his answers to her entreaties always gentle, and he invariably managed to persuade the directors to advance Mary something. It was never enough, and by June 1855 she was reduced to writing from Epsom: 'I have not a shilling to go on with.'

How much she wrote of her plight to her husband, and how often, is impossible to establish. Livingstone complained she never wrote to him, but even he knew that letters would find him only with difficulty, and might well be lost on the way, as were so many that he wrote to her. One of his got through, though, acknowledging a letter of hers that was a year old when it reached him. In a letter dated September 1855 (when in June that year she had not a shilling) he brought himself to apologise for 'a delay I could not shorten. But as you are a merciful kind-hearted dame, I expect you will write out an apology in proper form and I shall read it before you with as long a face as I can exhibit.' His main excuse for not joining her within the year or so he had promised was his illnesses – he had had many attacks of fever. 'I have written to you by every opportunity and am very sorry your letters have miscarried ... I cannot be long now.'

He had a different idea of 'long' from his wife. It was almost another year before news came that her husband had reached Quelimane, on the east coast of Africa, after his extraordinary trek right across the continent, exploring along the way the magnificent waterfalls he named the Victoria Falls. He put to sea at last, arriving at Dover on 9 December 1856 to a hero's welcome. Unfortunately, Mary had gone to Southampton, where his ship was supposed to land, so their reunion, in London, was delayed. When finally they met, on 11 December, Mary had something to give him. Not used to expressing her feelings in writing (she struggled even with letters), she had, however, composed a poem:

A hundred thousand welcomes, and it's time for you to come
From the far land of the foreigner, to your country and your
    home.
Oh, long as we were parted, ever since you went away.
I never passed an easy night, or knew an easy day.

Do you think I would reproach you with the sorrows that I
    bore?
Since the sorrow is all over now I have you here once more.
And there's nothing but the gladness and the love within my
    heart,
And hope so sweet and certain that never again we'll part.

A hundred thousand welcomes! How my heart is gushing
    o'er
With the love and joy and wonder just to see your face once
    more.

How did I live without you all those long long years of woe?
It seems as if t'would kill me to be parted from you now.

You'll never part me, darling, there's a promise in your eye;
I may tend you while I'm living, you will watch me when I
    die.
And if death but kindly lead me to the blessed home on high,
What a hundred thousand welcomes will await you in the
    sky!

If Livingstone managed to read it without being moved then
he must have had a heart of stone. For Mary, always so
reticent, its sentiments were overwhelmingly extravagant and
clear: she adored her husband, could not do without him,
blamed him for nothing, found happiness only with him. He
could give her what neither parents nor children could,
confidence in herself, that sense of emotional security she so
needed. And attitudes, of course, changed dramatically towards
her. Livingstone was heaped with honours – a Victorian public
hungry for excitement could not get enough of this slight, dour-
looking Scot who had triumphantly crossed Africa exposing on
the way the horrors of the continuing slave trade, tracing the
Zambesi to the sea, and everywhere identifying areas in which
missions to save thousands of souls could be established. The
great and the good, including the Queen, were as intrigued by
him as was the general public. Everyone wanted to see him,
everyone wanted to hear him. And his wife. From being utterly
neglected, except by her parents' friends, Mary was now being
fawned over by people she had never heard of. Being the wife of
a hero made her suddenly sociably desirable.

This new respect mattered hardly at all to her. She neither
hated nor loved it, remaining apparently impassive and
unmoved. Those who observed her in company at the functions
she attended with her husband, when praise was heaped on her
as well as him – and there were plenty of beady-eyed observers
about who later scribbled their impressions – were fascinated
by Mary's blank expression. She reacted to no compliment,
moved not a muscle at any applause for her. When eminent
men such as Lord Shaftesbury spoke in her honour (at the
Royal Geographical Society meeting, to award her husband the

Victoria Medal) and praised her self-sacrifice – 'she . . . surrendered her best feelings . . . her own private interests to the . . . great interests of Christianity' – or when Livingstone himself referred to her publicly as 'my guardian angel' she sat like a sphinx. A nod was the most she ever managed, when urged to acknowledge tributes. Praise belonged to her husband. She had no use for it. A wife's job was to keep in the background. In her own opinion, she had merely behaved as a good wife should. The fact that in none of the audiences who gathered to see her husband was there a single woman who had endured what she had endured was of no interest to her.

This was fortunate because it protected her from being aware of how she was patronised. Those who tried to talk to her found she had little to say and was incapable of the kind of conversation they sought. Society judged her as either dull or stupid, because of her lack of small-talk, as well as graceless. Worse, and more cruel, was how she was judged on her appearance. She was sniggered at as vulgar – not in the sense of being showy but in the sense of looking common. Then, even more than now, clothes were the measure of the man or woman, and Mary's signified that she had absolutely no fashion sense. Oswell, knowing how appalled people would be by Mrs Livingstone's tramp-like apparel, had of course kitted her out, but that was in Cape Town four years previously, a lifetime in terms of fashion. The mid-Victorian period was renowned for dresses that became yearly more extravagant and elaborate, covered in flounces and needing vast numbers of petticoats underneath. The year 1856 was when the crinoline came in – every truly fashionable woman wore one at grand assemblies. Mary had no crinoline and would not have worn one even if she had. Her figure was not made for such clothes – she had no waist to cinch in above the absurd skirt. Nor was her modest dress of silk or satin with lace trimmings: it was of a 'stout linsey' (thick cotton) and plain. She wore her unbecoming bonnet indoors as well as outside, even when other women were in ball-gowns and had their hair fashionably dressed. Remarks were made about her weight, as they always had been, and about what a sorry figure she cut as wife of the nation's most famous man-of-the-moment.

He looked little better himself, but he was a man, a missionary, a doctor and, above all, an explorer, so it did not matter that he, too, cut a slightly absurd figure in funny clothes more suited to tradesman than hero. He was judged on his achievements, not his costume, and it was in his favour that he had not decked himself out splendidly – he was given full marks for humility and modesty. Mary was given none for the same virtues in dress. Instead, she was despised for her shabbiness and for not attempting to 'make something of herself'. It was felt she let her husband down, that she was not a wife he could be proud to have on his arm. But Livingstone experienced no such embarrassment. He hadn't fallen in love with Mary's looks or clothes, and her appearance didn't matter to him now he was famous either. The public must take both of them as they found them, no concessions would be made to the folly of fashion.

And yet Mary tried to make other adjustments during this period when her husband was lionised. Her role as wife, after almost twelve years of marriage, changed and she found it difficult to adapt. When she'd been at her husband's side on the ox-wagon travelling through dangerous unknown territory, she had had to be first and foremost a stoic, a role suited to her temperament. Now, in London, being stoical was not enough. She was required to be animated in company, she needed the ability to protect him from the exhausting attentions of admirers, she wanted to be able to extricate him from tricky social encounters – and she could do none of these things. She was not, and never would become, a society wife. She was not an asset to him, as she had been in the wilds of Africa where, in every sense, she knew the language. She didn't understand fashionable London's peculiar language and was useless as an interpreter. She couldn't smooth his way or relieve him of crushing obligations. All she could do was what she had always tried (though not always successfully) to do: to provide him with a well-ordered domestic background to which he could return and be refreshed.

Nevertheless, there were some happy times for Mary during those fifteen months she and her husband were in England with their children, even though she had no more settled a home than she had had during their four years of separation. Her husband's presence was the vital factor, but money made a huge difference too. She was no longer poor to the point of not having a shilling. The London Missionary Society did not provide much, but the publisher John Murray gave Livingstone an advance to write about his travels; and once the book, *Missionary Travels and Researches in Southern Africa*, was published, it was such a huge success that more money flowed in. After all those months of moving around, staying with her parents' friends, they could finally rent a house at Hadley Green, then a pretty village to the north of London. There the children could play freely, and, surprisingly, Livingstone played with them, showing a side of himself never revealed before, while Mary supervised the running of the house, as she liked to do. England did not seem such a bleak and terrible place any more, and even when her husband went off on lecture tours she could bear it. He, on the other hand, minded not taking her, writing from Dublin that it had been a mistake not to bring her with him.

It was a mistake he knew he could not afford to make again. He must take Mary back to Africa with him, though it would mean sharing hardships more extreme than those she had yet faced. For her part, Mary could not contemplate being abandoned. It would make her ill again. But as Livingstone made plans for them to return to Africa in the January of 1858, there was the painful problem of what to do about the children, Robert now twelve, Agnes ten, Thomas nine and Oswell six. Mary could not possibly submit them to the dangers of exploring the region of the upper Zambesi, which was her husband's new ambition. It was obvious – to her, to him – that a choice would have to be made. She had obeyed her husband's decision before on this subject (rather than make a choice of her own) and had come to England with them; now, she had to think about her children and her own mental health, as well as her husband. Could she be a good mother if she were on her own, even with financial support? Livingstone, from all he had been told by observers during those previous four years (including the objective Tidman of the London Missionary Society), as well as the evidence of Mary's own account, knew she could not manage on her own. She had said it all in her poem – 'It seems as if t'would kill me to be parted from you now / You'll never part me, darling, there's a promise in your eye.' Whether there had been that 'promise' or not, he realised that to leave his wife again could well end in disaster.

But there was a new way out of the dilemma. Relations between Mary and his family in Scotland had finally improved. It had taken a death to achieve this harmony – Neil Livingstone's. He had died as his son was on the way home and, though this had distressed Livingstone greatly, it changed everything. In the test of loyalty with which he would have been faced – to his father or to his wife – it is by no means certain Mary would have won. But with Neil Livingstone dead, their differences were forgotten. Agnes Livingstone and her two daughters had, since his death, been happy to receive Mary. They would also be happy to provide a home on a long-term basis for the children while other appointed guardians looked after the financing of their care.

But it was agreed that Mary should take one child with her, the youngest, Oswell; fortunately by temperament he was the best suited to travel. To take Robert would have been insane. His stubbornness and moods had intensified during the years in Britain and he would have been a demanding companion, doomed to clash with his father. Besides, there was the question of his schooling, endlessly disrupted and only now settling down at the Hamilton Academy. Yet Mary also knew that Robert was likely to suffer most through being left behind. The most unruly and least charming of her children, he would find that with his mother gone nobody would love him enough to make allowances and give him the unconditional affection he craved. Agnes would fare much better. There had been no question of taking an almost eleven-year-old girl on such an expedition – yet to leave her would be painful for Mary. She was close to her daughter, in a way she was not close to her sons. To leave Agnes, not so far off puberty, was a different kind of betrayal. As for nine-year-old Thomas, his frequent illnesses barred him from accompanying her – his health was much less robust than the others' – but his very frailty made him precious to her. Who would give him the special tender attention he needed? He was the one, so used to his mother's care and nursing, who would find himself the most bereft physically.

It was agony for Mary to leave her children but there would have been far greater agony had she herself been left there by her husband. She could not even console herself with the thought that she would be back with them soon. Her husband had intended to rejoin her 'soon' and that had turned out to be four years. She was too experienced a traveller in and resident of Africa not to be aware that she might well *never* see them again – and then they would always know that being a good wife had been more important to her than being a good mother. Nevertheless, whatever others thought, she herself felt she had no choice – happiness, health, mental and emotional serenity, all depended on her going with her husband. Only one thing could stop her: another pregnancy. This was her greatest terror. In the autumn of 1857, at the age of thirty-six, she became pregnant again but had a miscarriage, the only miscarriage she ever had. Since she knew that pregnancy would bar her absolutely from going with her husband it is tempting to speculate that her anxiety may well have contributed to the miscarriage. Whatever the cause, she was safe – unless, of course, she were to become pregnant again before the date of departure . . .

This was set for March 1858. There was a grand farewell banquet for Livingstone during which three cheers were called for his wife. This made her feel awkward, as always among such company. In Africa, she was 'MaRobert' (the Africans called mothers by their first-born's name), respected and admired by all for her competence and skills, held by the Africans to be an eminently suitable wife for David Livingstone. There were plenty who thought him the lucky one. In England, she was that odd little fat woman, so badly dressed, so lacking in refinement, almost a disgrace to her famous husband. She was not sad to be leaving this world, but she was heartbroken at parting from her children. Livingstone too found it hard. The farewells were painful and protracted, taking place in Hamilton at the Livingstone family home, where the children were to stay. Then Mary and her husband and the excited Oswell departed for Birkenhead to board the *Pearl*. The weather was bitterly cold and as they stood on deck waving goodbye to the dignitaries who had come to see them off, flurries of snow whirled round them.

Mary was now the wife of one of Her Majesty's Consuls. Her husband had been appointed Consul at Quelimane (the town on the east coast of Africa, near the mouth of the Zambesi, where his cross-continent trek had ended). He was granted a generous stipend plus £5,000 in provisions for the Zambesi Expedition, which he now headed. He had all but severed links with the London Missionary Society, though he still considered himself a missionary. The government was sponsoring his expedition not from a noble desire to convert Africans to Christianity, but for the possible commercial gain, as his commission made plain. His parents-in-law would not be pleased – 'Christianity through Commerce' was not a gospel they had ever preached or expected their son-in-law to preach. But none of this made any difference to Mary. She was his wife, whatever new career path he had taken, at his side, as she liked to be, and ready for anything.

Except another baby.

IV

On board the SS *Pearl*, as medical adviser to the Zambesi Expedition, was Dr John Kirk who got to know Mary rather better than he had expected during the voyage to the Cape. Kirk was a shy young man, ten years younger than she was. In spite of his youth, he was an experienced doctor who had served in the Crimea and been Royal Physician at Edinburgh Infirmary before a spell at Kew researching rare plants. He'd accepted Livingstone's invitation to join the Zambesi Expedition with alacrity – Livingstone was a hero to him as to so many others. But right from the start his opinion of Mary Livingstone was not high and he seems to have developed a prejudice against her which coloured everything he wrote about her in his journal.

His first encounter with her came a week after the *Pearl* sailed, when Oswell injured his little finger, and Kirk had to cut half the cartilage off the joint. He was impressed that Oswell 'never uttered a cry' but less impressed by his mother, who was so prostrate with seasickness she could scarcely supervise her energetic son. On 11 April, a month into the voyage and the day before Mary's thirty-seventh birthday, Kirk was called to attend her and diagnosed a condition rather more serious than seasickness: Mrs Livingstone, in his opinion, was undoubtedly pregnant. The suspicion is that she must have known this before she set sail otherwise Kirk could never, within a mere four weeks, have been so certain in his diagnosis. But desperate though she was to accompany her husband, would Mary knowingly have set sail in a condition of early pregnancy? She would have realised exactly what it would mean: being left at the Cape, condemned either to find somewhere to live there or else to go to her parents in Kuruman, the very fate she had always rejected. It is far more likely that after her previous miscarriage and more recently the distress of parting with three of her children her menstrual cycle was upset, and she simply did not know. Or, of course, it could have been a case of wishful thinking: since being pregnant would wreck everything, she refused to acknowledge that she might be.

An awful birthday, then. Kirk noted unsympathetically: 'she and the young 'un will be left at Cape Town . . . I cannot but think that this is a lucky move for the expedition.' Livingstone himself did not think it lucky any more than did Mary. He was appalled at the implications, and also embarrassed. What would folk think of a fellow, a doctor no less, who got his wife pregnant at the same time as agreeing to take her on a dangerous expedition? No comments about birth control ever enter his letters or journals, but since Livingstone made a feature of keeping up with medical advances by having Mrs Sewell send medical journals out to him he cannot have been unaware that there were in existence pamphlets on this tricky subject. By this stage of his marriage, with four children, he certainly hadn't wanted Mary to become pregnant again, and the miscarriage had served as a timely warning of the ever-present danger, so it seems likely that he would then think about ways of avoiding this calamity and decide on some method, or perhaps, because of his religious beliefs, abstain from sexual intercourse. But he obviously had not abstained, so whatever his preventative tactics, if any, they failed.

In his correspondence, he shows himself in a poor light (as he often did) seeming to have little sympathy for Mary and also, in his use of certain casual phrases ('this is a great trial to me') to blame her. She would now be 'a hindrance'. And as a hindrance, she would be dumped at the Cape, because of course nothing must be allowed to get in the way of the expedition. Mary knew, for the rest of that long voyage, what would happen. She went on being sick and feeling wretched, stirring herself only to minister to her husband who in May developed a complaint which resulted in his 'opening his bowels thirty times' at night. In these circumstances, arrival at the Cape was a relief, even though for her it spelled misery.

Exactly what kind of misery was at first unclear, and now Livingstone expressed genuine concern and anxiety, though a good measure of his worry was for himself and not for her. He wanted to leave her in good hands, otherwise concern for her would prey on his mind and it was essential that he should not be distracted – all his energies, mental and emotional as well as physical, must go into leading the expedition. It was not within Mary's power to smile and assure him she could look after herself while he did his so-important work. She was sick, and incapable of deciding what to do. So once again he decided for her: she should return to Kuruman with her parents, who fortuitously had come to Cape Town to meet another ship bringing their daughter Jane home to Africa. There Mary could have her baby and once she was recovered she could rejoin him (How? No mention of that). Livingstone was vastly relieved.

The other members of the expedition, when they heard what was to happen to Mrs Livingstone, were to a man pleased. She had, in their uninformed opinion, been an encumbrance. Their hero was well rid of her. None of them had the slightest idea of her true value to him, never having seen how she aided her husband on the expeditions they had already made. (William Cotton Oswell could have told them a thing or two.) Her pregnancy was hailed as a blessing in disguise and they watched the parting of her and her husband, perhaps not with anything quite as malicious as pleasure, but with something close to it. Livingstone himself, however, seemed dreadfully distressed. 'It was a bitter parting with my wife,' he wrote, 'like tearing the heart out of one.' Mary herself was inconsolable.

Mary remained at the Cape until August, by which time she was six months pregnant and dreaded the long, rough trek to Kuruman. They were waiting not for Jane, who had arrived, but for her brother John, who was also due from England with his new wife Emily. It was almost the end of August before everyone was ready to go. A cavalcade of three ox-wagons, each pulled by a dozen oxen, set out. John's and Emily's wagon took the lead, followed by the Moffat parents', and then came Mary's. It was a terrible journey, one of the worst the senior Moffats had ever made. The rain for the first part was heavy, turning the ground to mud – 'surely we shall be drowned', wrote Emily to her father. Then, crossing a swollen river, Mary's wagon became stuck and when finally it was extricated her team of oxen began to fail – 'we do literally creep', Emily observed. She, too, was pregnant but, unlike her sister-in-law, not ill. Regularly, she got down and walked alongside the wagons while Mary cowered inside. To Emily, everything was new and exciting; to Mary, horribly familiar and depressing.

By October, Mary was drawing perilously near her time, and the nights were bitterly cold. Another of Mary's oxen died, and with three already dead she had only eight to pull her wagon. Crossing a river, one of the remaining animals became restive, kicking and plunging, and the whole span was disarranged. With unwitting irony, Livingstone wrote to John and Emily at this very time: 'I wish I had taken Mary with me. She would have been more comfortable . . .' Comfort was the last thing his wife enjoyed on that last stretch before reaching Kuruman. Emily notes, nervously, that Mary 'though far from well . . . must go on . . .' She remained in her wagon, ill, looked after by her parents and sister, simply getting through the days by doing what she had always done: enduring.

The party arrived exhausted at Kuruman on 10 November. Mary gave birth six days later to a daughter, named Anna (after Mrs Braithwaite of Kendal, to whom she owed much). It was the first time she had gone through childbirth without her husband, but she had plenty of close relations around her this time, all willing to help and support her. Apart from her capable if overpowering mother, there were her two youngest sisters, Bessie and Jane, her brothers Robert and John, and her sisters-in-law Ellen and Emily. For Oswell there was plenty of company too – Robert had two boys and a baby girl. The mission station had never been more busy, or more crowded, with two other missionary couples there, the Ashtons and the Prices, as well as all the Moffats. Yet from the moment Anna was born Mary was agitating to leave this reassuring group of friends and relatives. She wanted to join her husband and rejected the sensible idea of spending her time waiting in the security of Kuruman till he had finished his exploring.

At first, she considered going overland, through Makololo

country, with a missionary, Holloway Helmore, but this plan fell through. She was still stuck at Kuruman under her mother's rule as the new year came in, and the atmosphere was not good. Her sister Bessie was rebelling, in a way Mary herself had never done, against her mother's expectations, and Jane was not settling down well after her ten-year absence in England. At the beginning of February, Mrs Ashton died in childbirth. As if this did not cause enough misery, rumours grew that the Boers were planning to attack. Mary wanted to get away, far from the quarrels erupting between her sisters and her mother, from the tensions existing between her sisters-in-law and her mother, and from the encircling Boers who might prevent her leaving at all. But she was not going to be able to travel to the Zambesi to meet her husband. He, as usual, had moved beyond lines of easy communication and she did not know where to reach him. She had to do what she found so hard, which was to make her own decision. She decided to return to England and go on to Scotland. Shortly after her birthday in April, she was taken down to Hope Town by her brother John, and from there continued to the Cape coast where she embarked with five-month-old Anna.

Her reasoning, not so difficult to understand, was that if she could not be with her husband she could be reunited with her other children – a natural enough desire. But she had not thought out how she would manage, and seems to have suppressed all memories of how difficult she had found living in Britain. Her problems began as soon as she arrived. Even money was, after all, still a problem because, although she had access to it, she did not know how to handle it. As a wife on the three mission stations where she had lived with her husband there had not been much to handle – they were so poor that budgeting was pathetically straightforward. Her husband's small stipend came in and the list of what it should be spent on was simple, just the bare necessities. There was no rent to pay, and no bills in the European sense. When supplies ran out, they sent to Kuruman for more, to tide them over. Mary had had no training in how to run a household European-style, and unlike her mother had no natural aptitude for the task.

But far more serious than her inability to spend wisely was

her feeling of isolation in Britain. Her children, though of an age to be good company, were not enough. They kept her busy, and the baby Anna was a great physical comfort, there to be hugged and held, but like many a wife of her times, obliged to be separated from her husband, she craved adult society. She longed, in particular, for a gentle, reassuring masculine presence, a man with whom she could discuss problems, such as the children's education, some kindly man who could take the place of her husband so far as making decisions and offering guidance went. She needed a figure like her friend, the explorer Oswell, a man who would value her modesty and patience, and feel respect for her and sympathy. Such a man would not worry about their friendship being misunderstood – she was, after all, a solid, matronly figure, a middle-aged mother of five children.

The man who appeared to fill this role was James Stewart. He was a Scot, ten years younger than Mary, eighteen years younger than her husband. Tall, at 6 feet 2 inches (nearly 1.9 m) and well made, he was a young man who kept most people at arm's length and had a reputation for being aloof and distant. He'd trained as a medical missionary and, just before he met Mary, had applied to the Free Kirk Foreign Mission Committee for funds to inaugurate an industrial station in Central Africa – to develop the allegedly cotton-producing land there and convert the Africans. He was an independent spirit, in spite of his association with the Free Kirk, and determined to join Livingstone in his exploration of the Zambesi. Recommended to Mary as a suitable tutor for Thomas, now ten and still not strong enough to be sent away to school (except during his mother's absence), he saw this as providential – through Mrs Livingstone he would increase his chances of being allowed to join Livingstone himself. Mary was delighted with him. He listened to her and was willing to give advice when asked for it. She could, for example, discuss her eldest son Robert with him. Robert was now fourteen and on his mother's return had left the Quaker school in Kendal to join the rest of his family, in the pleasant house she had rented in Glasgow. There he was to train to be a doctor like his father. He started on a medical course but couldn't handle either the studying or the discipline, and to Mary's consternation simply played truant and disappeared. He was absent a whole week and when his distraught mother found him he refused to go back to medical school. She had written to his father, asking what should be done, but letters took months each way, and James Stewart, meanwhile, was at hand. When advice did come from Livingstone it was no help to her – he was exasperated with Robert and inclined to wash his hands of him, condemning his 'vagabond ways' and failing to see how his own restive spirit had contributed to Robert's waywardness.

But Livingstone had been receiving other letters too, about Mary's own behaviour. He was told by several friends that his wife was drinking enough to make her a spectacle occasionally in public. Though this meant no more than being a little unsteady and far too voluble all of a sudden, it was indefensible if true, as he believed it to be. He knew Mary drank alcohol, and he knew that their recent improvement in finances, plus an increase in the attendance at social functions at the same time, had encouraged the habit. After all, even he had succumbed, after a lifetime of abstinence, when fêted in London. His attitude to alcohol was not as rigidly hostile as his own father's had been – he knew very well the solace it could bring, and had been glad of that bottle of port wine for Mary during Oswell's birth. Women who endured what the wives of missionaries had to endure valued alcohol. Even prim Emily Moffat, Mary's sister-in-law, wrote to her father that '*entre-nous* and quite private' she had been glad of a bottle of port wine herself, and commented: 'wine is a real godsend, no matter what temperance friends say.'

Temperance friends said rather more to Livingstone in their letters and he felt obliged to take notice. Mary would have to come to him, since he could not leave the expedition to go to her. He was already being blamed for his wife's behaviour by influential friends like the philanthropist Angela Burdett-Coutts, one of the few influential women who had been kind to Mary. She wrote complaining of his neglect of his wife, and he was stung by her letter. Then there was the report from George Rae, the engineer from the Zambesi Expedition whom he had sent back to Scotland to arrange for a new boat to be sent out.

Rae, although dour, had a liking for gossip, and chose to insinuate that Mrs Livingstone's new friend James Stewart was perhaps not all he seemed. Livingstone decided Mary must join him and that Rae should bring her out.

But Mary, almost forty, was not quite so biddable. She no longer obeyed her husband without question, no longer had to be with him at whatever cost. Since her husband had left her, six months pregnant, at the Cape, her maternal duties seemed more important than her marital ones. She had finally realised what her desertion had meant for her children and that in turn allowed her to acknowledge what her husband's desertion had meant to her. All the misery of their being apart – herself apart from him, herself apart from her children – was supposed to be justified by the great work he was doing. But now she dared, nervously, to query whether his work *was* so great. She went even further, to the point of wondering how much she believed in God and in the work done in God's name. Perhaps it was all a waste of time, this missionary life, perhaps there were – the final heresy – more important things to care about, like one's own family happiness. Even without such philosophical confusion, there were so many practical matters to settle. Who would look after baby Anna, only eighteen months old and needing far more than the basic supervision given to the older children? Who would keep Robert under control?

So she hesitated, and did not go at once with Rae. Her excuse was that Anna was ill (true) and that she could not leave her yet. But then James Stewart informed her that he himself was at last going to the Cape, on the first leg of his proposed trip to the Zambesi, and this influenced her to join her husband, as instructed, after all. With Stewart accompanying her, the voyage would not be so daunting. But it was a hard decision, far harder than it had been to leave Robert, Agnes and Thomas almost four years before. Partly this was because of Anna's age – she was much younger than Thomas had been – but also partly because of having grown so much closer to all her children. Small children have their own needs but she saw, correctly, that adolescents' needs (like Robert's) were much more difficult to identify and satisfy. She worried about her baby Anna, but even more so about Robert, placing little faith in the ability of her sisters-in-law to stand in for her. She herself had not coped successfully with Robert, so how could his two spinster aunts be expected to do so? And she trusted them little more with her youngest, with Anna – they had no experience of babies. The faith she had to place in them, and in all the arrangements she had to make, brought her to the brink of cancelling her departure several times.

But in the end, good wife that she still struggled to be, she went. On 8 July 1861, she sailed with Stewart from Southampton, miserably unhappy and loaded with guilt. Her entire married life had been full of these agonising farewells, but this was quite the worst. From the beginning she was haunted by visions of Anna needing her and it was 'only with the utmost difficulty', she wrote to a friend, Mrs Fitch, 'that I can keep up heart'. But Stewart helped. He was 'kind and attentive, and will not allow me to mope'. All the same, 'my dear baby, how my heart yearns for her. I miss her so much.' There was nothing Stewart could do about that, except try to distract her. She fretted all the time over whether she was doing the right thing and could only persuade herself that she had had no real choice because she had been 'ordered' to join her husband. 'I received a letter from Livingstone dated 28 March 1861', she had written to Mrs Fitch earlier. 'In it he says, "embrace the first opportunity to come out . . ." So you see the orders have come.'

Gradually, as the voyage continued and the nightmares lessened (even if they never entirely ceased), she found some pleasure in it, once her usual seasickness was over. The captain was affable, the woman with whom she shared a cabin pleasant, and the weather good. When they landed at Cape Town on 13 August she was gratified to be 'most cordially welcomed' by missionary friends whom she hardly knew. She enjoyed showing Stewart around the town, and was of course seen doing this, thereby providing more fuel for gossip. It simply never entered Mary's innocent head that anyone could imagine she and Stewart were anything except friends; it never entered Stewart's either, but it was he who first heard the gossip and was outraged enough to pass it on to Mary, telling her that he was accused of being 'too intimate' with her. She was so appalled and furious that he recorded she left his company immediately without bidding him good-night. But she was angry rather than mortified and most certainly not cowed by this vulgar scandalmongering. Secure in the knowledge of her own incontestable virtue, she did not break with Stewart. She continued to be his friend, and proved her worth by supporting him in his attempt to go with the Universities Mission party, with whom she herself was to travel, when they sailed for the mouth of the Zambesi via Durban. Unless Stewart was allowed to accompany them, Mary said, she would not go, and if she did not go, there would be an irate Livingstone to face when they got there.

Mary's relations with this Universities Mission party (inspired, by Livingstone's example, to follow him) were already strained. She was looked down upon by its members, especially by Bishop Mackenzie's sister who had come out to Africa to look after him. The bishop had arrived at the mouth of the Zambesi in January, expecting to be taken to the new mission field by Livingstone, but had had to wait three months before going on to the Shire Highlands where nothing was as he had expected. He wanted his sister's help, and had written asking her to join him, much to Livingstone's annoyance. Anne Mackenzie was delighted to be asked, believing that, as her brother prophesied, she would be able to set a good example to the African women, of whom he had written: 'some of them [are] wild and rude, some of them worse.' Mary, brought up with African women, could be forgiven for feeling cynical about Miss Mackenzie's chances of success. This stiff, formidable Scottish lady had made it clear that she shrank from black people and thought herself infinitely superior to them. She did not really approve of her beloved brother's going among them and becoming a missionary (it was not quite a gentleman's role). Nor, in other ways apart from racial prejudice, was she suited to journeying up the Zambesi. She found heat enervating, spending days with blinding headaches lying on a sofa, and was terrified of even the most harmless insects. Within the larger party she had her own little 'household', made up of a housekeeper, Jessie Lennox, and a maid, Sarah, as well as Katie, a donkey.

From their first meeting – at the house of the Bishop of Cape

Town – she took a dislike to Mary, whom she judged far from being a lady. Miss Mackenzie knew David Livingstone's background and though his triumphs had lifted him above it, they had not lifted his wife, who looked and spoke like a lower-class woman. Then there were the rumours about her and James Stewart (whom she considered an intruder, trying to compete with her dear brother). Miss Mackenzie had heard all the gossip (from Rae, the engineer, among others) and was disposed to believe it. When finally the party, including Stewart and Mary, left for Durban, the first stage of their voyage to the Zambesi, the rumours grew and in Durban seemed to be confirmed. Mary stayed with her brother Robert, who was a trader there, but still saw a great deal of Stewart, with whom she defiantly went for walks along the beach. This was enough in itself to make Miss Mackenzie's eyebrows rise, but real damage was done one night when James Stewart was wakened by a servant telling him that Mrs Livingstone was very ill and asking him to come quickly. He went, deduced that Mary was drunk, gave her some laudanum and departed: it was not the first time he had been called in the night and responded – in Cape Town, he had done the same. But he had become tired of these emergencies, and of Mary, true friend though she had proved herself to be to him and his ambitions. He had been sympathetic to her in Glasgow, patient and attentive on the voyage out, but now that she was an embarrassment to him he had become disgusted with these scenes and had concluded that the cause of them, pure and simple, was alcohol.

But the case was neither pure nor simple. He records no details of Mary's condition, and if a careful examination of her distressed and fevered state was made he did not write it down. No medical notes were kept, and he does not mention any smell of alcohol – he just seems quite certain that, as he told Dr Kirk (who already disliked Mary), 'she drank freely so as to be utterly besotted at times'. Even if her night 'illnesses' were drunken stupors, the reasons for this 'drinking freely' were never gone into. The gossip about her and Stewart was enough in itself to drive her to drink. But what Stewart was also afraid of was that Mary had started to take him for granted. She alarmed him by showing signs of becoming dependent on him –

he had sensed that in the absence of her husband she was always in need of someone to support and guide her. He was embarrassed not only by her drinking and her leaning upon him but by her habit of expecting him to lend her money. Not well-off himself, he hated to be treated as a money-lender, especially when he was pretty sure where the money was going. The only reason he seems to have put up with it was that Mary was the wife of the man whose approval he was going to need and whose assistance he could not do without. For once in her life, being a famous man's wife gave Mary a lever, one she reached for desperately and foolishly, but without foreseeing the consequences.

By the time the party embarked for Durban in the dilapidated ship *Hetty Ellen*, Miss Mackenzie and company were frigid in their attitude towards Mary. She scarcely cared. On the contrary, she knew her hour was coming. In Cape Town, before they set off, she had written to a friend that she was expected by her husband to 'initiate them in the matter of housekeeping' – of the sort, that is, which would be needed on the journey to join the bishop and which would be a shock to their refined systems. It quite made her laugh to imagine how Miss Mackenzie, Jessie Lennox and Sarah, and also Mrs Burrup, the new bride of a missionary, would react to the conditions she knew they would have to endure. She was the only one with any experience, the only one unbothered by heat, insects and every other inconvenience the Zambesi would throw at them. And she, not they, was the wife of the leader of the expedition. She would be in her element, and they would be out of theirs.

The nearer the *Hetty Ellen* drew to the mouth of the Zambesi the more cheerful and excited Mary became. Even James Stewart was touched, and when Mary failed to make out her husband on board the *Pioneer* he kindly pointed him out, and noted her emotion. Livingstone, he thought, looked 'a great swell in white trousers' and was undoubtedly thrilled to see his wife. He felt a little sorry for the couple, unable to enjoy any privacy for their reunion, surrounded as they were by onlookers, and with Livingstone in such demand. Other scribblers were making observations too, Dr Kirk again and now W. C. Devereux, Assistant Paymaster on board the

Gorgon, the ship which had been ordered to proceed to assist Livingstone. Devereux was an intelligent young man (only twenty-four), with a keen eye, who was very curious to see Mrs Livingstone. He recorded that she was 'a motherly-looking lady' and that her husband seemed very fond of her. He was extremely impressed at how both she and her husband got up at dawn, turning out 'in easy déshabille' to help prepare for the trip up the river, setting such a good example. Neither of them stood on ceremony or pulled rank.

But Kirk had decided that Mary was 'a coarse, vulgar woman . . . cut out for rough work . . . a queer piece of furniture'. The very qualities that the unprejudiced Devereux admired in her (that she was not bothered about her appearance, worked alongside the sailors, was unconcerned about her dignity) Kirk despised. As far as he was concerned, she simply did not know how to behave like a lady, like the wife of a famous man. But he was hard to please, not to say misogynist. His estimation of Miss Mackenzie, though very different, wasn't much higher. 'She was unable to place one foot in front of the other', he recorded. 'If she decided to shift her position she had to get assistance.' The only woman in the party Kirk had any time for was Mrs Burrup, but then everyone liked her – she was pretty, cheerful and full of life.

Mary, unaware of Kirk's criticisms, was at last in excellent spirits. Her husband's pleasure in their reunion steadied and encouraged her, and she began to think perhaps it had been right to go through the agony of leaving her children to find such happiness with him again. She had told him of the malicious gossip about herself and Stewart which had circulated at the Cape and his attitude had been everything she could have wished – fury that such absurd tales should be repeated at all, sympathy for her hurt feelings, and above all complete and utter faith in her. He couldn't understand why she should have been so distressed by this nonsense. He himself was not going to give it five seconds of his time, and neither should she. As for Miss Mackenzie, he had not taken to her at all. Her very existence was a nuisance to him, and she for her part thought him 'abrupt and ungracious'. The sooner he could get rid of her and Mrs Burrup, the better.

But to do that he had to get them up the Zambesi to a point where they could go overland to join their menfolk. First he had to load them, with all the paraphernalia they had brought out for the new mission, on to the already crowded *Pioneer* which, apart from crew and passengers, was carrying sections of Rae's portable steamer from Scotland, to be assembled later and used in the higher reaches of the river. There was so little space to fit everything – it was like an impossible jigsaw puzzle – and yet Miss Mackenzie would leave nothing behind. Devereux couldn't believe how many parcels and packages she wanted transported, most of them containing useless items. Then there were the larger pieces – the mahogany wardrobe for one – which were almost impossible to store away and took so much effort to lift and manoeuvre. If the sailors had not been so willing to help the ladies – 'our fellows are continually . . . cheering and doing all they can to assist them' – nothing would have been managed. As it was, Devereux had grave doubts as to how these 'delicate creatures' would survive on the trip. 'I pity the ladies', he wrote in his journal, and said that he and others had tried to persuade them to return to the Cape before it was too late. 'It was cruel', he concluded, 'to allow them to come out here . . .'

Finally, far too heavily laden for the progress it hoped to make, the *Pioneer* got under way. The boat was low in the water and moved slowly as it negotiated its course between the slimy, muddy banks, densely covered with mangroves. The water itself was evil-looking, the colour of dirty beer, and it was easy to believe there were alligators and dangerous hippos just below the surface. There was nothing much for the women to see, except for the small shanty huts thatched with palmyra leaf and occasional groups of completely naked natives, a shock to every female eye except Mary's. Sometimes, the natives came to the ship in canoes and were allowed on board with the fruit they brought to barter. Devereux noted their astonishment at the sight of these white ladies, especially Sarah, the maid, who was considered the most beautiful. In the evening, they all ate together and Livingstone entertained the party with anecdotes of his adventures. Devereux took it upon himself to treat the company to 'a stiff bowl of punch . . . which the ladies love and want more of'. It became hotter and hotter – 120° Fahrenheit on 13 February (two weeks after they set off) – and the Livingstones were the only ones not affected. The mosquitoes were vicious, and Miss Mackenzie was bitten so badly and repeatedly that her left eye shut completely. She was heard (by Stewart) frequently enquiring if people died on boats. The nights were disturbed by the constant roars, howls and screeches of animals and nobody got much sleep, not even the Livingstones, accustomed though they were to the noises. They were in a small cabin by themselves, but this was no great privilege since it was even hotter there than on deck. Mary, though, had done her best to make it homely and never complained. She was the only woman on board who seemed relatively comfortable. The others, just as she had known they would, suffered agonies, encased as they were in tight bodices and corsets, their long dresses made even more stifling by the layers of petticoats underneath. They sweated furiously, though ladies were not supposed to do anything so vulgar, and their pale complexions reddened daily, despite the shelter of hats and parasols. Their hair was a particular trial, its sheer weight a curse in the heat, with the need to wind it up into coils or plait it, or somehow get rid of its burning bulk. Even when it was tamed into a bun and lifted off their necks, or pushed into a bonnet, the women still found it a burden, and it was the perfect resting place for insects.

None of them seemed to adapt to the climatic conditions, whereas Mary had grown up in them. Her complexion didn't redden. It was already darkened, from years in the sun, and her skin toughened. She always wore a cotton bonnet, hideously unfashionable, but it protected the crown of her head from the full glare of the sun – she had no thought of guarding against damage to her face. Utterly without vanity, she had developed stratagems over the years to keep as cool as possible and yet stay decent. Since she had no truck with fashion, tight clothes and fitted bodices were not in her wardrobe. She wore dresses as light and loose as possible, even if they exaggerated her stoutness. Miss Mackenzie, who was also fat, could not be persuaded to make the same concessions. She suffered most of all – getting dressed in the morning was an absurd performance as she struggled into her usual apparel. Dr Kirk noted irritably that part of the deck had to be screened off while she enrobed and that the business took an age.

What made the heat and the mosquito bites worse for these European women was the impossibility of taking a bath. Mary had grown up knowing how precious water was, far too precious to waste on bathing more than once in a while. Washing piece-meal was all that could be indulged in, and even then sharing water with another was obligatory. The men could risk taking dips in the Zambesi but it was unimaginable for the women. Mary did not fuss but the others longed for this most basic of comforts. No wife ever complained less than Mary about personal freshness being impossible to maintain, and that kind of femininity was never important to Livingstone any more than it was to Mary.

It was a relief when the *Pioneer* reached Shupunga House, on 18 February. This was an old Portuguese stone building, on the left bank of the river, built on a slightly higher piece of ground a couple of hundred yards (about 180 m) from the water's edge. It was only one storey, and in a poor state of repair, but it was a house with four solid walls, and seemed impressive after the cramped boat. There were trees all round it, making it pleasantly shady – lemon, orange and mango trees and a magnificent baobab measuring 75 feet (23 m) in circumference. On 1 March, there was a farewell party for Miss Mackenzie and those going on to join the Universities Mission. Devereux commented that 'with my usual ill-luck' he was 'let in for proposing the health of Mrs L.':

> I was very unprepared . . . began with stupid flattery and high compliments, holding her up to a giddy height for so devotedly following Dr L. . . . towards the middle and end found myself spluttering . . . sat down rather ashamed . . . thinking what a great ass I must appear more especially to Dr L. for the lady in question did not pay attention to it . . .

Mary was more used than the young naval officer could know to that kind of speech. She had taken no notice of Lord

Shaftesbury's praise and she took none now. The wife of a famous man simply had to become accustomed to such things, and if she had any sense, which Mary did have, rated them accordingly. She paid more attention to what was said about her husband, enjoying the praise given to him. But by then praise was not what the diarists were recording in secret. Instead, even Livingstone's most fervent admirers were having doubts about his ability to be in charge. Devereux, surprisingly, observed that he had 'rarely seen a man so easily led as Dr L.' and wondered at his distinct lack of competent leadership. Stewart, for his part, was shocked at his hero's short temper. But maybe, it was thought, things would improve once the mission party departed. It was decided that Captain Wilson and Dr Kirk would take Miss Mackenzie and Mrs Burrup ahead to meet their men, in an open boat up as far as the confluence of the Zambesi and the Shire rivers, and then on overland. They left on 2 March, and Mary looked forward to her husband's being much more relaxed now that this irritant had been removed. She even hoped to enjoy the rest of the expedition.

V

At the beginning, Mary quite relished the days spent waiting at Shupunga, as they prepared to continue upriver to the Murchison Cataracts and onwards to Lake Nyasa, but the atmosphere among the rest of the expedition party was tense. She alone had absolute faith in her husband's judgement. Everyone else was starting to think his stubbornness would lead them all to disaster – it was obvious that, with more than 300 miles (480 km) still to travel, and the level of the river falling (as it did every March) their objective would not be reached as easily as he had predicted. The new steamer, which was to be used beyond the cataracts, would have to be partially assembled and towed up the river. But Rae, the engineer, had still not even bolted the hull together and until he did so, no progress could be made. Everyone except Livingstone thought facts should be faced: they would fail to reach the Shire Highlands, this year anyway.

But Livingstone would not give up. He never gave up. If he changed plans, it was always because change was forced upon him. Mary was used to this trait of character, choosing to see it as one of her husband's strengths, and the chief reason for his previous successes. Whereas his iron determination scared others, it appears to have been reassuring to Mary, who rarely tried to influence its course. Many a wife would have seen it as her role to persuade her husband that he was being blindly obstinate and that he should rethink his position, but with few exceptions Mary was perfectly content to trust Livingstone without question – he was her man, he was her husband, he was the leader and as his wife, she was happy to follow. She undoubtedly heard the mutterings of concern, if not rebellion, but ignored them. What, after all, did the others know about the Zambesi compared with her husband? At his side, she felt superior to all of them. It never seemed to cross her mind either to do what so many wives did (and still do), which is to let him *think* he was getting his own way but meanwhile, in a subtle, behind-the-scenes fashion, manipulate him. Such wifely wiles, perhaps unfortunately, were not for Mary.

But even she, as the overwhelmingly loyal wife, had to admit there was a serious problem with supplies. When the expedition started, food had been plentiful and their meals were described with relish in the various journals. Mary was in charge of the cooking when encampments were made on the river-banks and had seen to it that everyone ate well. Devereux in particular was full of admiration for the dishes she produced from the iron pots on open fires – 'onions, venison . . . salt, coconut milk . . .' all combined to produce delicious stews and curries, and washed down with weak claret and water. But by the beginning of March, even though the Mackenzie party had left and there were six fewer mouths to feed, food was frighteningly short and complaints began. Mary was used to existing on very little if necessary, and so of course was her husband, and neither of them was particular or squeamish about what they ate – food was only fuel for the body in times of want. But food was more than that to Stewart and Devereux, and they watched anxiously as it diminished in quality and quantity. Mary, of course, had no experience of managing supplies for a large household. Stewart was appalled to find that by 8 March she had nothing to offer them but a little dried fish to be consumed with sweet biscuits. All the meat had gone. Nothing was left but flour, tea, coffee and sugar, and not a great deal of those. Mary, overwhelmed by the lack of provisions, was no longer so content.

As to the 'weak claret' that had accompanied other feasts, no mention is made of it, but Stewart rather suggestively reports at this point that 'Mrs L. said she was ill and lay on the deck most of the day' so maybe there was still some wine left at least. She worked on other days, however, even Stewart grudgingly giving her credit for tackling the washing. All their clothes were in a terrible state, soaked in sweat as well as dirt, so the pause at Shupunga was a good opportunity to get them clean. Mary's mother had never approved of what she termed 'lowering standards' by soaking clothes in the river and then spreading them to dry, but Mary herself had long ago given up on such high principles. She set about the washing with the assistance of several African helpers. At least she had soap, a commodity she had often been without on the treks she had made. It took a long time to complete the laundry, but between batches she walked with her husband round the grounds of the house, sometimes with Stewart, too, who would identify teak trees, and native ginger, and point out arrowroot growing and wild grapes.

The nights were uncomfortable, and disturbed by the chorus of hyenas and jackals all around, and, in Mary's case, by continuing nightmares about her children. These were not as frequent or as terrifying as they had been on the voyage out, but they were upsetting and not all her husband's reassurances could entirely banish them. They depressed her, and in the grip of this depression she lost hope that she and her husband would ever be reunited with the children. Always she'd sustained herself during the worst of times (and she'd had plenty of those) by looking forward to having a home such as she had had at Kolobeng, but now she saw that it would never happen. She had given everything up to be with her husband. He tried to reassure her that one day soon they would have a new home and could send for the children, but she was not disposed to believe him. She didn't believe other things either. He was shocked to hear doubts about her religious faith, which she had first confessed in letters to him, now voiced again more vehemently. This, to him, was worse than any other trial – his whole life and all he had asked of her would be worthless if his wife cast doubts on their beliefs. Her mother had once commented that Mary was never 'especially devout' but this was different. It was heresy and it horrified him. Patiently, he read the Bible with her, and prayed, late into the night, that she was once more on the path of righteousness with him. In the mornings he was often exhausted from the effort of guiding his troubled wife back to the path.

Curiously, this interlude refreshed them both. But it ended abruptly on 14 March with the return of the Mackenzie party. Their plan to join Bishop Mackenzie was never fulfilled – both the bishop and Mr Burrup had died of fever without ever reaching the Shire Highlands. The two women were brought back to Shupunga in a state of terrible grief and half-dead themselves after what they had endured on the journey upriver in an open boat. Livingstone was more furious than sympathetic, seeing the deaths only in terms of what it would mean for his own reputation (he'd be blamed for encouraging the Universities Mission and promising that the Shire Highlands were safe and healthy), and he expressed himself in some unfortunate words. Mary, though all compassion herself, did nothing to make him rephrase or retract them. She busied herself comforting and looking after the two prostrate women and impressed the crew of the *Pioneer* by 'proving to be a solid, strengthening, affectionate body upon whom Mrs B. could lean for comfort'. Officers who found poor Mrs Burrup weeping, 'hurried below to fetch Mrs L.' who 'took her head on her bosom and comforted her like a child'. It was what Mary was good at, and what she hoped some other woman would do for her own children.

After this disaster, Livingstone's decision was made easier. The grieving women would have to be escorted to the Cape, and so he and Mary would take them as far as the mouth of the Zambesi. Once there, he could collect more supplies and spend the next few fever-ridden months with Mary on the island of Johanna, off the eastern coast. By the time they returned to the Zambesi, the river would be high again and another effort could be made to get past the Murchison Cataracts. So the *Pioneer* set off, back down the river, everyone subdued and anxious to get both Miss Mackenzie and Mrs Burrup on a ship to the Cape before they, too, expired. When they reached the mouth of the Zambesi, however, there was no ship. They had to wait for the arrival of the *Gorgon*; not even Livingstone could leave the suffering women until they had been put into good hands. Meanwhile his long-term plans changed again. As soon as Miss Mackenzie and Mrs Burrup had been transferred from the *Pioneer* – 'two dark objects . . . borne on the crossed arms of two bluejackets ... not a word comes from them ... they are the ladies, not dead, but next to it ... poor Mrs Burrup covered with boils and ulcers' – the boat set off again, back up the Zambesi, with him and Mary on board.

It was 14 April before they reached Shupunga, which meant that they had been almost a month in the worst area for fever. Stewart, who had not accompanied them, had himself had malaria badly while they were away but was recovered by the time of their return. He was glad to see them. The nights had been long on his own and as the candles had run out he couldn't read. The heat was worse then ever and he was frequently wakened by 'impudent rats' and dozens of bats. All he had to eat was dry porridge oats and tea without sugar. The Livingstones brought new supplies, which was a relief, but they also brought the familiar tension. The old quartermaster of the *Pioneer* got drunk and had a fight with the engineer; and then there was the continuing uncertainty as to what exactly Livingstone intended to do. Would he still try to reach the cataracts and go on beyond them?

Meanwhile, Mary was not well. Dr Kirk, keeping his usual unfriendly eye on her, remarked that in spite of the meagre rations, she was 'getting very stout'. He seemed to hint that she might be pregnant again. He described her as having 'frequent febrile attacks consisting of flush and sweats lasting but for a few hours'. Were these malarial, or perhaps even menopausal, symptoms? She was now in her forties and an early menopause was possible. Kirk, however, had other theories. He was convinced her health had been, as he put it, 'undermined' by her 'indiscretions', both physical (drinking too much) and emotional (hearing the gossip about herself and Stewart). In short, he blamed her for her own condition. Luckily, her husband did not. He recognised fever when he saw it, but he knew there were different strains of malaria and not all of them responsive to the remedies available. Anxiously, he dosed Mary with massive amounts of quinine, but by 24 April she was no better and confined to the tent which they had pitched on the river-bank. Stewart had stopped entering in his journal that 'Mrs L. *said* she was ill' and even Kirk betrayed some genuine anxiety.

Mary lay in the stifling tent making no protest. She trusted her husband to look after her when she was ill, as he always had done, and obediently took whatever he gave her. Unfortunately, she vomited repeatedly and could not keep down medicine or anything else. Her complexion started to turn yellow and her hair was matted from the violent sweating of the fever. Livingstone tried to reduce the fever, but without success. On 26 April, at last Mary was moved out of the wretched tent into Shupunga House itself where a proper bed was prepared for her. Kirk and Stewart vacated their quarters to give her some privacy. Helping to carry her into the house, Stewart noted, 'I was struck by the altered expression of her face, but distrusted it as indicating anything serious.' Even now, there was the same prejudice against Mary, with the same uncharitable insinuation that she must be pretending and could not really be so ill.

But her husband was in no doubt that she was. He consulted with Kirk, desperate for any advice. Together the two of them applied poultices all over Mary – on her calves, on her stomach, on her neck – but she sank into a coma. Livingstone was frantic, but even in the middle of his intense distress what concerned him more than anything was that Mary might die without reaffirming her faith. He hoped that in the last few weeks he had brought her back to confidence in her religion, but he could not be sure. As she lay there, inert in the suffocating heat, her poor body ravaged by fever, by the application of poultices and by the final indignity of an enema, her husband bent over her and said, 'My dearie, my dearie, you are going to leave me. Are you resting on Jesus?' There is something grotesque about the scene, in his asking such a question of a woman who was barely breathing and who had not spoken for the last twenty-four hours, but to him it was a matter of damnation or salvation. He did not get an answer, but convinced himself that a slight upward movement of her eyes, the merest flicker, was an indication that she was indeed 'resting on Jesus'.

At seven o'clock on the evening of 17 April, an hour after dark, Mary died. Her husband was inconsolable. Nobody had ever seen him weep before but now he wept uncontrollably, first embarrassing and then frightening Kirk and Stewart. Neither of them in their journals expressed one word of sympathy for him or any regret over the death of his wife. Their entries are cold and clinical, Stewart observing how Mary's 'face after death [was] suffused with bile and even more yellow than in jaundice' and Kirk that her 'skin [was] tinged with deep yellow'. Their help was of a practical variety only. It was important, in that climate, to bury Mary as quickly as possible and they set themselves to see to it. The weather was 'dull, heavy, leaden' wrote Stewart, with black cloud massing to the east and a thick mist creeping ominously over the flatlands to the north. A grave was dug, very deep because of the fear that wild animals would dig the body up, and a rough coffin hammered together (though the ship's carpenter himself had fever and the job had to be done by Rae, the man who had spread the gossip about her). The grave was at the foot of the giant baobab tree, which alone gave some grandeur to the otherwise pathetic scene. All the way through the simple, hurried ceremony, which Stewart conducted, the geese screamed around the house, a final eerie salute to Mary. Four sailors mounted guard round the grave while a stone cairn was built over it. And now, for the first time in his life, Livingstone said he was willing to die himself. Without his wife, there was for the moment no joy in living.

Still in a state of shock as well as grief – because the fever had advanced so rapidly and he had not thought until the last two days that Mary would die – he applied himself to writing necessary letters. In all of them he expressed himself in almost the same way, though it was only to his eight-year-old son Oswell that he confessed he was writing 'with my tears running down my cheeks'. He went over, in each letter, the course of Mary's illness, emphasising its unexpectedly speedy nature, and over and over again repeating that he believed she knew she was dying and that she died full of faith. He made no attempt to hide his desolation, particularly in the letter to his mother-in-law with whom he had so often had disagreements over his treatment of Mary. 'My dear mother', he wrote:

> With a sore heart I give you the sad news that my dear Mary died here on the 27th. This unlooked for bereavement quite crushes and takes the heart out of me.

Everything else that happened in my career only made the mind rise to overcome it. But this takes away all my strength. If you know how I loved and trusted her you may realise my loss . . . There are regrets which will follow me to my dying day. If I had done so and so – etc. etc.

It was very rarely that he had acknowledged regret over anything, and never to his mother-in-law. But it was to a friend rather than a relative that he wrote not just of his sorrow and regret but of his true appreciation of what Mary had been, a good wife *par excellence*, the 'faithful companion of eighteen years' who when he looked back had worked so hard:

At Kolobeng she managed all the household affairs by native servants of her own training, made bread, butter and all the clothes of the family; taught her children most carefully; kept also an infant and sewing school – by far the most popular and best attended we had. It was a fine sight to see her day by day walking a quarter of a mile to the town, no matter how broiling the sun, to impart instruction to the heathen Bakwains. MaRobert's name is known throughout all that country and 1800 miles beyond . . . A brave, good woman was she.

Nobody, receiving these letters, was in any doubt how much his wife had meant to him. But what was not so clear was whether Livingstone realised how he had exploited Mary's natural tendency to obey and to put him first at all costs. He had expected far too much of her, justifying his expectations on the grounds of his great work. His dedication to it had robbed her of the opportunity to enjoy the quiet, married life she was made for.

His grief was profound and in his personal journal he tried to examine the change he felt had taken place within him. 'It is the first heavy stroke I have suffered,' he wrote, 'and quite takes away my strength. I wept over her who well deserved many tears. I loved her when I married her, and the longer I lived with her I loved her the more.' It was what he had said to her in a letter early in their marriage, that he had always loved her (no matter what people made of their marriage, branding it as one of 'convenience'). This love had not only grown but, as he now realised, become part of his own strength. Mary, his *good wife*, had made him feel complete. Her loss was his 'first heavy stroke', far worse than witnessing baby Elizabeth's death, or being attacked by a lion, or failing in his duty to make many converts. No other sort of adversity compared with it and he felt he had never been so sorely tested before. His misery burst out on the page – 'Oh Mary, my Mary! How often we have longed for a quiet home . . .' But it was she who had longed for it, he who had denied it to her, and the guilt lacerated his conscience.

The worst possible people for him to be with were Kirk and Stewart, one of whom had never liked Mary and the other who had grown to dislike her. All they were good for was to help him sort out her things. In the end, he had to leave them to do this themselves – he had not the heart. He tried 'for an hour', wrote Stewart, 'then says I can't stand it'. He was visibly, for the time being at least, a changed man 'peculiarly communicative and agreeable'. Stewart's opinion was that 'his recent loss seems to have had some effect of a softening kind on him'. This new 'softness' was remarked upon by all, but to Livingstone himself it was not softness but that loss of strength he had noted – he no longer felt invincible. As he wrote to Mary's brother John, 'I had got so into the habit of feeling her to be part of myself I did not fear but she would hold out.' They were a unit, strong together, man and wife joined for ever. Now that she had died, his own hold on life felt loosened. In spite of the long separations they had had during their eighteen-year marriage here was the evidence, in his letters and journal, that she had been essential to his sense of self, something no one had suspected. He had always seemed supremely independent and tough, obsessed with his work. Unemotional, self-disciplined, hugely ambitious, fearless – how could such a man be thought to *need* a wife?

The future looked infinitely bleak. What was a man who had lost such a wife to do? Find another? The idea never seems to have occurred to him. Much was later made of a comment he made years after Mary's death that he wished he had remained single, but I believe this was misinterpreted by Mary's detractors. The reason he wished he had remained single was twofold: guilt over what he had put his wife through, and despair after she had died. His marriage had brought him feelings he had never known; joy and pleasure, which he had lacked before he married Mary. His capacity to experience such light-hearted emotions had been buried so deep that he had hardly known it existed. Mary matched him in the strangest way – neither of them was fun-loving, both were known for their gravity, their serious demeanour, but together they could ignite joy in each other. Writing to a friend whose daughter was to be married, months after Mary's death, he wished the young couple 'as much pleasure as I enjoyed during eighteen years with my wife'. Enjoyment, pleasure, where would he find them now? In his journal, a month after her death, he remembered their pleasure in each other: 'I said to her a few days before her fatal illness, "We old bodies ought now to be more sober, and not play so much." "Oh, no," said she, "you must always be as playful as you have always been; I would not like you to be as grave as some folks I have seen."' The idea of his being *playful* with his wife would have astonished those sober folk (Stewart, Kirk) with whom they had lived at such close quarters. It might even have disgusted them.

The playfulness had gone. Only his children could give it back to him, in a different but still meaningful way, but he was a long way from them. Another two years went by, two years of more valiant exploration ending in the Zambesi Expedition's being ignominiously recalled, and reckoned a failure since no suitable places to establish either missions or trading stations had been found, before he was reunited with them. He had never seen Anna, the baby his wife had been compelled to leave in charge of her aunts in Glasgow, and the other children had grown so much that he felt he was meeting them all for the first time. It brought home to him at last how much they had suffered in losing a mother, just as much, if not more, than he had in losing a wife. But he did not give them a new mother. He never remarried.

David Livingstone had the wife he wanted. Mary Livingstone

did not have the husband she would have preferred. She never had a fault to find with him as a man, and was supremely happy to be with him, but as a husband he made of her a wife who was constantly called upon to obey too much and to her own detriment, eventually fatally. She never thought she had much choice when it came to the big decisions. Her husband said he had to go into the interior of southern Africa and so she went with him because she felt unable to function properly without him; he said she had to go to England with the children because they were hindering his work, so she went, dreading her fate; her husband summoned her to the Zambesi and she answered his call though knowing her children should have prior claim. At every turn her interpretation of 'wife' was 'one who obeys', which in her case meant following her husband to the ends of the earth, or at least the Zambesi, exposing herself, in his name, to extreme danger.

She was not alone – there was nothing unusual about Mary Livingstone as a wife in the mid-nineteenth century except the degree of obedience she gave. The wife as the chief mainstay, the 'rib', the 'main spoke in the wheel', the 'guardian angel', was an accepted image. The Victorian wife had few opportunities to define her role in any other way.

The doctrine of separate spheres for women and men prevailed and the woman's was domestic. The circumstances of Mary's marriage were exceptional but her status within it was mirrored in millions of other Victorian marriages. A bad marriage, in which a wife was not content to be as submissive as Mary was, or in which a man abused his power, was a hell from which there was virtually no escape. Spinsterhood, nevertheless, was rare. The vast majority of women preferred to risk marriage rather than remain single. Very few were prepared to believe Harriet Martineau the spinster was speaking the truth when she swore she was 'the happiest woman in England' (because 'the older I have grown . . . the more serious [I see] . . . the evils . . . of married life') but instead agreed with Queen Victoria, who said that 'being married gives one one's position which nothing else can'. It might turn out to be a position of absolute dependency, but it was still sought for precisely that reason.

Men, of course, also saw themselves as dependent, but in their case on making the right choice – marriage was risky. As the popular ditty ran:

> In many a marriage made for gold
> The bride is bought – and the bridegroom sold.

Men were led to believe that women would do anything to become wives and that they must therefore be on the look-out for every kind of trick. They must be suspicious of beauty – 'no man is so much to be pitied as the husband of a professional beauty' – and of wealth – 'the girl who brings to her husband a large dowry may also bring habits of luxury learned in a rich home'. A potential bride's intelligence must also be checked out. No man wanted a wife too obviously clever, one who would perhaps make him look stupid, but a foolish wife would also be a disaster for him because she would be incapable of running a household properly. All the handbooks on marriage at this time agreed that the qualities wanted in a wife were those of patience, frugality, punctuality, gentleness, charm and what was enigmatically described as 'a genius for affection'. Thackeray put it well: 'What we [men] want for the most part is a humble, flattering, smiling, child-loving, tea-making being, who laughs at our jokes however old they may be, coaxes and wheedles us in our humours, and fondly lies to us through life.' But even if such a paragon could not be found, marriage was still reckoned desirable for a man as well as for a woman. Dr Johnson was one of many who pontificated that 'marriage is the best state for man in general; and every man is a worse man in proportion as he is unfit for the married state'.

Judged by the standards of her own time, Mary Livingstone was undoubtedly a good wife. The ways in which she was considered by some not to score so highly were trivial: her appearance and clothes let her husband down in society, her drinking threatened to disgrace him, her friendship with Stewart called her reputation into question. But judged by other standards, those of our own time, Mary was not a good wife at all. She was a foolish wife, if a loving one, an indictment of all that was wrong with the stereotypical role of wife. Passive, humble, self-deprecating, with low expectations of her own rights, she makes the calling of 'wife' seem like a punishment. All the dreadful things that happened to her were because she was a wife. And yet her selflessness and that terrifying obedience of hers still lend her a certain dignity, a dignity and heroism she would never have attained without being married. She could never have been a 'partner'. Her relationship with Livingstone had little of that balance. He didn't want a partner. What he wanted was what he got, total commitment from an adoring wife. If she had been a partner, his whole life would have been different.

And so, of course, would hers, and the lives of her children. Livingstone sacrificed his family's happiness and security in the cause of his own self-fulfilment. Even after his wife's death, he did not go home immediately to his grieving children, (and when he did, he soon left them again) though he wrote to them much more often, constantly telling them how he loved them and how he mourned their mother. When he died, in 1872, soon after Stanley found him near Lake Ujiji, he had done nothing to compensate them for the loss of a mother who had chosen to put *him* first, and not them.

Reflections

There are very few points at which my experience as a wife touches Mary Livingstone's and yet there are some, some things that haven't changed much and which unite all wives. In-laws, for example. A wife has to face taking on her husband's family. Most women, unlike Mary, have met their prospective in-laws before they marry and a delicate and threatening business they find it. A wife automatically becomes part of a new family, when she takes its surname in place of hers, in a way a partner does not. She has to adapt, but Mary didn't or couldn't.

Unlike Mary, I met my parents-in-law long before I became a wife. It wasn't a meeting which went well. The very first meeting doesn't really count – it was New Year's Eve 1956 and the Davies house was crowded with people – but a week later I was taken to meet my future mother- and father-in-law properly. I can't say I was nervous, not being of a nervous disposition, but I was certainly curious, certainly aware, too, of how important this introduction was. I didn't then intend ever to get married, but I knew I would have to become involved with his family if, as we did intend, we were going to live together. Since his father was an invalid (he had multiple sclerosis and was by that time bedridden) his mother was the more significant parent. I had an image in my head of what she would look like: small, slight, dark-haired. Only the dark hair was right. She turned out to be tall and heavily built and looked nothing like her son except for her colouring. Her first words to me were, 'Would you like a cup of tea?' If I'd merely declined the offer politely that would've been bad enough – tea in this Scottish household was the magic word, the key to friendship, the essential social lubricant – but, stupidly, I found myself not only saying that I didn't want tea, but adding the inexplicable and offensive words, 'I hate tea.'

It was so unnecessary. Why on earth did I have to say it at all? I saw incredulity in Mrs Davies's face. 'You hate tea?' she gasped. 'But everyone likes a nice cup of tea, it's good for you, I've never heard of anyone hating tea . . .' She didn't know what to do. Hospitality demanded that the kettle be boiled, the tea-pot filled, the cups and saucers laid out, the milk and sugar brought, the sublime liquid poured. I'd made our meeting awkward. By insulting tea, I'd insulted her. Tea-less, we sat and tried to chat. Every remark I came out with damned me further in her eyes and it was all my fault. The trouble was, I could never let a pleasantry pass or respond to one with another, simple enough you'd have thought. 'It's been a nice day,' Mrs Davies offered, 'quite warm.' And I had to say, 'I don't like this kind of weather, it isn't warm actually, it's muggy. I like bracing weather.' Mrs Davies sniffed, helplessly, and said, 'Oh. Well.' So it went on, each exchange more excruciating than the last.

I got on better with Mr Davies, which was not what I'd expected. He was in a little front room, mainly confined to bed. The MS had not only made him unable to walk but had by then also affected his speech and eyesight. Whenever someone new came into the house, I later learned, he was always on his best behaviour, very much wanting to see and talk to visitors, many of whom found it quite hard to make out what he was saying. I managed fairly well. He'd had his wireless on when I was taken in and whatever programme it was gave me something to talk about. Oddly, I felt more at ease sitting at his bedside than I did in front of Mrs Davies, and I noticed she seemed surprised and pleased that I'd stayed with him so long. But I left the house knowing she and I were opposites – there was going to be no instant rapport. I imagine Mary felt much the same, in her case with disastrous consequences.

Later, after I'd become her son's wife, I tried hard to gain my mother-in-law's approval, though I'm not sure she would have thought so. I know that for years and years she didn't think I was the right wife for her son. She never, ever, said so and she was never, ever, hostile – she was much too benign a person for that. She wasn't jealous, either, she wasn't struggling to compete with me for her son's affection (and in fact, much though she loved him, it was her twin daughters who were far the more important to her). But all the same she let little hints drop, some of them funny. 'Keep £100 to yourself,' she told me, and when I asked why, she said, 'So you can run away.' Then, on another occasion, after she'd heard me yelling in some argument, she murmured that Hunter needed calm, because of his asthma. I wasn't calm, dear me, no. I was too volatile, too aggressive, and it worried her. Raised voices distressed her and she always read sinister undercurrents into what she heard. A wife should never shout, especially at her husband. She herself never shouted. And a wife should never call her husband stupid; that was unforgivable.

The only way I scored any points at all was by being a good, Mary Livingstone-style housekeeper, but one with more financial sense. She stayed with us often and marvelled at the speed with which I could clean the house and prepare good meals. She was slow and I was quick, and she was impressed; she was always in a muddle and I seemed organised, and she sighed with envy; she found making decisions (as simple, say, as what to have for tea) agony and I decided things, wrongly or rightly, in two seconds. She knew her son was being beautifully looked after in a practical sense and this relieved her. (Orderliness was after all also good for his asthma, a well-regulated existence extremely soothing.) I made a fuss of her when she stayed and since no one had ever done so, except for her beloved daughters, I think, this touched her. I took her tea in bed in the morning, together with the mug of boiling water she always needed to drink first ('for the bowels'). I told her to put her feet up and become a lady of leisure – though this was a mistake. She felt uncomfortable when idle, endlessly drifting round the house, looking for jobs to do. I learned to let her do them. The way she did them was not how I did them. Everything would take her ages and she'd get in a great mess doing the simplest task, though it would be done to far higher standards than my own. Cleaning drains was her speciality. I'd occasionally chuck a bucket of boiling washing soda down, followed by some disinfectant, and that was that, but she'd lift the grid off the drain and go back and forth with brushes scrubbing inside as far down as she could get and then there would be much scraping of the grid itself with a variety of implements which she would collect around her and end up tripping over. I couldn't bear to witness all this and had to go and hide till she was finished.

But we made a go of our relationship over the decades. Both of us wanted to, both of us thought we had a duty to, so we did, overcoming differences of temperament and clashes of personality. I admired my mother-in-law – anyone would have done so, when she was so kind and had performed marvels against the greatest odds, to bring up her family almost single-handed. But there were some tricky moments. She could feel isolated sometimes and become paranoid. With her daughters around, she was invincible, but alone with us before we had children she could occasionally feel squeezed out. Once, in the middle of Hampstead High Street, after a silly incident over a banana (she'd wanted to buy over-ripe ones, I'd said they were uneatable, and Hunter had agreed) she said, 'I'm going home, I'm not wanted here,' and she suddenly crossed the road and started walking away. We ran after her, apologising, begging her to forgive us, ready to thrust a ton of black bananas into her arms if it would persuade her to stay. I remember feeling absolute panic at the thought of her going back home to Carlisle (though she'd never have managed it). I felt a total failure as a wife – it was awful to have caused such unusual anger. But she was quickly mollified and the little storm blew away with, what else, a nice cup of tea.

Nothing is said in the marriage service about its being a wife's duty to be a good daughter-in-law, but it is implicit in the contract. No one 'takes' a husband on his own, unless he is an orphan – the bride 'takes' his family too. I never thought that was unfair, though I can see some wives might. My husband owed an incredible amount to his family, especially to his mother.

But how I would have coped with Neil Livingstone, I dread to think.

*

Most of Mary's years as a wife seem so desperately serious that it was a relief to find her touching on an essentially frivolous duty, one I could identify with strongly: trying to choose David's clothes. She couldn't bear his always looking scruffy and, though no stylist herself, she saw it as part of her duty as a wife to try to smarten him up, hence the plea to his sisters to send a new jacket.

I know how she felt, and yet at the same time I can't agree with her. I wish my husband didn't seem to concentrate most of the time on trying to look like a tramp, but if that's how he wants to look, fine. 'How do I look?' he asks as he is leaving the house. 'Like a seedy old tramp,' I say, to which he always replies, 'I think I look very nice,' and I reply, 'Fine,' again, then this little charade is over. I *care* how he looks, but I don't care enough to do what Mary did, and many wives still do: try to make him get some decent clothes. Plenty of wives see shopping for their husband's clothes as one of their wifely duties. I don't. I might buy him an article of clothing as a present occasionally, but that's it. It's bad enough shopping for myself without the boredom of trailing round shops for him. He can do it himself, but he rarely does and then he has neither the patience nor the interest to search for what he wants. He regularly buys what he does not want just to have the task over with. He even buys things he knows won't fit. 'You're a 36-inch waist,' I point out when he comes home with a new pair of trousers, size 34. 'I know,' he says, 'but they didn't have size 36.'

What he likes to wear are not trousers anyway, but shorts. All the time. When he was a boy, he longed to get out of short pants and into long trousers, but now he's a man he says he hates trousers. He has six pairs of shorts, ranging from what are solemnly called Town shorts to Gardening shorts, and all of them would give even Mary Livingstone a fit. They are all virtually the same in style – style! – but different in colour and with slight variations in type of material. He buys them from Lands End's or Hawkshead's mail-order catalogues. Enough said. He wears them with a collection of vile T-shirts, unless he is trying to look smart when he wears them with short-sleeved seersucker shirts (yes, same catalogues). On his feet he has sandals. 'They are Reeboks,' he says, and waits, in vain, for my admiration. I don't care what they are, they are awful. He spends every walk we take together stopping every ten yards to fiddle with the fastenings. Sometimes, he wears socks with them and then I absolutely refuse to accompany him. When it rains, he pulls over his feet but *under* his sandals a pair of thin, green, rubber galoshes. He looks exactly like a caricature of a frog and the noise his feet make is dreadful.

In the winter, the clothes situation is even more dire. It is a matter of the Coat. This is an extremely heavyweight, good-quality herring-bone tweed coat, bought at what he thinks of as vast expense some years ago at Aquascutum. It was far too big for him when he bought it and at sixty he wasn't going to grow into it, as I felt obliged to point out. After he'd tripped up a couple of times, because it was so long, he took it to our little local dry-cleaning shop to have it shortened. There was a woman there, never actually seen, who did alterations. What-ever the alteration required, her Greek husband, who fronted the shop, always confidently announced, 'She do it.' She did it. It made very little difference. He still looks drowned in it, but he loves it. 'I look distinguished in it,' he says. He wears it with a woollen hat, the sort men wear on building sites. When it rains, the coat smells like a wet dog. But he is happy. The marvellous thing is, what a good self-image he has. Now why, in that case, should I bully him to change his clothes? A good wife, in my opinion, makes it clear what she thinks her husband looks like, but only if asked, then stays silent.

Sometimes, my clothes-conscious, elegant daughter says, 'Mum, why do you let him go out like that?' I say because it isn't my business to dictate what he should wear. 'But he *can* look good,' she wails. True. He can look good. In a suit. He loathes suits, however, making the most absurd fuss about wearing one, except for a battered off-white thing he boasts is a designer item (the designed part being the thousands of wrinkles in the material which gives this suit the appearance of having been slept in). But it isn't this suit I'm thinking of. The suit he looks good in is a dark suit, worn with a pristine white shirt – which transforms him. I think he's worn it twice since I bought it for him years ago – a birthday present less than rapturously received. He wouldn't wear it for his son's wedding, a Christmas wedding, but clung instead to his white summer suit which next to the bridegroom's Paul Smith number looked even more of a rag than usual.

But I leave him to dress as he likes, not as *I* like. I am not his mother, he is not a child, and I am not, just because I am his wife, responsible for his appearance. I don't want to be. I reject this as being part of my role. I reject, too, that the way *I* dress should reflect on him. Those criticisms of Mary because she didn't look as a famous man's wife should were based on the pernicious idea that a wife's appearance should enhance her husband's reputation and standing. It's an idea still heavily in evidence. Look at what the wives of recent Prime Ministers have had to put up with – poor Norma Major, sneered at for wearing the same blue suit two days running when her husband won the election, and Cherie Blair, ridiculed for a pair of trousers worn to some public event as well as for countless other so-called sartorial gaffes. Wives are still thought of as trophies, which have to glitter and shine and do credit to a husband by the way they look. It takes a brave wife to ignore the sniping and rise above the attacks.

I've never had to, but on those few occasions when I've attended functions as a wife, I've never worried about how I will look, though I've always taken trouble. I like clothes, though I don't like shopping for them. He always seems pleased with how I look, but I doubt if I would change if he didn't. He did once say, many years ago, that he wouldn't like me to have grey hair, which I thought a liberty and laughed. When I was fifty-five, the first grey hairs started to appear and as a joke my sister-in-law gave me one of those easy-to-use colour rinses. I'd always wished that when I was young I'd had the fun of dyeing my hair the way one of my daughters dyed hers as a teenager – a wonderful purple, then green, then orange – so I used these rinses until I was sixty. Then I thought, this will become serious soon. The rinses won't be enough in a year or so because the grey is gaining ground. So I stopped. He now has a growing-daily-greyer wife. I haven't asked him if he minds being seen with me and as yet he hasn't dared to say he wants me to dye my hair. Luckily, he professed not to like make-up so he accepted my unpainted face, though I do recall that he expressed the solemn opinion when I was twenty that he thought the time would come, around the age of forty, when I might benefit from it. Forty came, and though I might have benefited I didn't choose to.

I remember only once, and that was before I was married, feeling distressed because I knew I looked wrong and – I can hardly bear to acknowledge this – *let him down* by my appearance. It was a ball, in his final year at Durham University. I'd never been to a ball (nor ever wanted to go, except out of curiosity) but was told evening dress was essential – he'd be in the full rig-out, and I should wear a long dress. I didn't have a long dress, so I made one. I couldn't sew, but in Carlisle in the 1950s there were few dress shops and none had the sort of long dress I liked or could afford. I bought yards of blue taffeta and set to. I looked terrible in the resulting horror but, by God, it was long, long and full and sleeveless and entirely wrong for me. I could hardly breathe and tripped up when I walked and I felt a fool. I scowled even more than I usually do and the whole night was the most awful ordeal. He said I looked lovely and he knew I knew he knew it was a lie. Never again. Thank God, times have changed and women can wear anything and even if I had to go to another ball – as if! – I wouldn't have to wear a long dress. But fate has been kind to me, shielding me from the kind of scrutiny a public wife still faces.

Mary's dependency upon him was a great trial to David Livingstone. In one way, a Victorian way, it was also, of course, flattering – he was the strong man, the paterfamilias, she was the little woman who needed him. Better by far was the kind of wife Livingstone's mother-in-law had proved to be, able to function perfectly well on her own. Robert Moffat never needed to worry that everything would go to pieces when he left his wife in charge. He knew it would not.

I think a good wife is very definitely an independent wife, one who does not rely entirely on her husband for sustenance of every kind. It makes me uneasy somehow to hear the words 'I can't do without him' from any wife. I feel that she should be able to do without him even if that is not doing as well as when she is with him. It isn't so much a matter of being able to run a household herself in all the practical ways but in being able to stand alone mentally and emotionally if necessary. Mary's inability to keep herself together when apart from her husband was finally a terrible handicap and made her a bad wife for him.

Maybe I go too much the other way, maybe I am too much of a Mrs Moffat and a threat to a husband's ego. I've been too fond of being determined to manage on my own even when I've known I was struggling – independence has been of such vital importance to me that I've perhaps made it into a rod with which to beat my back. 'Please help me' are not words I've found easy, which has often made me a foolish wife and not a good one. Husbands should not be allowed to think their wives can do everything. I learned at last, though only after several years, that however kind my husband was, however amiable and willing, he did indeed have to be programmed to help – it was up to me to carve out the time to myself which I needed. So programme him I did. I stole Mondays from him when family life was at its most hectic. It was his day off then, since he worked on a Sunday newspaper, and I handed the children over to him for most of the day. It gave me about six hours on my own and I seized it deliriously. If I didn't actually leave the house I pretended to do so – left loudly, door banging, and then sneaked back in and up to the top of the house where I lurked contentedly. What a way for a man to spend his day off, some people might think, but I didn't and neither did he. He hadn't suggested this little plot, though. I had. He'd only readily agreed.

But I've never claimed the same kind of emotional ground as Mary did in her poem. During bad times, I seem to have to battle away in my own head, to close up rather than open up, which is not to say that he hasn't done everything possible to help but more that nothing much *is* possible. I can't look to other people, not even to him, to whom I am so close, for that sort of help.

The worst part of being a wife such as Mary Livingstone was the way in which she seemed forced to put being a wife before being a mother. I've never had to face the agonising choices she had to make, but I've always known I would have put the children first in any clash of loyalties. Easy to say, at this distance of time, that I could never have left Anna behind, that I would never have obeyed those 'orders' that came. Some wives, though, still make that choice today, feeling there is no alternative, that they have to go with their husbands and leave their children behind (if they are diplomatic or service wives, for example). Like Mary, they are able to put husband, marriage, before the needs of the children.

For wives like me, those women who haven't been put to the test, there are only the small battles of allegiances, but these can be quite telling. Being a good mother seems to me so much harder than being a good wife – I've worried so much more about the welfare and happiness of my children than I've done over my husband's. He's big and strong (well, not very big or very strong, but still . . .) and can take care of himself. They couldn't when they were young. I found it almost impossible to leave them when they were babies, which he found annoying – surely finding someone to be in the house in the evening for three or four hours while we went to the cinema and had a meal in a restaurant wasn't asking too much? No, it wasn't, but the baby might wake and scream and the babysitter not know what to do. All the more reason, said he, to go out regularly so that the baby becomes accustomed to the babysitter – oh, he was so sensible and I was so silly. I tried. The sitting tenant in our house, Mrs Hall, had a friend who had been a nurse. This friend, always referred to as 'Nursey', came and went all the time and often paused in the hall to admire my baby. Why not ask Nursey to babysit? She was delighted to oblige. Aged seventy, but seeming fit and strong, she was duly collected from her flat by car and brought to our house to babysit. I left milk, and precise instructions as to where we would be, and off we went to the cinema in Camden Town. Halfway through the film, the manager walked down the aisle, shouting 'Emergency call for Mrs Davies! Is there a Mrs Davies with a baby?' I was out of my seat in a flash, rushing in a panic after the manager who had disappeared once he'd made his startling announcement. Nursey had phoned to say my baby was in agony and I should come at once. The drive home was torment – but the moment I picked her up, I knew there was nothing wrong with her. She stopped screaming at once. Nursey was shame-faced but defiant – never, it seemed, in all her years of experience had she seen a child so demented. We never, of course, used her services again, but it took me a long time to learn to laugh at the absurdity of the incident.

I got better about the babysitting problem eventually, but not much better. There were teenagers in plenty wanting to earn money, and other people's *au pair* girls too. I never really trusted any of them (and when years later my own children were babysitting I couldn't credit that they were trusted either). Clearly, I had what would be termed 'separation difficulties', having confidence only in my own caring. That may have made me a good, if over-protective, mother but it made me a bad wife. *He* had no trouble leaving his babies with someone else – he simply couldn't understand my attitude. More important than trips to the cinema were the chances of going away for weekends. I refused absolutely to go abroad without my children when they were very young. Trips were offered to him, journalistic freebies, fun weekends to the south of France, or New York, but I would never go. I put what I thought of as the best interests of my children before his pleasure. And he didn't like it. Husbands don't. They dislike playing second fiddle to their own children, however devoted they are as fathers. They don't see the need for it or the sense. Many a tussle we had over this sort of thing, especially when times were rough, when we had nights so broken they just ran into the days and there was no sleep ever to be had. Then I would be told that what we needed was a week in the sun away from bawling babies. He was right. We did need it. But I couldn't do it. There was no one I could trust who was available to take my place, and I wouldn't engage a stranger from an agency no matter how brilliant the references. I couldn't go. I wouldn't go, not for years and years. So far as I was concerned, being a good-enough wife never included giving way to a husband's wishes if these might mean upsetting a child by leaving it.

It's hard to justify. It sounds so ridiculous now. But it is how I felt at the time. To have been put in Mary's position would have crucified me. I would have refused to go, I know I would, and the knowledge that David Livingstone might have had, in those times, the *power* to make me leave my baby is too painful to contemplate. Without money Mary had no power and no apparent choice. So when I state so stoutly that I would never have left my children, as ordered, to join my husband, what would I, realistically, have been able to do? Go on being ill and unable to travel, I think. Subterfuge was the only resort of the good wife in Mary's situation. But then there is the other side of the coin: she *wanted* to be with her husband at least as much as she wanted to remain with all her children. The idea that she could, as his wife, exert enough influence on him to force him to arrange his work so that they might all be safely together never occurred to her. She couldn't challenge him. She didn't have the courage. And being a good wife is surely about making those kind of challenges, not allowing the husband to believe that *his* work, *his* wishes, *his* convenience are more important than the needs of his children. It isn't a question of wanting him to sacrifice his ambition, or his sense of a higher duty, on the altar of family harmony, but of expecting him to accommodate what becoming a husband and father really means.

Nothing in the marriage service gives a job description of the role of wife and yet the tasks she is expected to accomplish, then as now, are many and varied in a way for which no woman can be prepared.

Mary had to take on far more than her share of jobs within the marriage simply through the force of her circumstances. There was very little she did not have to do, enough to make most modern wives turn pale at the thought, and far more than her own contemporaries in England had to contemplate. So what Mary did could never have been taken as normal for anyone but a missionary's wife. What was the norm then, and remained so for many years afterwards, was that the wife would do the 'feminine' jobs and the husband the 'masculine'. Cooking, housework, needlework, shopping and childcare were feminine; finance, house maintenance, heavy gardening, and any kind of sawing, chopping and hammering were masculine. These roles are not so rigidly defined now (especially in marriages where the wife works outside the home) and yet I see how I followed the traditional pattern without thinking about it or challenging it. I couldn't cook, he couldn't cook, yet because I was the wife I was the one who automatically learned to cook. It took me long enough, solemnly following recipes from a *Good Housekeeping* volume and then moving on to Elizabeth David. I'd been brought up on a rigid pattern where meals were concerned: in a typical week, Sunday was roast meat, potatoes and cabbage; Monday was the remains of this fried up; Tuesday was sausage and chips; Wednesday was shepherd's pie; Thursday was tattie pot; Friday was fish and chips; Saturday was cold ham and salad. I hated all those meals and was called 'faddy'. Now, as a wife in my own kitchen, it was my chance to cook the sort of food I did like but it took me a while and a lot of frustration to get it right. I certainly thought it was my job to do so, even when we were both working and there was no real justification for the cooking to fall to me.

But then there was also no reason for the driving to fall to him. I couldn't drive, he couldn't drive, but there was never any question as to who should be the one to learn. He took lessons, and failed the test. He took more, and finally passed. He hated driving, but he drove, and I didn't. I'd no desire or need to – we lived in London – so I didn't. But of course part of having no 'need' was my reliance on him. I was a bad wife, not learning to drive so that I could do my share. He didn't do his share of cooking but that seemed different because I soon liked cooking and found it easy, whereas he hated driving and found it stressful. But we'd fallen into the traditional roles and stayed stuck in them.

New jobs come up in marriages all the time, of course, and get allotted in the most inconsistent ways. Sometimes one or other of us has complained – 'Why should *I* be the one doing this?' – and the explanation is never logical. For years I looked after the boiler which runs our central heating. I was the one who knew how to change its setting and organised the servicing. This doesn't sound much of a job, but it was a temperamental boiler, always going wrong, and there were certain tricks that could persuade it to work. I knew them, he didn't. It had become mine only because I was the one at home when it was installed, and the one there when the servicing was done, and so I'd been taught how it worked. A lot of these dreary little tasks have fallen to wives precisely because of the wives' availability, of course, and have nothing to do with their being traditionally feminine or masculine jobs. Housework is the same. Women at home are expected to do the housework precisely because they are at home; and when they, too, work outside the home, it still often falls to them.

I've never minded that. It's true I took it on originally because of how I'd been brought up, but I found I liked it, it never seemed a burden. I would have chosen to do it, though in fact, on the rare occasions he's been obliged to turn his hand to Hoovering and washing floors and cleaning sinks, he's proved himself a little treasure – but he hasn't liked it. Jobs within a marriage which a wife chooses to do, which she positively wants to do, can hardly be said to amount to an unfair burden. It's all about suitability and balance, the allotting of tasks within marriage, or it should be. Mary Livingstone was allotted far too many and never complained about any of them, but had she had the choice, I'm sure she would have chosen to retain at least three quarters of them. But in her day she would never have thought of suggesting to her husband that he should share equally in the housework and childcare. It was women's work, and no argument possible. Today, plenty of argument is not only possible but essential. Legions of researchers regularly come up with surveys showing that even when wife and husband both work equal hours outside the home it is the wife who does the majority of the work within it. It is also alleged that men don't 'do' lavatory-cleaning and other mundane but necessary jobs – they think they are contributing if they do the easy stuff, like pushing a Hoover around. If all this is true, then each individual wife has a battle on her hands. She has to fight hard to win it, however much it exhausts her; but it is a battle that can be won. In Mary Livingstone's day it was a battle that would not even be fought.

I would never have been able to endure the hardships Mary did. Five minutes in an ox-wagon and I'd have been screaming to be sent home, lashing David Livingstone with my MaMary type tongue for his thoughtlessness and selfishness. I thought about her in Botswana as we trundled slowly but comfortably, in a four-wheel drive vehicle, through desert areas, in the oppressive heat. When we stopped, it was to sleep in luxurious tents and to eat delicious meals prepared by others, but even then we thought we were roughing it. In the dead of night, lying awake, listening to lions roar around the camp, or flinching as an elephant brushed the canvas with its trunk, I'd think of Mary, having to feed and care for her children in conditions so primitive that merely surviving was a struggle and the danger all round her was an added torture. If 'wife' had gone on meaning what it was taken to mean by her, then who would want to marry?

It had to change, this assumption that being a wife was first and foremost to be submissive (fatally so, in Mary's case), and it did. But never for all women, or never enough. My own mother, though very far from being a weak person, was submissive as a wife. Her marriage was not a happy one, but I am absolutely sure that it never crossed her mind to contemplate divorce. The laws relating to divorce had changed dramatically in the interval between Mary Livingstone's era and her own but she would never have thought of freeing herself from her marriage. Divorce horrified her. Every bit as much as Mary, she believed marriage vows were for life. She wouldn't have been able to justify a divorce. My father was not cruel, he did not in any way mistreat her. On the contrary, he was a good, hard-working, loyal husband, who was devoted to her. The idea that she might have a right to divorce him because she was *unhappy* would have seemed preposterous to her (in any case, mere unhappiness was not yet, in the 1940s and 1950s, when she was at her most miserable, grounds for divorce). What had her own unhappiness to do with anything? She'd married in the first place not for love, and certainly not for economic security, but because she wanted children. Children, in her opinion, had to have their father. She was clever, and could have returned to her pre-marriage job, a job better paid than my father's, so theoretically she could have supported herself and her children. But I am certain she never thought of doing such a scandalous thing. Another sort of life was not possible for her. What she was submissive to was a promise, made when she married in church on 11 April 1931.

PART TWO

Fanny Stevenson
1840–1914

I

Fanny Stevenson was married twice (the second time to Robert Louis Stevenson), and in both cases it was a challenge for a woman like her to be a 'good' wife according to the standards of her times. Her times were different from those of Mary Livingstone, though their lives overlapped – the status of women had already begun to change, and marriage as an institution was also in the process of changing. When Fanny was eight years old, a Married Women's Property Bill was passed in America, where she was born, and the Seneca Falls Convention had seen the first public declaration of women's rights; by the time she was twenty-seven, the National Women's Suffrage Association had been formed and two years later in 1869 Wyoming gave women the vote. Things were happening, and happening fast. Women were no longer willing to be as submissive and subservient as wives. Nothing had yet altered in the marriage service – women were still bound to promise to obey – but the spirit in which this promise was made had begun to change. Brides no longer went so humbly to the altar.

But the first time, in spite of not being in the least docile by nature, Fanny went quite humbly. She married aged seventeen, as though becoming a wife had been her destiny. Born on 10 March 1840, in Indiana, she'd grown up in a boisterous family, the eldest of six children (five girls, one boy). Her mother Esther was of Swedish descent and her father, Jacob Vandergrift, of Dutch origin. He was a powerfully built man, said to have striking eyes, who was adored by all his children. Successful in the lumber business, he was affluent enough to live with his family in a large, red-brick house on the corner of the main street of Indianapolis, then a small town. Esther and Jacob were, it seems, happily married, and so Fanny, like Mary Livingstone, grew up in a household where the role of wife didn't seem particularly oppressive. Fanny's father was the dominant partner but her mother seemed entirely content to minister to his needs and those of her children. Fanny was trained, like Mary, to be a competent housewife. She learned to sew, to cook and to garden like a model daughter, only revealing an adventurous, tomboyish side in her love of horse-riding and her enjoyment of climbing trees and playing games. Interestingly, her parents did not try to make her more ladylike – they appeared proud of her athleticism, and liked to show off her daring. She was also artistic, drawing well, and wrote her own stories to read to her sisters. At school, she excelled at Composition but otherwise did not shine academically. There was never any hint that she might have a 'career' other than that of wife and, in due course, mother.

Marriage came sooner than her family had anticipated, all the same. Fanny was not thought of as a beauty – she was dark-complexioned and dark-haired – so it was a surprise when the conventionally handsome, blond Samuel Osbourne proposed. He was only eighteen himself, a law student from Kentucky and a member of an old plantation family, who when he graduated had become Secretary to the Governor of Indiana. He and Fanny were instantly attracted to each other and married in December 1857. It was a big wedding (unlike Mary Livingstone's quiet ceremony), with all the town notables present, and the young couple dazzling in their finery. The bride wore a gown of heavy white satin with a long skirt and train, and her low-necked, revealing bodice was trimmed with old lace. The bridegroom was hardly less splendid. Six feet tall (1.8 m) and towering over the diminutive Fanny, he looked impressive in a bright blue, brass-buttoned coat worn over a white shirt and white brocade waistcoat sprigged with tiny lavender flowers, which matched his high, lavender silk stock, and set off his immaculate tight fawn trousers. They looked the ideal bridal pair – young, healthy, attractive and very much in love. They had their own house from the beginning, and here, nine months later, their daughter Isobel was born. It seemed Fanny had settled down nicely to be a wife and that her happiness was surely complete.

But then, in 1861, not quite four years into the marriage, Sam went off to fight in the Civil War (on the side of the North). He couldn't resist the challenge and Fanny scarcely expected him to – she was only one of many wives left at home to look after house and child. Unlike Mary Livingstone, she was no clinging vine, but in spite of her independent spirit she found being without her husband far more difficult than she had anticipated. She missed Sam terribly. He, on the other hand, relished his freedom, though not enough to stay with his regiment. He left it after six months to go prospecting for silver in Nevada, expecting Fanny and Isobel to join him. The long, arduous and downright dangerous journey tested Fanny to the limit but she managed it, though the misery and difficulty of the travelling was as nothing compared to the shock of arrival. Nevada was a scene of desolation, an endless vista of rock and sand and thorn-bushes, a place where the dust blew in the eyes all the time and there was no shelter to be had. Reese River, where Sam was prospecting with some four thousand other hopefuls, was a rough miners' camp. There were only fifty-seven women there, twelve of them prostitutes, and five of them girls under ten years old. Here Fanny was supposed to adapt to the hardship of her new circumstances and learn to be a different kind of wife from the one she had been in cosy Indianapolis.

She did. She made the log cabin in which she lived into a home and adapted to the circumstances in which she found herself. They were tough. The cabin had a stove, a table and bunks to sleep in. It was freezing in winter when the snow lay thick on the rocky ground for months, and stiflingly hot in the summer. Everything to do with the way of life there was primitive. Fuel for the stove had to be searched for, then chopped, water had to be carried in metal pails from a standpipe, food had to be brought in from a great distance. Fanny managed. She learned how to cook beef fifteen different ways and how to improvise with the few other ingredients at her disposal. This kind of pioneer existence would have been hard enough, but what made it even more challenging was the constant fear of attack. There were Indians around (naturally, since it was their country) and from time to time there would be raids, which were terrifying. Anxious that something would spark off hostility, when she and Belle (as Isobel was always called) were alone in the cabin Fanny set herself to placate the Indians, offering them coffee when they appeared at her door, and gradually losing her fear. But as a precaution, she learned to use a revolver (and soon enjoyed the thrill of being able to shoot straight).

She also learned to smoke. It helped dull the boredom, and her days, though busy, were very boring. Sam and the other men, nearly all of them like him college-educated and adventurous, were under ground prospecting and when they came home they were exhausted. There were no libraries or meeting-houses, no shops, no entertainment of any kind – Reese River was a mining-camp, after all. Being a wife there was a permanent endurance test, one Fanny passed with flying colours, but she was far from contented. Everything depended on Sam. If he found no silver, their prospects were grim. Sam gave it a year, and then admitted defeat. The three of them left the camp and moved to Virginia City where he became clerk of the local court to support his family. All that they could afford to rent was a shack, little better than the Reese River cabin, and in some ways not as secure. Fanny found that the desolation and gruelling hardship of living in the camp were replaced by the ugliness and squalor of living in what she soon learned was one of the most brutal and dissolute towns in the West. It was no place to bring up a child. Sam didn't like it any more than she did but felt he had the harder time, doing a dull job he hated instead of prospecting for silver. Doubtless, with both of them miserable, there were rows – Fanny was not a wife like Mary Livingstone, who believed she had no right to criticise or point out the error of a husband's ways.

They began quarrelling, and soon Sam went in search of comfort and distraction, and found them. When Fanny discovered he was sleeping with other women, she was furious. She could put up with anything so long as she had Sam, but his unfaithfulness humiliated and disgusted her. Not for Fanny the game of keeping up appearances rather than have everyone know the reason she'd quarrelled with her husband. Unusually for her times, pride did not mean she would sanction any behaviour for the sake of her marriage. She would rather be on her own than be the wife of a womaniser. Very soon, she was – Sam threw up his job and went off prospecting again to Montana. He was away months, and Fanny decided she had had enough. If she was to be a deserted wife she would have to fend for herself and Virginia City was no place to do it. So she and Belle left, and went to San Francisco, where, posing as a widow, she set out to make her living as a seamstress. Then news reached her that Sam had been killed. She believed it, dressed herself in black, and prepared for a future as a genuine widow. She and Belle lived in a cheap boarding-house in a run-down area, and Fanny spent her time crocheting baby clothes and embroidering pillow slips. Whenever she went out, to collect and deliver her sewing, she had to take Belle with her. Fortunately the child, now seven, was obedient and docile, but Fanny was well aware that her daughter was being denied the happy family life she had enjoyed herself. She could, of course, have gone home to Indiana but that would have been to admit defeat. Fanny would not be defeated.

But then, dramatically, Sam reappeared – the report of his death had been a mistake. Instantly, Fanny's hard times were over. There is no doubt that she was overjoyed to be reunited with her handsome husband, whom she loved in spite of his transgressions, and that Belle was ecstatic to have her father back. Promising that he was reformed, Sam got a good job as a court stenographer and moved his family into Fifth Street and to a pleasant cottage. There, in April 1868, just after Fanny's twenty-eighth birthday, a son was born, named Samuel Lloyd. As a well-looked-after wife with no need to scrimp and save to make ends meet, Fanny was happy in San Francisco. But her contentment was short-lived – Sam could not resist other women. This time, Fanny didn't wait for him to leave her. She left him. She went to the only place open to her, her family home in Indiana, ostensibly on a long-overdue visit to show her children to their grandparents. Sam pleaded for them to come back, promising once more to be faithful. Eventually, Fanny returned, but bringing her younger sister Cora as an ally. They bought a cottage in East Oakland, and there she settled down once more, with her errant but chastened husband. In some ways her married life had never been better. She loved the cottage, particularly its garden to which she devoted herself with gratifying results. She was happy as a mother, teaching Belle how to recite poetry, and making sure that she was proud of her unusual swarthy skin and dark eyes and hair, and not ashamed as she herself had been made to feel. She was a devoted but not a fussy mother, strict over manners but ready to encourage all kinds of imaginative games. Another son was born, in 1871, named Hervey, and it seemed that at last the stormy period of her marriage was over and that she and Sam and their three children had many happy, settled years ahead.

It was at this stage of her marriage, when she was thirty-two and had been a wife for fourteen years, that Fanny discovered something about herself which she should perhaps have suspected earlier. Put simply, it was that by becoming a wife and mother so very young she had missed out on developing other parts of herself. Living in San Francisco had brought her into touch with the sort of people she had never known in Indianapolis, Reese River or Virginia City – artists, cultured people, bohemians who were sophisticated in her eyes and to whom she was greatly attracted. She wanted not only to become a part of their world but also to discover if she had their talent. She had always liked to draw, as well as to write, and now she wanted to test herself, to see if she could be trained. Belle, aged fourteen, had just left school (which she'd hated) to go to the School of Design. Fanny, aged thirty-two, decided to join her there. The director was Virgil Williams, and the class he taught had twenty pupils, of all ages. She quickly became friends both with him and his wife Dora. A governess was engaged to look after Lloyd and Hervey, and suddenly Fanny was in her element, even winning a medal for her drawings. Sam apparently made no objection to having a wife who was now an art student. (He was in no position to – he had another mistress. Unwisely, this woman once came to the cottage and was sent packing by an outraged Fanny.)

But this time her rage was much more dangerous than it had been before. In the Virginia City days, she had learned how to survive on her own and she knew that if she had to she could do it again. If Sam forced her hand, she was quite prepared to stand alone. But more than that, she had lately realised that she might even have career prospects. She might not need to rely on essentially menial work such as sewing. In short, Fanny had become ambitious, she had new and daring aspirations, and if Sam was going to have his freedom she was determined to have a chance to expand her own horizons in a quite different direction. She would go to Europe and train further to be an artist. She would take her children and travel with them to Antwerp and change her life. The only obstacle, as she saw it, was the usual one for wives who wanted independence from husbands: money. She had none of her own. But Sam should surely pay for his sins. He could be persuaded to give her an allowance. In time, she might be able to support herself, if not through selling her paintings, then by writing stories. Another new friend of hers was Timothy Rearden, head of the Mercantile Library, who encouraged her to think she wrote well enough for a magazine to buy her work. There were all sorts of possibilities in her head and she was excited by them.

But it was none the less a mad idea. Not for a moment does Fanny appear to have thought out the implications of crossing the Atlantic with three children, to indulge her own whims. She had made no enquiries about the art colleges in Antwerp and had no idea that they did not admit women. She had nowhere to stay, no contacts there at all. But Sam, instead of being scandalised and refusing to finance this crazy project, gave in to it. Maybe it suited him to have his family out of the way for a while (his mistress moved into the cottage pretty soon after Fanny left). He was by no means wealthy, but he agreed to a small allowance, just enough for his wife to manage on if she lived frugally. At the end of April 1875, she and the children and Miss Kate, the governess, left San Francisco on their exhausting journey to Europe. Fanny, who looked a decade younger than her thirty-five years, was taken for Belle's sister, and a charming pair they appeared to all on board the ship. Offers of help were plentiful and Fanny accepted them – 'When in difficulty', she told her daughter, 'look bewildered and gallant strangers will leap to our assistance.' The same ploy worked once they arrived in Antwerp. Fanny spoke not a word of any foreign language (and never bothered to learn any), but this proved no handicap. The Gerhardt family, who ran the inn she was directed to, took her and the children to their hearts and helped her find a house to rent. It was a little stone house, with four small rooms one on top of each other, but Fanny was delighted with it and ready to start her new life in Antwerp.

Her delight was short-lived. Antwerp itself was a shock – with its narrow, cobbled lanes, so unlike American streets, its milk-carts drawn by dogs, and the clothes of the people (baggy trousers and smocks for men, wide-winged head-dresses and long cloaks for women) – but a far greater shock was her discovery that the Academy would not admit her and Belle. There was no point in staying in Antwerp – she would have to move on, to Paris, where she was told there were certain studios which accepted women. The thought of travelling to Paris was daunting enough – she felt so secure living near the Gerhardts – but what made it worse was that Hervey was ill. He needed rest and stability. But somehow they made the transition from Antwerp to Paris, and rented a sunny little apartment in the rue de Naples. Hervey was still sick, but no worse than he had been in Antwerp, and Fanny felt encouraged enough to leave the devoted Miss Kate in charge while she enrolled at Julien's Atelier des Dames. It was crowded with women, some of them American like herself, all trying to find space for their easels, all solemnly drawing the nude models. Fanny felt comfortable there and made friends, but had no social life. Her evenings were quiet and long. She sat with Hervey, and sewed, and wrote to her friends back in San Francisco. Sometimes, but rarely, she wrote to her husband. He was still sending her money, without which she could not have survived. It confused her to have to confess to Timothy Rearden that she missed Sam and that he said he missed her and his children. She didn't like to think what this might mean. Did it mean they still loved each other? Did it mean that it was not only in the strictly legal sense that she was his wife? She was a woman on her own and yet she was not. Back in America she had a husband to whom she appeared to be still emotionally tied.

Belle and Lloyd were happy enough in Paris, though they

both missed their father, especially Belle, but Hervey did not thrive. His illness was diagnosed as scrofulous TB, a particularly virulent and ugly disease. He grew worse, in spite of Fanny's and Miss Kate's nursing, and in his delirium called for his father. As the child grew weaker and weaker Fanny sent for Sam, telling him to come quickly if he wanted to see Hervey alive. Sam came, and was not just appalled but also frightened by the sight of his little boy vomiting blood and covered in oozing sores. Much as he loved him, he could hardly bear to look at him. Inevitably, in the middle of all this horror, there hung over the dying Hervey the question of whether he would ever have come to this if his mother had stayed at home with him in San Francisco. On 5 April 1876, aged four, Hervey died a hideous and painful death. There was no money to bury him with any dignity. His heart-broken parents and his brother and sister followed the little white coffin to a common grave. Fanny was catatonic with grief, barely able to function. Sam was hardly in a better state, but he was not as exhausted as his wife, who had nursed her son through his final weeks. Sam and Belle walked about Paris, holding hands tightly but saying little, while Fanny sat silently in her room. As his wife, she was his responsibility and he still felt keenly for her. But she would not return with him to San Francisco. She was incapable, too worn out to consider such a journey. She needed rest, an opportunity if not to get over Hervey's death (which she never would) at least to recuperate strength.

Concerned friends told the Osbournes of a quiet little village called Grez, about two hours from Paris, where Fanny could convalesce. It was frequented in the summer by artists and she, like them, would find it a congenial environment. Sam went with her to inspect the place and was relieved that it appealed to her. On 14 April, Sam left to go back to America. Belle alone saw him off, hating his departure and almost afraid to be left in charge of her mother who grew paler and paler and seldom spoke – it was like being with a ghost. She didn't know what the situation was now between her parents and didn't ask. Neither of them would have been able to give her a satisfactory answer. Hervey's death might have been expected either to bring them closer or finally to part them but the tragedy did neither. Fanny was too numb to feel anything, Sam too distanced from her to be able to sort out his own confusion.

At first, life at Grez was dull, but its very monotony was what Fanny needed. She was well fed at the inn and its simple comforts suited her sombre mood. She didn't want luxury. She liked the spartan arrangements. Miss Kate did not. As soon as they were settled, she left the Osbournes and went off to another post in Paris. Fanny and Belle sketched, Lloyd fished, and they all benefited from country life. The inn was a stone house with a large garden and was empty except for them, its two rows of bedrooms, with a single bathroom at the end, waiting for the arrival of the annual summer influx of artists. By the time the first of them came, Fanny was not quite so pale, though she had not yet recovered her usual energy. She appeared 'in no sense ordinary' to Birge Harrison, one of the first to arrive. Bob Stevenson, Walter Simpson and Frank O'Meara, the next arrivals, were captivated and intrigued by the sad-faced, quiet American woman and her pretty daughter. If she was a married woman, where was her husband? And was she pale because she had been ill, or for some other reason? Was she a real artist, or just playing? How would she fit in when the rest of the colony was complete? And the most interesting speculation of all: how would Stevenson's cousin Louis react to her?

Years later, Robert Louis Stevenson vowed he fell in love with Mrs Fanny Osbourne the moment he saw her. That moment was vividly described by Belle, who said she remembered very well glancing at her mother, as the assembled guests sat eating, and saw that she was looking intently towards the window opposite, where a young, slender man with a high colour had just appeared. He was leaning forward, 'staring with a look of surprised admiration' at Fanny, and she stared back at him. The mutual attraction was as instant, and as physical, as that – love, it seemed, at thrilling first sight. But love between a young, unattached man and a woman who was a wife and mother of two children. There was never any secret about Fanny's status. The artists at Grez now knew that the mysterious Mrs Osbourne had an absent husband, who had put in at least one appearance at the inn. If Louis did indeed fall in love with Fanny the moment he saw her, he was bold to imagine he had a chance of declaring or fulfilling that love.

But perhaps he was particularly susceptible to experienced women, to wives. The only other woman he had loved was also a wife, Mrs Fanny Sitwell, with whom he had been infatuated for years. She was separated from her husband by the time he met her in 1873, when he was twenty-three and she was thirty-four, and within a year he was regularly writing letters of adoration, declaring that he was 'only happy in the thought of you' and that she had all his heart. But Mrs Sitwell hadn't wanted his heart. There followed, before he saw Fanny Osbourne at Grez, two miserable years in which he continued to declare to Mrs Sitwell that he would never love anyone else, but at the same time concluded that 'a good dull marriage with a good dull girl would be a good move'. Fanny Osbourne was neither a girl nor was she dull. She was, on the contrary, extremely unusual both in looks and in personality. There had been a clue to what attracted Louis in a woman in his admiration for a Miss Ward whom he'd met in the south of France – 'I was greatly pleased with her manner. She came in so *directly* and shook my hand . . . and sate herself down in a chair and crossed her legs with quite amusing nonchalance. It is a blessing to see a girl who looks like a woman, after so many young ladies.'

Fanny Osbourne looked like a woman. She was not an unobtainable goddess like the beautiful, elegant Mrs Sitwell, but, like Miss Ward, was direct and unaffected and in appearance casual and lacking in artifice. Her body was womanly, full-breasted, round-hipped, and though she was small, just over 5 feet (1.5 m), she had a presence. Her dark eyes were watchful, and she did not smile much, but when she did her whole face became animated and glowing. Louis set himself to make her smile more often. He brought into Fanny's life what Belle called 'a sort of joyousness' to which, in spite of her grief, she could not help but respond. Belle noticed, as the weeks of May and June went by, that her mother was beginning to look prettier, especially when, as the weather grew hotter, she wore a bathing suit to go boating with Louis and Bob and the others. It had sleeves, and a little skirt which reached below her knees; she tucked her curly dark hair under a scarlet kerchief and on her feet she had red espadrilles. She couldn't swim, but she was fearless, loving the boisterous games on the river. It was as though she were discovering her lost youth, as though she were back in Indianapolis, the tomboy she had been before ever she became a wife. She regained some gaiety, and when they were all eating supper – delicious *pot-au-feu* served in a big yellow bowl, yards of bread, lettuce salads flavoured with garlic and tarragon – and drinking red wine, she joined in the conversation, full of opinions, capable of startling the men with her originality and critical insight, her voice low and even but commanding. Bob, as well as Louis, was under her spell, and she began to realise it. And she was attracted to them, at first to Bob and then, increasingly, to Louis. But where could these feelings end? In an affair? And where would *that* end? In disgrace, most probably, and complete rejection by Sam, which in turn would hurt and injure her children.

The summer came to a close, the first of the autumn winds heralding the exodus of the artists back to their studios in Paris. Fanny left too, renting an apartment in Montmartre where an American friend already lived with her two children. Sam's allowance was still coming in, enough to live on if they ate bread and herrings most of the time. Louis was also in Paris, almost penniless (though his ever-indulgent father Thomas constantly sent him money) and trying to write. He'd had one book published (*The Pentland Rising* – a slim historical pamphlet), but had made no money. By November, he was writing to his friend and mentor Sidney Colvin: 'Life is very hard day by day . . . when I know so well I am making another tie about my heart.' To another friend, Charles Baxter, he was by the end of that month speaking even more plainly – 'I am damnably in love.' So what was to be done?

For that winter, nothing. Louis didn't live with Fanny and her children but he used her address for post and was with her a great deal of the time. He wrote to Baxter, at the beginning of spring 1877, that 'love . . . plays mighty hell . . . nothing will satisfy . . . but marriage'. But how could that be? Fanny was already married. And her husband made her life in Paris, such as it was, financially possible. But in March came the news that

Sam was in financial difficulties and could no longer send money. Fanny should come home. In May, he arrived in Paris himself but whatever passed between him and his wife, she did not go back to America with him. Instead, he went with her and his children to Grez where once more the artists had gathered. According to Belle, they all – all the Osbournes – had a happy week there before Sam went home alone. Ten days after he left, Louis arrived. What were people to think?

What they thought is what anyone would think: here were a couple visibly in love but not free to be together. They were in a mess, and some might say it was of their own making. To marry Stevenson, Fanny would have to be divorced from Osbourne, a lengthy and difficult process to which he would have to agree, for she had neither the funds nor the appetite for a legal battle. Divorce, in late-nineteenth-century America, was just as much a matter of shame and scandal as it was in Britain. Her own family would be horrified, her children marked by her disgrace. The future as a divorced wife would be very bleak indeed, especially as Louis would be unable to support her and her family.

Money, money, money – the lack of it complicated an affair that was already complex enough. Love would not feed and house Belle and Lloyd. The third winter in Paris was miserable (and the summer in Grez had not been so good either because of the poor weather). By this time, they had given up all pretence that they were not living together. Louis had moved in with Fanny and if they had not been lovers before, by then they were. Fanny was taking a terrifying risk. Louis's long-suffering parents were intensely religious and their tolerance of their son's wayward behaviour would certainly have limits. It was hard enough for them to send money to a son infatuated with another man's wife, but if this woman bore him a child they might very well cast him off.

In the summer of 1878, Louis was ill. He was frequently ill, as Fanny now knew, but this was different. There was something wrong with his eyes, and when she thought he was threatened with blindness Fanny acted. She took him to London to see a doctor whom he trusted. While there, she met his friends, Sidney Colvin and Mrs Sitwell, who were polite and kind to her, recognising the sincerity of her love for Louis and her concern for his welfare. She was being a good 'wife' to their talented young friend even if she was, in reality, a bad wife to her own husband. The strain made Fanny herself ill. She had to stay in bed, in Colvin's house where she and Louis were staying, and was embarrassed to have 'the solemn Mr Colvin . . . and the stately . . . Mrs Sitwell sit by me and talk in the most correct English about the progress of literature and the arts. I was rather afraid of them . . . but they . . . came down to my level and petted me as one would a kitten.'

As soon as Louis had seen the specialist and his eyes were improving, he went home to Edinburgh and Fanny back to her children in Paris. He hated being apart from her – 'no dear head upon the pillow' – and couldn't sleep for being so miserable. It was nearly two months before he could get himself back to Paris, with money given, yet again, by his parents. 'I want coin so badly', he wrote to Colvin. So did Fanny. 'Her nerves are quite gone', Louis wrote to Mrs Sitwell, and there was another cause for concern. 'We have many strong reasons for getting her out of Paris in about a month', he wrote, and asked Mrs Sitwell if she knew of some cheap farmhouse they could rent in the English countryside. Why would he specify the timing, unless for some reason it was crucial? Perhaps Fanny suspected she was pregnant, but if so she was either mistaken or had an early miscarriage. Whatever the reason for the sudden desire to hide away in the country, this move was never made. Instead, Fanny prepared herself to face the inevitable. Sam had not sent any money for a long time and Louis had very little, not nearly enough to support her. She would have to return to America or face real poverty. She would have to go back anyway, to face Sam and discuss with him what was to be done. If she was to stay with Louis she had to get Sam to release her from marriage to him. There was really no alternative, unless she was to be Louis's mistress but never his wife.

In July, she came to London with her children to find a ship to take them home. Belle said she was never told why they were going – Fanny did not discuss matters with her, offered no explanation at all. They stayed in cheap lodgings in Chelsea until they sailed. Louis took them to the station where they boarded a train to take them to Liverpool from where they would sail on a Royal Mail steamer. Lloyd, aged ten, and already devoted to Louis (though he still loved his own father), remembered Louis saying goodbye then walking down the platform without once looking back. Nobody knew what, if anything, had been agreed. Was Fanny going to seek a divorce? Or had they agreed on some sort of trial separation? The precise details of the parting were never revealed. All that is known is that it was painful and that Fanny went back to resume life as a legally bound wife.

II

It is easy enough to discover how Louis felt once he and Fanny had parted – he wrote enough letters to friends describing his absolute misery and sense of loss; but it is hard to judge Fanny's state of mind. He was on his own, she was not. She went back to being truly a wife after three years of being a wife in name only. From all the evidence that is available, which consists of other people's observations, she did not descend into the state of wretchedness endured by Louis. Instead, she seems to have made a determined effort to be a wife once more. Sam's behaviour over the past twenty years might have become repugnant to her, but Sam himself had not. And Sam didn't want a divorce. What he wanted was to persuade his wife, in the well-worn tradition of deceiving husbands, that his affairs meant nothing.

But to Fanny, of course, they did mean something. They meant that Sam preferred other women to herself on one level, and a very important level, at least. And now that she had had as her lover a man who did not so much as glance at another woman, a man to whom she was all, she had someone to measure Sam by. This measuring took a long time and was far more painful than it appeared on the surface to those around her. Fanny took her children home to Indianapolis when she arrived in America and it was obvious that her family thought she and Sam had patched up their differences and were once more to be united. They wanted her to stay married for reasons of respectability. Their attitude to divorce was no different from that of Louis's parents, however different as people they might be. Fanny saw at once that she could expect little sympathy and absolutely no encouragement here. Her young sister Nellie (aged twenty-two), whom she took with her when she joined Sam in San Francisco, had no notion that Fanny was brooding over what she should do.

There was no one to whom Fanny could talk freely. For six months, she did not write to Louis, not even a note, which caused him great distress. He was ill (with a swollen testicle) and rather oddly put the 'true cause of my illness' down to 'that rough time when letters did not come'. Fanny had decided that she must see if she could survive completely without him. According to Belle and Nellie, she seemed to get on rather well. Sam had rented a house in Monterey after he and Fanny had spent a week's holiday there and the family loved it. Fanny took up riding again and became sunburned and healthy-looking as she rode her mustang to rodeos and slept in barns in the hay with a group of friends she had made. It was an active, outdoor life in the sun and it suited her in a way city life never had done. She liked the rented house they lived in – it was a simple, two-storey adobe house, sparsely furnished – and she liked her neighbours. There was an artists' colony in Monterey, as there had been in Grez, and congenial company for her. Belle loved it too and began to forget O'Meara, one of the artists in Grez, with whom she had been infatuated, much to Fanny's disapproval – she didn't want her daughter to marry too young, as she herself had done, though Belle was already four years older than she had been, nearly twenty-one. What her mother had not realised, however, was that Belle had fallen in love with another artist, Joe Strong. Joe proposed to her but Belle didn't dare tell her mother who, she was convinced, would disapprove – even though she liked Joe, and made use of him by telling Louis to write to her at his address so that Sam wouldn't find out.

But Joe would not be put off. Something Fanny said (of which there is no record, so it could well have been bluff on Joe's part) convinced him that she was planning another marriage for Belle. There seemed to him only one course of action: to appeal to Sam, which he did. Sam was sympathetic and gave his approval, Joe bought a special marriage licence, and the two of them were married secretly, the bride so unprepared for the elopement that she was wearing an old grey dress and scuffed shoes. As soon as the hasty service was over, they went to San Francisco, where Sam had found them an apartment. Fanny was furious. She went at once to San Francisco to confront her daughter and it was, said Belle, 'a painful interview'. Whereas Sam had given his blessing (and some money), Fanny was contemptuous – Belle had been a fool, becoming the wife of a man she had known for only one summer (though she had, strictly speaking, known him very briefly before ever she was taken to Europe).

It appalled Fanny that Belle could make the same mistake she had made herself and, in her haste to become a wife, fail entirely to consider either the consequences or properly assess the qualities of the man she was marrying. But more importantly, Joe had no money. Fanny knew what having no money would lead to. Sam's generosity would not last, and when her father failed her Belle would turn to her mother. And if there were children . . . Fanny could hardly bear the thought. It depressed her to witness the mess she felt Belle was making of her young life, but then she was becoming depressed anyway and the joys of Monterey no longer cheered her. She had tried so hard to go back to being a good wife to Sam but it was becoming harder and harder to succeed.

Louis had written to Colvin that year that 'perhaps I have been spoiled by a very perfect relation and my heart having been coddled in a home grows delicate'. Beautifully put, and exactly how Fanny herself appears to have felt. She had tried to stifle memories of her 'perfect relation' with Louis but had failed. Sam did not help. At first indulgent, renting the Monterey house because Fanny loved it, and willing to commute to San Francisco where he worked, Sam grew less and less interested in visiting her. When he arrived for a weekend, there were arguments, often noisy and, in a relatively small house, easily overheard. Lloyd heard one in which his mother burst out, 'Oh Sam, forgive me!' He didn't know for what. Fanny had plenty to forgive Sam for, but why would she be moved to ask his forgiveness unless it was because she had confessed her love for Louis? Belle, before she ran away with Joe, recalled hearing the word 'divorce' used, and she was aware her mother had mentioned the possibility of divorce to her own family in Indianapolis. They were violently opposed to it, as she'd known they would be, not only her parents but also her brother and four sisters. They were concerned about the disgrace, the shame, the effect on the children, and not least the question of who would support her.

Surprisingly, this worried Fanny least. She'd supported herself years ago and believed she could do it again. Sam was devoted to Lloyd, so she knew he would always contribute to his son's welfare. The economics of divorce, which in the nineteenth century made it a terrifying prospect for women, and which was the strongest of deterrents, no longer seemed to frighten Fanny. Living in Paris, virtually penniless, she had been afraid, but in Monterey, with Sam working in San Francisco, and very close to his children, she did not think she would starve or be homeless. What caused her more anguish was her own indecision about the future. Was she asking for a divorce to free her from Sam, in order to regain her independence? Or did she want a divorce to free her to marry Louis?

By the end of that summer of 1879, with Fanny gone fourteen months, Louis was also feeling desperate. His life, he wrote, was 'the impersonation of waiting'. He waited for a letter 'to clinch things'. It never came. Instead, a ten-word telegram arrived. Nobody knows what those crucial words were, but Louis cabled back, 'Hold tight. I will be with you in one month', suggesting that Fanny's words had been ones of desperation, a sudden outburst of longing for him. He wrote to his cousin Bob that 'Fanny seems to be very ill' and to his literary friend W. E. Henley that she seemed to have 'inflammation of the brain'. He sailed for New York within a week of receiving the famous telegram, 'a little off my nut' as he put it. His friends were appalled (and so were his parents, who did not know of his departure till they read the letter he'd left). Henley went so far as to blame Fanny – 'I hoped she would be brave and generous enough to give him up.' He didn't want to see Louis 'get mixed up once more in a miserable life of alarms and lies and intrigues that he led in Paris'.

But Louis did want it. He didn't see his life with Fanny as being like that at all. From New York, Louis went on to

Monterey, arriving there exhausted and ill, kept going only by the thought of the passionate reunion awaiting him. It was a terrible let-down. Fanny, instead of being ecstatic, seemed almost embarrassed to see him, as though she had never really expected him to come and, now that he had, was overwhelmed by the implications of his arrival. He looked awful. He'd lost a stone (6.3 kg) on the journey and was haggard and weak. Fanny let it be known to her Monterey friends that the visitor was a well-known writer on a lecture tour. But as suddenly as he arrived, Louis disappeared, to go off on his own into the surrounding hills, camping. Ostensibly, this was for his own good, because Fanny's sister Nellie was suspected of having diphtheria. But there was more to his abrupt departure. Within a week of his reunion with Fanny, before he went wandering off, he had written to Colvin that 'all is in the wind, things might turn out well or might not' and that there was 'frankly no decided news'. To Baxter, he went so far as to write that he had 'a broken heart'.

So what was Fanny playing at? Having apparently sent him a telegram which he interpreted as a cry for him to come to her (though there is no knowing if this interpretation was intended by her) she now hustled him out of her house as quickly as possible. Maybe she was afraid Sam was about to arrive on one of his erratic visits, maybe the diphtheria scare was genuine, but whatever the reason her lack of any convincing welcome hurt and bewildered Louis. Within a few days of starting to camp, he fell ill with a fever and only through the kindness of two rancheros, who found him 18 miles (29 km) from Monterey in a state of collapse and took him to their ranch, did he survive. When he was better, he returned to Monterey where he boarded with a French doctor rather than stay with Fanny. After a month, seeing Fanny daily but not living with her, he was more confident that everything would turn out well and that he had been right to come, however strange his reception. 'The effect of my arrival', he wrote to Baxter, 'straightened everything out.' There was, after all, it seemed, to be a divorce and then he would marry Fanny and live happily ever after. He longed for her to be his *wife* as well as his lover – the distinction was important to him. But he admitted that he had been in a state of terrible anxiety for the first weeks in Monterey, not knowing if Fanny could or would bring herself to the point of insisting on a divorce, or if her husband would agree to one. The impression he gave was that without an agreement between the Osbournes to divorce, he would have gone home. This time, it was to be all or nothing.

The strain seems to have made Fanny ill again. Her 'inflammation of the brain' flared up and the doctor, according to Louis, gave him 'the worst account of her health'. At this point, he received a telegram from his distraught mother, saying that his father was seriously ill and he must return. But Louis would not return. Fanny was more important to him than his parents, much though he loved them, much though he acknowledged he owed to them. In his own eyes, however, Fanny was already his wife – 'I won't desert my wife', he wrote to Henley – and her illness was of more concern to him than his father's. He now expected to be cut off without a shilling and even boasted that he didn't care, Fanny was worth it. The divorce was expected to go through soon, but for the sake of decency months must elapse before he could actually make her his legitimate wife. On 12 December, according to Louis, Fanny would obtain her divorce, freeing her from Sam. Louis told Colvin that Sam behaved well, and commented, rather oddly, that in return he and Fanny would wait to marry to avoid scandal for him. Sam was willing to support Fanny until she remarried, which in Louis's straitened circumstances (earning nothing and thinking his parents would no longer send him money) was vital. But then Sam lost his job and could give Fanny nothing. She had left Monterey and was back in the East Oakland cottage, which Sam let her live in, so had a roof over her head, but otherwise must fend for herself and Lloyd.

Louis's friends back in England were almost as distressed as his parents. In their opinion, any marriage between him and Fanny would seal his doom as a writer. He was about to burden himself with what one of them described as 'a divorced invalid' and they saw it as their duty to try to get him to come home before this happened. Colvin, like Henley earlier, thought Fanny should have cared enough 'to leave him to forget her'. Everyone saw her as a schemer, always intent on trapping

Louis, and attributed to her the most base of motives: greed. She knew he had wealthy parents and was said to be after his inheritance. But what they left out of their reckoning was that Fanny no longer expected Louis's parents to give him anything. She thought they hated her and that once their son had made her his wife their hatred would deepen. A future as Louis's wife could never have been thought by her to be a financially secure position. His own income was paltry, despite three books and some praise from critics – 'the want of coin' was more pressing than ever. Fanny would not be marrying for money or glory, whatever his friends thought. She would be marrying for love, and a love that might not endure for long because Louis was a very sick man (with a lung complaint never properly identified).

Meanwhile, he was living in rooms in San Francisco trying to write and seeing Fanny only when she managed to come over from East Oakland. It was an unsatisfactory arrangement, frustrating for both of them, but part of that waiting-game they had agreed to. In a way, it pleased them both to be putting themselves through this test – as Louis wrote to his friend Edmund Gosse: 'few people before marriage have known each other so long or made more trials of each other's tenderness and constancy. I do not think many wives are better loved than mine will be.' This time, Fanny would enter into marriage with a thorough knowledge of her husband and absolute confidence in his devotion. Knowing this, her own health improved markedly during the early part of 1880. She had no more 'fits', no more 'inflammation of the brain' (which may have been only symptoms of depression). But Louis's always perilous health worsened. He wasn't eating properly and he found the strain of waiting much more difficult than Fanny. He had an attack of malaria in January and then, in March, his first lung haemorrhage.

Fanny thought he was dying. Dismissing all considerations of propriety, she moved Louis into her cottage and nursed him devotedly, determined not to allow him to die. She was a good nurse, efficient but not fussy, knowing the importance of nursing mind and spirits as well as body. For five weeks she looked after him and then he began really to recover, though he was very frail and announced he would make 'a very withered bridegroom'. But the shock of the haemorrhage had decided both of them that they should delay their marriage no longer. Louis needed mountain air to convalesce and if they were to seek it they must go together as man and wife. They would marry in May and go to the mountains. He still had no money to cover the expense, but in mid-April his parents cabled the news 'Count on £250 annually.' Far from cutting him off, they had already paid for his medicines and now they capitulated completely. Fanny was going to be their son's wife and they finally accepted this. Perhaps Louis had counted on their love for him working this miracle all along, but Fanny had never expected it, and now it became important to her to be a 'good wife' for the Stevenson parents' sake as well as his.

The marriage took place on 19 May 1880, but the couple did not leave for the mountains immediately. Louis, unromantically, had to have some false teeth made; and then the weather was bad. But by the end of June he and his wife and stepson had travelled to the Napa Valley and were camping in Silverado. Fanny did all the work, literally hammering together planks of wood to make a shack and struggling to make stools out of the wooden packing cases in which they had brought their belongings. She was endlessly resourceful whereas Louis, even when well, could barely bang in a nail. She made him rest in the sun all day, on a platform she erected among the trees, and there he relaxed, recovering. All meals were eaten out of doors. Fanny had found an entrance to an old mine which was cold enough to serve as an ice-chest and here she hung up pigeons and wild ducks, purchased from trappers who supplied the one store down on the toll road above which they lived. She drew water from a nearby spring and there was plenty of wood around to burn. Mid-morning and mid-afternoon Fanny made Louis and herself rum-punches. It was a physically hard life for her, but compared to the Reese River days the daily toil was easy. In any case, there could be no comparison – she was a happy woman now, striving to bring back to health a husband she loved and who loved her more than ever. But they could not stay on the mountainside for ever and, anyway, Louis was homesick for Europe. Besides, he wanted to introduce his wife to his parents. Fanny, not unnaturally, dreaded this meeting. She was apprehensive that the Stevenson parents would be unable to hide their disappointment and that the magnanimity they had shown on paper would vanish.

But unlike Mary Livingstone, she wisely set herself to woo her parents-in-law. Her letters to them were clever and careful, full of a modest assessment of herself and freely acknowledging how attached their son was to them. One which she wrote jointly with her husband to his mother was a masterpiece of tact. Louis, she said, was obviously a mother's boy, and she made it clear that, far from dismaying her, this pleased her and she did not see herself in any kind of competition. She was sure Louis even looked like his mother and only wished she had been sent a photograph so that she could see if this was true. She sent her own photograph, about which she was self-deprecating, warning Mrs Stevenson that it flattered her and she must not expect her to look as good. But Fanny instinctively knew that the way to her mother-in-law's heart was to stress how well she was looking after Louis, how his health was her prime concern. 'I do try to take care of him; the old doctor insists that my nursing saved him', she wrote, adding that she herself must know that this taking care was 'very like angling for sly trout . . . I am becoming most expert'. But she didn't boast – if she had had 'a sad time of it', she said, she knew it had been far worse for his mother, so far away and unable to do anything. Gently, she tried to establish a bond of sympathy between them, both united in care of their 'boy'. Her desire for Mrs Stevenson to like her was openly expressed – 'I do so earnestly hope you will like me, but that can only be for what I am to you after you know me . . .'

No wife could have done more to prepare the way for a difficult encounter, but in spite of Mrs Stevenson's swift and friendly response, saying she liked the photograph and that she was not going to look backwards – 'I don't care for ancient history at all' – Fanny still worried. Louis didn't. He had none of his wife's fears. He loved his parents and had no doubt they would share his love for Fanny. What worried him was securing her future if he died. Her own family had been strongly opposed to this second marriage and he knew none of them was in a position to support her should he fail her. So he wrote to

Jacob Vandergrift, Fanny's only brother, who alone had written to him. He confessed his anxieties about his own health and explained that this was one of the reasons he was in such a hurry to take her to meet his parents – 'They are well off, thank God; and even suppose that I die, Fanny will be better off than she had much chance of being otherwise.' It was a letter which, if they had known about it, his London literary friends could have used in support of their theory that Fanny was a fortune-hunter. But she had never looked to Sam's family for help when she needed it and even if she had been set to take advantage of Louis's she would never have counted on it when the Stevensons had every reason to resent her.

Fanny, Louis and the twelve-year-old Lloyd arrived in Liverpool on 17 August 1880, met first by Colvin and immediately afterwards by the Stevensons who had come from Edinburgh. They all had lunch together, Lloyd endearing himself to the Stevensons by eating an enormous amount with obvious relish and showing himself 'a true boy', and there was remarkably little tension. Louis, though horribly thin, looked well, his new teeth filling out his face and improving his appearance. Colvin, writing to Henley, wondered rather nastily if he would ever grow to like what he described as Fanny's 'little determined brown face ... and grizzling hair', but Thomas and Margaret Stevenson seemed to have no reserva-tions. It was in Margaret's nature to like everyone if she could, though Thomas was much more critical, much more inclined to be suspicious and reserve judgement. Fanny knew he would be the harder parent to win over – he would not be fooled by a display of charm and would, she knew, be scrutinising her every word and expression. She was ten years older than Louis, a divorcée, mother of two children, penniless, not conventionally beautiful, foreign – any parent could be forgiven for fearing the worst. Yet within three weeks Louis was writing to his cousin Bob that Fanny was getting on with 'the old folks' better than he had ever dared to hope, and Fanny herself was writing that to her delight she was on very friendly terms with the parents and liked them exceedingly.

This happy state of affairs was a credit to all of them but perhaps most of all to Fanny. She had pulled off something many a daughter-in-law with far more in her favour could never manage to achieve. Far more wives fail, as Mary Livingstone failed, to make a successful relationship with a husband's parents and the husband can end up torn between the two rivals for his affections. Fanny worked hard to fit in with the Stevensons' tastes, allowing her mother-in-law to dress her smartly and enduring hours of shopping with her, though neither clothes nor shopping for them was of any real interest to her. Mrs Stevenson had never had a daughter, and Fanny realised she wanted to do with her what she would have done with a daughter – 'his mother, I am sure, plays dolls with me', she wrote to a friend. Fanny was no doll, but she was prepared to allow herself to be used as one if it would make her mother-in-law happy. Thomas Stevenson, on the other hand, had no use for a doll-like daughter-in-law. He liked independent minds and hated those who meekly bowed to the opinions of others. Like many men who appear domineering, he liked people who stood up to him and Fanny certainly did that. She was not afraid to argue with him and even to correct him, which amused him and endeared her to him. But at the same time Fanny had the sense to defer to her father-in-law in matters that were unimportant to her, presenting him with little victories. He disliked black stockings, so Fanny, who regularly wore them, immediately changed the colour of hers. And she tried to take up what the Stevensons thought women should do, such as embroidery and going to church.

But it was in the care of Louis that Fanny scored most highly. They saw how she protected Louis from himself, quietly and cunningly persuading him to husband his energies in such a way that he hardly realised he had been manipulated. She thought and planned *for* him, and they saw her as an excellent influence, one he had long needed. He respected her opinion as they had regretfully to admit he had never respected theirs, however much he had loved them. Then there was young Lloyd, who gave them so much pleasure and was a credit to Fanny's mothering. They saw how Louis loved the boy and it seemed right that he should now have a stepson, a child to satisfy his well-known love of children. Fanny was forty and though it was just possible she might yet give them a grandchild, it was probably unlikely. Altogether, Fanny brought into the lives of the Stevenson parents a sense of family which they had long wanted to see their son enjoy. Suddenly, he was rooted, no longer quite such a wayward spirit forever dashing off on mad whims and often forgetting to write to them.

But what they didn't appreciate was something Fanny realised very quickly. Louis had told her often enough that though he loved his parents and was profoundly grateful to them, he couldn't stand being in their company for long. He had confessed that he always felt conscious of loneliness when he was with his parents. Once, to Mrs Sitwell, he had expressed the opinion that 'the children of lovers are orphans' but now he found himself irritated by his parents and oppressed by their need of him. Even their indulgence towards him made him restless – he felt, perversely, that somehow they shouldn't indulge him so much. Fanny, who had no such difficulty with her own parents, understood very well, once she had lived in Heriot Row for a while, that though Louis's parents were wonderful, they smothered their son. Louis was not to be blamed for finding the atmosphere at home claustrophobic and she saw how he needed constant respite from their eager involvement. It was up to her, as his wife, to manage some daily degree of separation without hurting them or making them suspect the truth. Even his health was affected by living in their household and this was not all to do with Edinburgh's climate.

The climate – the cold, the damp, the biting wind – at least provided the excuse to leave the Stevensons and go south, not to France, which Louis would have preferred and to which Fanny was attracted, but to Davos in Switzerland. The doctors had decreed that only the climate of this relatively new alpine spa would cure Louis's lung complaint and, though the thought of snow and the high altitude made Fanny apprehensive, she was ready to try anything. But they had to pass through London on the way, and this meant her husband's meeting up with his friends which she quickly discovered was far worse for his health. Henley, Colvin, Baxter, Gosse – they all came to see him and stayed far too long, smoking and drinking and talking for hours. Fanny sat in a corner and listened and kept quiet, but she disapproved strongly. The morning after one of these sessions found him worn out – but still eager for more. It was bad enough when his friends came to their hotel but worse still when Louis went to visit them and Fanny could exercise no control. She was furious one evening, when Louis, who obviously wasn't well, insisted on going to dine with the Gosses. She had, of course, been invited too, but refused to accompany him. He went alone, seeming to want to be with his friends more than with her, for that evening at least. It made her miserable. As Louis's wife, she felt her judgement should matter, but in London he rejected it. He wanted to see his friends and that was that. Anyone who thought he was under Fanny's thumb was greatly mistaken.

Henley (whom Fanny disliked the most of Louis's old friends) realised eventually that Louis was stronger-willed than his wife, whatever the appearance to the contrary. He decided they were a 'couple of Babes in the Wood ... the male Babe is the principal'. In fact, he felt sorry for Fanny, seeing, over the course of time, that when Louis had made up his mind, she could do nothing with him. Henley judged her 'indolent, impractical and feckless' but Louis was worse. Both of them were extravagant but Louis was the more thoughtless – Fanny was only 'careless and thriftless' but at least spent nothing on herself. It was Louis who should have realised, for example, the cost of staying at the expensive Grosvenor Hotel while they were in London, but who gaily ran up enormous bills, which his parents had to settle. Henley, while considering that Fanny, as a good wife, should have curbed her husband's expenditure, at least did not lay the blame directly upon her.

Fanny herself felt ill by the time she and Louis departed for Davos, and wrote to her parents-in-law that if they had stayed any longer she would have become an embittered woman, full of hate for her husband's friends who went on refusing to notice what damage they were doing to him. At least, once in Davos, he was free of them, though nothing about their arrival on a bleak, bitterly cold evening after a tedious and dreadfully long journey made the place seem otherwise attractive, and Fanny was dismayed. Davos was 5,000 feet (1525 m) above sea-level, situated in the most easterly canton of Switzerland. A massive mountain wall at the end of the wedge-shaped valley in which it lay formed part of the border with Austria. It was, Fanny wrote, like 'living in a well of desolation'. The Belvedere, where they stayed, was a good hotel, only fifteen years old, and with above-average sanitary arrangements and extremely effective steam-heating. They would be comfortable there, but still Fanny was depressed by the gloom of the place. There wasn't even any snow, only frost in November when they arrived. Everything seemed grey and forlorn.

What lifted her spirits after a few weeks was the vast improvement in Louis's health. There was no doubt that Dr Karl Ruedi's treatment was working, though it consisted of little more than keeping Louis in the open air. She liked Dr Ruedi, a tall, genial man who had learned his excellent English in Colorado, and quickly had faith in him, so much so that she allowed him to put her on a diet. Fanny had become decidedly plump – or, as her husband bluntly put it, fat. He made constant jokes in letters about 'this fat woman at my elbow', called her 'a barrel of butter' and reported with glee that she had burst a button off her dress. He didn't seem to mind Fanny's being fat, rather relishing her plumpness as a sign that she was thriving, but Fanny minded. She'd weighed 131 lb (59.4 kg) in California (which, for her height, was quite heavy), and had since put on much more weight. Dr Ruedi had no doubt that the weight gain was the cause of her not feeling well and, according to Louis, threatened her with being obese. 'The word OBESITY', observed her very thin husband, 'was like a dart through her liver.' She obeyed Dr Ruedi's dietary advice: no bread, no butter, no potatoes, nothing but meat and wine. Soon, she was feeling much better and yet was puzzled to find that, though she had become much thinner, she appeared to weigh the same.

Davos was dull for her. Louis spent his time tobogganing with Lloyd once the snow came, and he had made a congenial friend, the scholar John Addington Symonds (who'd arrived in 1877 and spent the rest of his life there), but she pined for the Californian sun and wondered restlessly how long she would have to endure this cold, remote prison. By the following June, Dr Ruedi pronounced Louis well enough to spend the summer in Scotland with his parents and, though the prospect depressed

Fanny, it was preferable to Davos. Unfortunately, the summer of 1881 in Scotland turned out to be atrocious. The rain never stopped. 'The nice little Highland cottage' near Pitlochry, which Mrs Stevenson had rented, practically floated in the torrential downpour. It did Louis's lungs no good to be there. Soon, he was prostrate with a heavy cold and all the good done by wintering in Davos seemed undone. They needed to get away, but they only moved to another cottage near Braemar. The rain still fell there too, great squalls of it, and the black clouds never lifted. But here, kept inside by the weather, Louis began to write a story to amuse his stepson Lloyd. He was weak, easily tired and spitting blood but his boredom was so acute that only writing seemed to lift it. Fanny watched apprehensively. She was glad to see Louis absorbed, and more cheerful, and glad to have Lloyd entertained, but she thought Louis was wasting his creative energies by writing a children's story instead of attempting more serious stuff.

By October, when the return to Davos was made – reluctantly, but of necessity – Louis had found a magazine, *Young Folks*, to publish the story, in episodes. Fanny was proved wrong to doubt its worth. The story was *Treasure Island*, and its success, when published in book form in November 1883, was to transform their lives.

III

The second winter in Davos was an abnormally mild one, with very little snow and almost continuous sunshine. They lived not in the Hotel Belvedere but in a chalet on a hillside above it. With her own home around her, Fanny felt able to make her husband more comfortable (though there were plenty of visitors who remarked on how untidy and chaotic was their household). She hoped that the right atmosphere would enable him to write and be more successfully productive than he had been since their marriage. It irritated her that Louis had fooled around with a children's story all summer and that he was also now expending precious energy on a history of the Highland clans. Her faith in his talent was absolute but she felt he needed direction and stringent criticism to produce his best work.

This she was eager to supply. Almost everything about Fanny annoyed Louis's friends, but the way she set herself up as a judge of his writing infuriated them most. Where were her literary credentials? Non-existent. But the lack of either a proper education or experience of publishing did not seem to deter her from giving her opinion of her husband's work. She had no embarrassment about damning or praising it. What seemed astonishing to them was that Louis ever showed her his writing. The phrase 'Fanny thinks' in Louis's letters enraged them – what Fanny, just a little housewife, thought was of no importance, and it alarmed them to have evidence that Louis was listening to her. So far away from them, cooped up in Davos, she had a dangerous literary power which she was entirely unequipped to exercise.

Then there were her own literary ambitions which Louis

appeared to encourage in a misguided way. Colvin was told, while the Stevensons were at Pitlochry, that Fanny had finished a story, *The Shadow on the Bed*, and was busy completing a second. She very much wanted to see them published. Henley, to whom Louis sent the first story, when he sent his own *The Merry Men*, saying that as it was his wife's he didn't feel in a position to judge it but he felt it had something, pronounced it good and thought a magazine editor might buy it. Fanny was naturally thrilled and became hopeful, feeling (rightly) that Henley would not lie. It gave her, she wrote, 'a great lift'. But it also worried her that Louis, as a consequence, had decided that *The Shadow on the Bed* should appear not in a magazine on its own but in a volume with his own stories. She was not stupid. Unless her story really was good, people, she knew, would say it was only there because she was Louis's wife. It would, she wrote to Henley, 'be brought into such prominence by appearing with Louis's that I feel doubtful whether it is not foolish'. And yet she could not resist the idea of being a published writer alongside her already published and well-noticed, husband.

In fact, Louis had not yet written a great deal and nothing which had earned him real money or fame. *Treasure Island* was not published in book form until two years later, after Davos had been given up. Ten years before meeting Fanny, he'd published a slim historical pamphlet *The Pentland Rising*; two years after he met her, *An Inland Voyage* appeared and a year later *Travels with a Donkey*. Apart from these two travel books, some of his essays had appeared in book form but there had been no fiction yet. He had spent a great deal of time on trying to write plays, in collaboration with Henley, and Fanny had spent hours reading them and making suggestions as to how they could be improved. She did the same with the children's story, about which she had been so dismissive, writing to her in-laws that she was trying 'to see if I can help to find out where it breaks down'. Louis was happy for her to do so, reporting cheerfully to Henley that 'the pert and hypercritical Fanny Van der Grift after reading the whole of *Treasure Island* has eaten much of her venom; thinks the end quite good and only wants a chapter or so rewritten'.

So whatever his friends thought, Louis himself welcomed and encouraged his wife in the role of critic. He talked about his work with her, the pattern of their days becoming one of his writing in the mornings and then in the evenings discussing the manuscript with Fanny after she had read it. There was, at this stage anyway, nothing secretive about his work – it was open to Fanny all the time. She was completely involved in all he did because this was how he wanted it. Their marriage was indeed a meeting of minds as well as bodies and no matter what others thought of his wife's critical faculties he himself respected them. So did his father, quickly becoming convinced that not only should Fanny be listened to but that she should have control over what Louis submitted to editors and publishers. She accepted the responsibility willingly, even eagerly, and applied herself diligently to the task of vetting Louis's writing without any apparent qualms. There was a slight note of self-importance in her observations to some correspondents as to her own usefulness and significance, but this was balanced by her anxiety to do the job properly. She never said she was too tired to do the reading (even of the tedious plays), or too bored to analyse what she had read, and she never felt Louis was patronising her. On the contrary, she knew he needed her as a sounding board just as he needed her in so many other, more common, ways as a wife.

Her own needs in this second marriage were never of first importance, though like many strong women she had a yearning to be cared for herself, for someone to take charge of her welfare as she took care of so many others'. Louis certainly wasn't capable of this. He couldn't nurse himself never mind his wife, and Fanny felt the lack of this in that second Davos winter. The altitude didn't suit her. She had endless headaches, was what Louis called 'seedy', and then became quite seriously ill with what he first described as 'drain-poisoning' and then suspected was cancer. He wrote to his mother that he was miserably aware 'I am not fit to help her these bad nights and besides she scruples to call me till she is worse than she perhaps need have been.' Things got so bad that Fanny was transported to Zürich to be seen by a specialist, who finally decided the stomach pain she'd experienced and the passing of 'stools of pure bile' indicated gallstones. She returned to Davos, was dosed with laudanum, and, after nearly two months in bed, she recovered.

But, clearly, Davos would not do. However much good it did Louis's lungs – and, temporarily at least, it did them a great deal – the place made Fanny ill (her heart was affected) and depressed Louis. And it was so expensive. 'I am eaten up with shame,' Louis told Henley, '. . . hot blushes consume me . . . all Davos has swindled me.' He was still dependent on his parents, and reported them nearly 'dry of coins'. He and Fanny would have to live somewhere warmer and cheaper when the next winter came. Spain attracted him – he had a dream of the Balearic Isles – but if not Spain, then the south of France where he and his mother had gone for their health when he was a child. But first another summer in Scotland with his parents had to be endured, the weather every bit as bad as the year before and the effect on Louis worse. He had a haemorrhage and feared that the doctor, whom he went to London to consult, would banish him to Davos again. But mercifully, the south of France was agreed to as a winter destination, so long as they were somewhere near pine woods. But who was going to find such a place? Fanny was too weak, still not completely recovered both from the gallstones episodes and what she referred to as 'congestion of the brain'. Louis was hardly in a better state but at the same time desperate to get to France and so he went off with his cousin Bob to look around.

Fanny didn't really want to let them out of her sight, not trusting either him or Bob to be sensible. She knew perfectly well how dependent he had become on her. During the time at Davos, when she'd gone to Zürich, and once to Paris, he had become depressed and said he no longer seemed to take the pleasure in his own company which he had once done – 'the results, I suppose, of marriage'. But Louis spoke French, as did Bob, and both of them were familiar with the Riviera, which she was not, so she persuaded herself that no harm could after all come from allowing him out of her sight while she gathered her strength. She stayed in Edinburgh, with his parents, and he and Bob went off as arranged, first of all to Montpellier. There, Louis had another haemorrhage. As soon as she heard, Fanny was decided: she must join him. Her mother-in-law was appalled at the thought of her travelling such a distance alone and still in poor health, but off she went, finally meeting up with Louis in Marseilles.

The relief of being once more together was great, but the greater relief of finding somewhere to live was yet to come. They made a mistake, renting what seemed a perfect house near Saint-Marcel only to find the climate deadly. It was March before they were settled at Hyères, near Toulon, in the Chalet la Solitude, which Fanny described as being like a doll's house, with rooms so small they could hardly turn round in them. But in compensation the garden was large and wild, with extensive views, and perfectly secluded. A day's outing to Toulon was a delightful ride through lanes where the hedgerows were thick with roses and violets, the scents intoxicating. Toulon provided them with diversion, if they wanted it, but they did not want it often. This was their first real home, far superior to the rented chalet in Davos, and Fanny relished making it attractive. She had one maid, but did all the cooking herself, thrilled at the variety of local ingredients, but her real joy was the garden. She'd missed the cottage garden she'd had in East Oakland ever since she'd left it, and there had been no opportunity since to indulge her passion for growing things. Now, she was in the garden every day, planting herbs and vegetables as well as flowers, doing her own digging and raking and experimenting with different kinds of cultivation.

Their life, that spring and summer of 1883, was simple and tranquil. In the morning, Louis wrote as usual while she attended to household duties; in the afternoon, after a good lunch (usually of salad from the garden) and a rest, he read his morning's work aloud and they talked it over before Fanny made suggestions and offered criticisms; late afternoon they had a gentle walk until dinner (lots of fish), then they read and talked. The routine, and the climate, did them both good but not as much as it should have done. Louis had built up no resistance to germs and in May caught what he labelled an 'influenza cold'. Fanny was back to being a full-time nurse again, ever her primary duty as a wife. This time, she had help. Valentine, the local young woman she trained to share the nursing (as well as much else) soon proved skilled and took her turn at Louis's bedside. In addition to the usual symptoms, and the haemorrhages, Louis was again threatened with blindness, a severe case of ophthalmia. He couldn't read, a deprivation of the very worst kind, much worse than being told not to move – he could tolerate that, as he had been obliged to do many times, but not to be able to read was almost insupportable. To help him endure this punishment (and he was quite surprised to find it actually was possible to be alive and not read) Fanny was instructed to go for their usual walk in the afternoons and make up some story to repeat when she returned. She'd read of several outrages involving dynamite in London at that time, and so made up a tale about dynamiters to entertain Louis. He was very amused, so much so that he added to the story, as though playing consequences, and it became the basis for a book (which, when published two years later, bore both their names). Slowly, Louis recovered, but Fanny had her own worries. She was afraid she might be pregnant, which from every point of view – her age (forty-three), their financial situation (still perilous), Louis's health (poor, requiring all her energy and time to safeguard it) – would be disastrous. But it was more than that, far more. Fanny was quite passionately against bearing any more children. When her daughter Belle gave birth to a son, Austin, while the Stevensons were in Davos, she wrote to her old friend Dora Williams that she was extremely glad Belle was so far away because otherwise she might have had this baby left on her doorstep: 'And I *don't want* a baby.' Curiously, she added, 'I have a moral conviction borne in upon my soul that that baby is mine . . . it is pretty hard, isn't it, when one hasn't the courage to venture upon one for oneself that someone else should do it for you.' Belle's baby was a 'misfortune'. If she now had one herself, the misfortune would be hugely magnified. For her husband, it was a different sort of anxiety. He'd always adored children and even though he had claimed, after the deaths of several children he knew, that he didn't want a family because he wouldn't be able to stand the pain of such tragedy if it happened to any child of his, there was a lingering regret in his mind. And of course his parents had no grandchildren. They loved Lloyd, but a grandchild given to them by Louis and Fanny would satisfy and thrill them in a way Lloyd never could. He began to fantasise the having of a son or daughter and his excitement grew as did the tension. But Fanny was not pregnant. When this became clear, the relief was mixed with a sort of sadness, on his part at least.

There had been hints before of pregnancy scares and there were to be more to come but Fanny was not prepared to accept these as simply part of married life, about which nothing could be done – she was not Mary Livingstone, and times had changed. Contraception was not efficient, nor was knowledge of it freely available, but Fanny had lived in Paris where ways and means of preventing pregnancy were certainly more talked about than anywhere else. In 1879, the Mensinga diaphragm had been invented and in 1881 the first birth control clinic opened. This was in Holland, but the advice it made available spread quickly so that, though unable to go to any such clinic, Fanny had the opportunity to benefit from the advances in contraception. She had taken great risks even before she was married to Louis, sleeping with him in Paris, but in a strange way the risks did not lessen after their marriage but grew greater. In Victorian terms, she was old at forty-three and her health had not been good. Pregnancy would mean a threat to her strength and she had begun to believe she could not face it. There was no question, in the kind of relationship she had with her husband, of her being *obliged* to grant him his conjugal rights. Fanny never had to submit to Louis, as so many wives had to (and no doubt still have to). But at the same time, she was the one in whose interest it was to take every precaution available. The onus was on her, and she felt it. Her close reading of *The Lancet*, which she had sent out from London, was not only to keep up-to-date on possible treatments for Louis's illnesses but to be on the look-out for new information to help herself. She was avid for all medical knowledge.

She was also ever vigilant over possible epidemics – the very mention of the words 'typhoid' or 'scarlet fever' had her alert and ready to take Louis away. Cholera was what drove her and Louis from Hyères, where they had been so happy in spite of illness. Fanny swore she could see a cloud hanging over Toulon which meant cholera had swept through it (the cloud being of smoke from all the fires burning to clear out infected houses). Lloyd, who was staying with them on holiday from the English school where he had been sent this time when they moved abroad, said she panicked and insisted it was too dangerous for Louis to live any longer at Hyères. She forced him to leave, by easy stages, for London, partly to escape the cholera and partly to see specialists who could assess the state of his health and determine where they should live next. Once in London Louis was examined by a Dr Mennell, but there followed some confusion over the verdict. Dr Mennell thought Louis could safely live in England now, but another medical man, Dr Fox, ordered him back to Switzerland, and Dr Lauder Brunton and the eminent Sir Andrew Clark agreed with Fox. Neither Fanny nor Louis wanted to return to Davos, but by not doing so were they risking Louis's already fragile health? Should they return to the south of France, avoiding unhealthy areas? Or should they risk a winter in England?

Fanny, rapidly coming to believe she knew as much as the doctors, convinced herself that the blood Louis had been spitting, which she had seen but they had not, was bright red, not dark red, and therefore more likely to be from blood-vessels broken through coughing than from the lungs. She was sure a winter somewhere in the south of England, though certainly not London, would be feasible. The Stevenson parents were of course all for this – if they couldn't have Louis in Edinburgh, at least they would have him in England and could visit easily. And Lloyd's school was in Bournemouth, another attraction. It was to Bournemouth they went, first to see Lloyd, and then to stay, renting in November 1884 a house among pine trees (they were reputed to be good for lung diseases). Neither of them was well, though Louis thought Fanny's poor health was a direct result of worrying over his coughing and dizziness and blood-spitting. What dramatically changed things for her was the news from Thomas Stevenson that he would like to buy a house for her. Fanny was ecstatic, hardly able to sleep for thinking that she was about to own a house. She was tired of renting properties, transforming their gardens, making dreary rooms attractive – and then moving on. Now, there would be a point to all her hard work.

It took time and determination to find and then buy a suitable house, but in April Fanny concluded the purchase in Bournemouth of what was named Skerryvore, a two-storey, yellow-brick house in half an acre of ground. The garden was mostly at the back, with a lawn sloping down towards a small ravine full of rhododendrons and with a stream at the bottom. Suddenly energetic again, Fanny rushed to London to meet her in-laws and begin the delightful task of buying furniture. She bought three old oak boxes upon which she put cushions covered with yellow damask, and a cabinet and an oak coffer for a window seat and a beautiful convex mirror. Louis complained she wasn't buying the necessary, ordinary things like tables and chairs, but he was pleased to see her so happy and busy. Soon, he had to admit that she had made the drawing-room 'so beautiful that it is like eating to sit in it. No other room is so lovely in the world.' There was colour, especially yellow, everywhere. Now, at last, they could behave like any other married couple and entertain if they wished, and have friends and family to stay.

This new freedom proved a source of conflict before long. Louis, still in poor health and often bored, wanted his old friends to come and entertain him, and they were only too willing to oblige, but Fanny, as ever, thought these chums exhausted her husband and she resented their presence. Then there were new local friends, people who arrived to introduce themselves, wishing to establish some social intercourse with the author of the by now famous *Treasure Island*. According to Fanny, they poured into Skerryvore 'in droves' and she found none of them interesting or amusing. She announced that she was breaking down under the strain. Her in-laws increased it. They, of course, were welcome, and she had spent a lot of time and energy on making Louis into a more appreciative son. 'We have had,' he wrote to his father, 'a dreadful overhauling of my conduct as a son the other night, and the daft wife stripped me of my illusions and made me admit I had been a detestable bad one . . .' Fanny said he should *show* his parents how much he loved them and he was determined to try. But when they did come to stay, their presence was oppressive and, worse still, his mother arrived with a cold which Louis promptly caught. It was one thing for Fanny to turn Louis's friends out if they had colds, but she could hardly exert the same power over his mother, who did not in any case share the belief that coughs and sneezes spread diseases. She wrote to Colvin that she was so furious that suppressing her rage with her mother-in-law made her have one fainting-fit after another. If Louis died as a result of this infection she vowed it would be murder and his mother the murderess.

Louis survived, and eventually the Stevenson parents left (though returning all too quickly), but still the visitors Fanny found so tedious kept coming. Louis found her resentment irritating. He even lectured her on her arrogance, telling her, 'It is the mark of dull people to loathe others.' She was not being a good wife to sit in the corner of the room, silently glaring at his friends and complaining bitterly about them as soon as they left. But the truth was he found their social life pretty dreary too and longed for diversion of a different kind. His writing was not going well – he was trying to write some short stories for a new collection – and the couple began to have rows, some of them violent enough to alarm any witness to them. A neighbour, Adelaide Boodle, who became a regular caller, confessed she sometimes used to turn away when she approached Skerryvore and heard the shouting. But though these loud arguments at first alarmed her – 'the casual looker-on might have felt it his duty to shout for the police' – she soon realised that they signified not a real hostility between the couple but instead a complete freedom. They could, and did, say what they liked to each other – there was nothing suppressed, nor did either of them feel the need to keep up any kind of front. They could be themselves to each other. Arguing furiously was a distinct part of their marriage and one they both relished. Fanny said Louis's obstinacy opposed her firmness of character and it was only natural that sparks should occasionally fly.

But boredom was another matter, not nearly so easy to handle and far more difficult to do something about. Both of them suffered various forms of depression while in Bourne-mouth and had to find remedies. Louis was ill much of the time and couldn't be as active as he wished. He wrote to his cousin

Margaret Forster and Hunter Davies on their
wedding day, 11 June 1960.

David Livingstone, aged 39, a few years after his marriage.

Mary Livingstone, in her thirties. The cameo at her throat seems to testify to her wifely devotion.

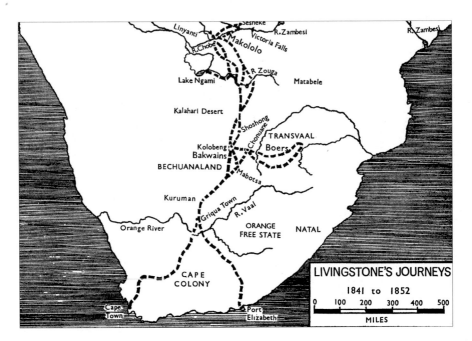

LIVINGSTONE'S JOURNEYS

1841 to 1852

0   100   200   300   400   500

MILES

Map showing how far Livingstone travelled between 1841 and 1852, and the missions at Kuruman, Mabotsa and Chonuane.

The Livingstone family in 1857: left to right, Oswell, David, Thomas, Agnes, Mary, Robert.

(*Right*) Fanny Osbourne, aged 36, around the time she met Robert Louis Stevenson in 1876.

(*Below*) Portrait of Robert Louis Stevenson, c. 1880, still boyish looking in his forties.

(*Above*) The Stevenson family in 1891, on the veranda at Vailima, Samoa: left to right, Lloyd Osbourne (Fanny's son), Mrs Mary Stevenson (RLS's mother), Isobel Strong ('Belle', Fanny's daughter), RLS, Austin Strong (Belle's son), Fanny, Joe Strong (Belle's husband).

(*Below*) The Stevensons photographed on a trip to Sydney in 1893: left to right, Fanny, RLS, Belle and Mrs Stevenson.

Jennie Lee,
newly elected MP for
North Lanark, on her way
to the House of Commons
for the first time, 1929.

Jennie Lee and Aneuran
Bevin on their wedding
day, 25 October 1934.

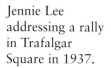

Jennie Lee
addressing a rally
in Trafalgar
Square in 1937.

Jennie and
Aneuran Bevin,
married
for over 25 years,
in the spring of
1960, shortly
before Nye's
death.

(*Inset*)
Margaret and Hunter
Davies, silver wedding
anniversary, June 1985.

(*Main picture*)
Margaret and Hunter
Davies, June 2001.

Bob that the climate required more exercise but he hadn't the strength to run around in the cold and wind. He was hardly in the open air at all and began to think even Davos preferable – at least there he had been able to toboggan and skate. It frustrated him terribly to be stuck inside, and made him irritable, which in turn made him an even more difficult patient for Fanny and Valentine to look after. They tried a little excursion together, but this trip ended in disaster when Louis had a haemorrhage in a hotel in Dorchester. Fanny had a dreadful night trying to follow his instructions to lift him into a kneeling position, his face to the pillow, so that he could breathe better. She was glad to get back to Skerryvore, but being at home didn't seem to improve Louis's health. He had awful headaches and terrible nightmares which exhausted his wife as well as him. The only good thing was that out of these disturbed nights came the story *Dr Jekyll and Mr Hyde*. He wrote a draft of it in three days, ill though he was, and presented it eagerly to Fanny. She criticised it heavily, pointing out that he had missed the allegory inherent in the story. Furious with her he threw the whole thing in the fire. She felt guilty, but then, realising she was right, he rewrote the tale in another three days. This time, Fanny approved and he went happily to work on it.

Work, as ever, made him feel better, and also made him easier to live with. But Fanny, though she tried to carry on writing her own stories and had her garden to occupy her, did not have the same stimulus and needed it. The obvious solution was to go away on her own, something she didn't like to do, preferring to be with Louis and fearing to leave him even with the capable Valentine. Should a good wife leave a sick husband? She found it hard to do, but in the end, feeling weak and run-down herself, she went to stay with the Henleys in London, in Shepherd's Bush. 'Do for God's sake amuse yourself', Louis wrote to her, and she did. Later, she went to Bath too, and the change of scene did her a great deal of good. She was learning that total devotion between husband and wife did not have to mean living like Siamese twins – each could, and did, benefit from time on their own. But Fanny benefited more than Louis. He couldn't sleep when she was away, whereas she slept better (hardly surprising, since her nights were uninterrupted when alone).

Coming home from her brief outings, Fanny looked at Louis afresh and was troubled at what she saw. She began to think he was much more seriously ill than he realised and suddenly was convinced that he was indeed consumptive. She had never thought him a handsome man (whereas Sam had been) but now, so very frail, he looked more like a boy in his teens than a thirty-five-year-old. But his powers of recuperation were tremendous, and by the spring of 1886, after a year in Skerryvore (a terrible year) there were signs they were working again. He returned to writing a boys' story, commissioned by the editor of *Young Folks* (who had published *Treasure Island*). In the spring of 1885 it hadn't gone well, but now it suddenly began to flow from his pen. But he wanted to go to London and have some fun. So off they both went, joining his parents at an hotel in Fitzroy Square. Unfortunately, Thomas Stevenson was ill, and much against her better judgement Fanny had to agree that Louis should take him to a spa. She'd worked hard to make him a better son, and could not, at this test of devotion, tell him to put himself before his father.

The spa was in Derbyshire and once installed there with his ailing father Louis was homesick. He described the women there, and the other patients were mostly women, as 'dreary bitches'. Convinced Louis was breaking down under the strain, Fanny organised his release from duty, writing in the most tactful terms to her mother-in-law, who started at once for the spa to take her husband home. Predictably, Louis took to his bed once he returned to Bournemouth, but free of his father, he recovered his own spirits rapidly. The good news that *Dr Jekyll and Mr Hyde* was selling well cheered him further and he began agitating for some kind of proper holiday. Not Scotland with his parents, though, and not even London. He was 'weary of England' and wanted to go abroad. *Kidnapped* was to be published in book form in July and the money he'd got for it, first from the serialisation and then from Cassell's, made him feel flush. But where to go? Fanny thought France 'hot and unhealthy' but he had set his heart on Paris at least and so she capitulated. They went via London, where Louis indulged his taste for mingling with the famous, writing to his mother that he had dined with Browning and lunched with Burne-Jones and was having a capital holiday. Paris was even better, except for an interview he gave to an American journalist, Olive Logan, who then wrote an inaccurate and unflattering piece, causing Fanny to remark when she read it that it was 'comic' not only in the 'hideous picture' it presented of him but in its 'summary disposal of me'.

She was feeling low anyway. London and Paris may have made Louis feel astonishingly well, but the holiday had done nothing for her. Her limbs ached and it pained her to walk. This was diagnosed as rheumatism for which there was currently a new treatment consisting of massage. It wasn't available in Bournemouth, so Louis returned alone – since he was feeling wonderful she wasn't so worried about him – and she began her treatment in London. Louis mocked it mercilessly. He wrote to his parents that Fanny was 'being pinched by Swedes' and to a friend that 'my wife is away being pinched and slapped and mauled by certain powerful Scandinavians . . . they twitch every part, the nose included'. It was all, he reported gleefully, a bit like a prize fight, but if it helped make Fanny feel better he was all for it however much he missed her. He wrote to her he could cope without her during the days but, as ever, found the nights hard – 'I have remorse when I wake alone – see how marriage relaxes a man's fibre!'

When she did go home, Fanny was furious to find that her housemaid (not Valentine) had made a poor job of looking after Louis. The mattresses were damp and the chops the girl had bought were all fat. To make matters worse, Fanny's in-laws were arriving the next day, to find a house to rent so that they could spend the winter near their dear Louis. Their search for a suitable house went on and on, the weather was bleak and grey (it was November), and she wrote to Colvin that she spent her time acting as a buffer between her husband and his parents – 'A buffer's life is a wearisome one,' she moaned to Louis, and he accused her of always looking on the dark side of everything, to which she riposted that he was like a canary bird, always twittering brightly. He retorted that it was no use turning life into a tragedy on the scale of *King Lear*. He was the optimist, she the pessimist, and though these different philosophies usually balanced out within their marriage this was a case when, instead, they got on each other's nerves.

Fanny was rescued by the need once more to take Thomas Stevenson to a spa, but though it released her from acting as a buffer, it was depressing. She took her father-in-law to Salisbury, but lasted only four days and afterwards needed another jaunt to London, alone, to recover. She was taken to the theatre by friends, and met George Bernard Shaw at someone's house and 'enjoyed herself hugely' according to her husband. It seemed as though a pattern was emerging which would be followed indefinitely, one in which life in Bournemouth could only be tolerated if it was broken up, especially in the winter, with trips to London, either together or separately. But it was a pattern Louis resented, writing, 'I do not love this health-tending, housekeeping life of mine.' Fanny liked it better, taking pleasure in her house and in tending her garden, but even she was not entirely content. There was the feeling that something would have to change before another winter.

The change which came was not of their own making but it set in motion a course of events which was to end in their quitting Bournemouth. On 7 May 1887, Thomas Stevenson died. Fanny and Louis were both in Edinburgh, in answer to Margaret Stevenson's urgent summons, but had arrived only the day before, by which time the dying Thomas was unable to recognise his son. The funeral was on 13 May, but by then Louis had a cold and was too ill to attend. The moment it was over, there were legal matters to be dealt with, cold or not. Louis, who had trained and qualified as a lawyer, even though he had never practised as one, should have found this task easy, but it proved complicated. At first, he thought it looked as though 'the Church of Scotland might walk off with the whole' but luckily this proved not to be the case. His mother was well provided for, though in her lifetime he himself didn't actually inherit anything. Margaret Stevenson bore up well, determined to be as cheerful as ever whatever her grief, but it felt wrong to leave her alone in the Heriot Row house when they returned to Bournemouth. But she had her own suggestion to make. Dr Balfour, called in for Louis's cold, had expressed the opinion that what he needed was a winter not in Davos but in Colorado. He'd even gone so far as to promise this would effect a complete cure. With about £20,000 capital at her disposal, his mother proposed that Louis and Fanny should try a few months in Colorado and she would pay.

The idea fired Louis's imagination at once – the thought of the sea-voyage alone thrilled him – and of course for Fanny it would mean a chance to visit her own family whom she had not seen for seven years. Thomas Stevenson had included Fanny and her son Lloyd in his will and her £3,000 legacy would pay for a visit to Indianapolis in comfort. But still there was the problem of leaving Louis's mother, widowed and alone in Edinburgh. Louis wrote to her 'if you won't go to Amerikee, no more will we' but it was Fanny's letter which was the more persuasive. She proved herself a kind woman and a good daughter-in-law, writing that since Margaret had only Louis left now 'I could not take him away from you even for his own good.' Margaret had apparently confessed she would only spoil everything by being so miserable because Fanny wrote, 'As to your being a wet blanket, how do you think we should feel knowing we had left you behind with your sad heart?' It was not to be thought of. 'Come with us, dear,' she urged, 'and let us try to be to you what we can, even though that may be little.' In fact, both Louis and Fanny wanted her to come to them immediately without waiting for the Colorado plans to be finalised. The change would do her good – 'and your presence might cheer us up.' It was nicely put, and so was Louis's final word, 'I have been a bad enough son all round; I would now be a decently good one if possible.' She was persuaded.

On 21 August, having let the Bournemouth house, Fanny, Louis, Lloyd, Margaret Stevenson and Valentine the maid set sail for New York.

IV

If Fanny had any misgivings about travelling with her mother-in-law, she did not express them. She had always liked Margaret Stevenson, now known as Aunt Maggie (for Lloyd's sake), and she had noted that it was only the *joint* presence of the Stevenson parents that had a bad effect on Louis. His mother on her own would be a different matter, especially since she was so amenable and less likely to impose her will. There was every hope that she would fit in well and not come between her son and daughter-in-law.

So it proved. Margaret Stevenson enjoyed the voyage to America, not minding a bit that Fanny had mistakenly booked their passage on a cargo ship carrying animals. Louis, she wrote to her sister, looked as young and gay as a schoolboy – he was 'a hardy mariner' and so was she. Both of them were on deck all the time, while Fanny was obliged to lurk in her cabin much of the way, suffering from seasickness. Aunt Maggie taught her to knit socks, to pass the time, but she had to struggle to turn the heel and Louis vowed she'd secretly asked help from every member of the crew. Mother and son formed an alliance on board ship which slightly excluded Fanny but caused her no distress. She'd always been able to see Louis in his mother, and since she herself had a good relationship with her own son she was never silly enough to be in competition with her mother-in-law. On the contrary, it pleased her to see the two of them so close.

Once established, not in Colorado but in Saranac in the Adirondack mountains, things were a little different. Arriving in New York, Louis had received an astonishingly rapturous welcome from an American public, who loved both *Dr Jekyll and Mr Hyde* and *Kidnapped* (published the year before) and were intensely curious about him. He was suddenly a success, but success brought with it problems Fanny had never had to handle for him before. She'd had practice as a guard-dog when his friends threatened to exhaust him, but in New York she had to protect him from the press and from publishers frantic to sign him up. It was all very flattering, but also tiring, and she couldn't wait to get him away to the peace and healthy climate of the mountains.

In Saranac, they were living in what was little better than a shack, a house built of wooden boards with four rooms and a kitchen, ten minutes from the village. It was primitive in the extreme, far more primitive than the chalet in Davos, but Louis liked the simplicity and lack of comfort. He wouldn't let his mother put a cloth on the bare wooden table and he saw no need for the footstools she craved. The draughts were terrible, but he thought them healthy, and as for the lack of tea- and coffee-pots and egg-cups he was exasperated that she should want such fripperies.

It was a freezing cold winter, far colder than the winters at Davos, so cold that ink froze and food had to be thawed before it could be eaten. Unlike Davos, there was little sun but instead lots of grey days which were depressing for all of them, cooped up in such a comfortless home. As soon as they were settled, Fanny left Louis in charge of his mother and went off to Indiana to visit her mother and sister (her father had died) but she was back before the real snows began. Just as well because the snow became so deep that the shack was almost buried and they had to clear pathways to get in and out. She made another quick trip to Montreal to buy furs for them all to wear; and then they simply had to hole up and see the winter out, hoping the hardship was worth it for Louis's health – everything, always, was for the sake of Louis, both mother and wife willing to put up with anything to benefit him. Fanny pined for warmth and sunlight, but struggled on in the snow, not feeling at all well herself, but pleased that Louis was thriving and had begun to write (*The Master of Ballantrae*). She kept a close eye on her mother-in-law, not allowing her in the same room as her son when she had a cold. Aunt Maggie complained that she felt like a figure in a weather-box – when she came out, Louis had to go in, and vice versa.

But they survived the cold and the claustrophobic conditions and at last spring came. Fanny went, as soon as it was possible to travel easily, to San Francisco. Ostensibly, she was going ahead to see if a boat could be chartered to fulfil Louis's ambition to sail to the South Seas, but she was also going to seek medical advice and maybe treatment. She had a growth in her throat and was anxious about it. At that time no connection was made between smoking and cancer, but Fanny, who had smoked since her Reese River days, was suspicious. She had the growth removed and luckily it proved benign, but she went on to Monterey to convalesce, staying with her sister Nellie. It was such a pleasure to be in the sun again, and beside the sea, and she hoped she would never have to endure another winter, of ice and snow and biting winds. Cruising in the South Seas was Louis's idea, but it was one to which she was attracted, in spite of being a poor sailor, simply by the prospect of warmth.

There was a great deal for Fanny to organise before this adventurous cruise could start, but she was more than equal to the task. Organisation of this sort, putting together a Grand Plan as it were, was far more to her taste than, say, sorting out their financial affairs. Louis cabled that she was his 'blessed girl' for finding and hiring the *Casco*, a schooner of 70 tons which came complete with captain and crew. He knew, as did his mother, how Fanny dreaded sailing, how seasick she would undoubtedly be, and that she was agreeing to this adventure for his sake – she would have been far happier settling for sun in stable California instead of sailing thousands of miles in search of it. But she entered into the spirit of this enterprise enthusiastically, refusing to worry about the possible danger and looking ahead to what would be required once the South Seas were reached. Different clothes, for one thing. Her mother-in-law was startled to find Fanny was having made for her and for herself and Valentine the most extraordinary gowns, little more than chemises with a flounce round the lower edge and a sort of loose gown worn over it, so that it was like wearing two nightdresses, one sleeveless. This made Aunt Maggie distinctly uncomfortable – she didn't know if she ever would be able to discard her corsets and fitted bodices, but Fanny couldn't wait. She'd never liked tight, formal gowns and loved the idea of such freedom from restraint (especially as she was now overweight again).

She gave equal care to the matter of drugs. Her mother-in-law was impressed at how Fanny consulted with medical opinion before they set off and had everyone vaccinated against smallpox except Louis, for whom the vaccine was not considered safe. Knowing this, Fanny took with her a syringe and what his mother referred to as 'lymph' so that if he did contract the disease she could inject him herself, since in that case it would be necessary. She also took two medical reference books and a wide variety of remedies for all kinds of ailments. In effect, she equipped herself to be the ship's doctor. Fanny also supervised the stores brought on board, even though she was not the ship's cook, and made sure the party would be properly nourished. By the time they sailed from San Francisco on 28 June 1888, she was exhausted and soon, of course, violently seasick. She spent hours lying in her berth – the three women were 'laid away on shelves to sleep' concealed by white lace curtains, as Aunt Maggie described it to her sister – willing herself to conquer the nausea, but it never entirely disappeared before they reached the Marquesas Islands where, thankfully, they went on shore.

At last Fanny felt her suffering had been worthwhile – Louis was looking tanned and fit, as was Lloyd, and once she had land under her feet she, too, revelled in the island life. The islands were beautiful and the islanders friendly. Whole days were spent swimming and picnicking; even Aunt Maggie donned a bathing suit and had her first swim for twenty-six years. They were soon 'red as lobsters' and rather ashamed of 'our own plain white legs' when they looked at the lovely brown limbs of the islanders. They were in the open air all day long, ending with walks on the beaches in moonlight when Louis played his pipe. Everything was perfect, until they sailed on to Tahiti where, inexplicably considering how superbly well he had been, Louis was taken ill again. At the same time it was found that a mast was rotten on the *Casco* and the boat had to leave them there to go and be refitted. Fanny was as resourceful as ever, finding a house in which she could nurse Louis. Here he spent weeks recuperating, before moving eventually to the house of Princess Moë (ex-queen of the island) and becoming great friends with her and her family. Fanny was happy living like an islander (once Louis was on the mend) but his mother was not at ease. She was amazed that her daughter-in-law had gone so 'native', describing how she lay on a pillow in the chief's smoking-room, taking a whiff of a native cigarette and passing it on in the approved way. She sat cross-legged with the women, too, and learned how to weave hats and baskets. Fanny relished every local dish, but it was not enough for her to enjoy the food – she was determined to learn how to make various specialities and wrote the recipes down in a special notebook where she'd written those for bouillabaisse in France and noodle soup in Indiana. She'd always been a good cook, but now her repertoire extended to include the exotic. Her mother-in-law was impressed – how lucky her son was to have a wife who was an excellent nurse and a good cook.

Fanny was indeed a 'good wife', but she had children and that complicated her marriage to Louis. And as the Stevensons set sail on the refitted *Casco* for Honolulu, these complications hove into view. Louis had taken responsibility for Lloyd when he married Fanny and had been delighted to do so – he loved the boy, thought he was 'dam fine', and felt that if he was to have no children of his own Lloyd was as close as he could get to paternity. But Fanny's daughter Belle was a different matter. Lloyd was twelve when Louis married Fanny, Belle twenty-two, herself married and therefore legally not his responsibility. But, however much her daughter's marriage to the artist Joe Strong had angered Fanny, she could not entirely cast Belle off and neither could Louis. The Strongs' marriage had had its problems almost from the beginning, and financial help had been requested, just as Fanny knew it would be. Reluctantly Louis had given it. Belle and Joe and their son Austin (born in 1881) had been living in Honolulu for the last seven years. Joe painted and Belle taught, and both of them enjoyed the life of the island – until Joe began to enjoy it a bit too much. He was drinking heavily and became ill. Belle maintained that the cause of his collapse was sunburn leading to blood-poisoning, which in turn caused a nervous breakdown. The two of them were in debt, and no longer getting on (and a second child had been born and died). It was towards this domestic situation that Fanny and Louis were now sailing.

When the *Casco* swept into the harbour and the Stevenson party disembarked, Belle couldn't get over how well and brown Louis looked and was equally bowled over by the change in her brother. Lloyd was now, at nineteen, thoroughly English in his speech and manner, though she also noted the gold rings in his ears – decidedly un-English. During the next four months the house Fanny rented on Waikiki beach became the centre of a new kind of family life, of which the Strongs were very much a part. Belle observed how her mother 'managed' her husband, protecting him from, as she put it, 'draughts, colds, bores and fatigue' without his even noticing it. But she also realised what Henley had noted long before, that under it all, Fanny was only a wife. Louis was emphatically head of the house, with his own rules which had to be obeyed, even by Fanny. (These rules were simple enough – talk within his house was to be confidential, no irritating topics were to be brought up at mealtimes, books must be treated respectfully – but they were real.) Louis was the breadwinner, his word was law in the Waikiki household, just as if he were a paterfamilias in Edinburgh. Belle liked him – she and Lloyd had always liked him – but she was wary of him. He and Fanny together had the power to dominate her and make her do what she might not want to do.

In this, she was right. Fanny and Louis had decided that Joe Strong needed to be straightened out, and Belle and Austin to be brought under their wing. A week before the Stevensons were due to depart, on another ship, Belle was summoned by Louis and told she was to go to Sydney and wait for their arrival there. It was an order. Her mother, she observed bitterly, agreed to everything her husband said, while letting him be the one to say it. Belle wept and pleaded – she loved Honolulu and had wanted to stay there for ever – but it was useless. Saying of herself that she had always, unlike her mother, been 'rather a meek person' who 'always obeyed the

nearest man' she dried her tears and started making preparations to leave for Sydney with the nine-year-old Austin. Joe
would be separated from them, taken on the cruise with the
Stevensons.

Fanny was just as reluctant to leave Honolulu – 'I hate the
sea,' she had vowed many times and on reaching Honolulu
she'd told her mother-in-law she would never leave land again.
But Louis loved the sea, and never felt better than when sailing.
Besides, they had not yet found an island where they felt they
could settle. Fanny, the great organiser, had failed to make
progress on that one. Her mother-in-law, going back to
Scotland alone to visit her sister, was told that Louis and Fanny
would follow for a visit soon. Belle noted that Mrs Stevenson
didn't shed a tear when she departed, confident she would see
her son the following year and that meanwhile his health would
go on improving in the warm climate of the South Seas.
Meanwhile, Louis wanted to buy a schooner of his own, but
Fanny persuaded him to charter one, the *Equator*, for the
meantime, and this they did, sailing from Honolulu in June
1889, taking Joe Strong with them. Fanny was the only woman
on board, never having replaced Valentine (who had returned
to California soon after reaching Honolulu) and feeling no need
for female help or company.

One of the qualities that Louis loved and admired most in his
wife was this lack of a feeble side to her femininity. She was
perfectly comfortable in an all-male environment, objecting
only that all decisions about cooking should be referred to her.
Seasick though she was, barely able to face the sight of food,
she found herself having to choose menus for the cook to
follow. At least this task grew simpler as they sailed first to the
Gilbert Islands and supplies dwindled. The *Equator* was
actually a trading vessel and it had been agreed that trading for
copra could continue while the Stevenson party was settled
temporarily on an island. They were put ashore at Apemana,
where they spent six weeks. Fanny loved it. She always had
seeds with her, and sowed onions and radishes here, which
flourished in record time giving them fresh vegetables, a much
needed addition to their diet. Louis had been heard to say, 'I

think I could shed tears over a dish of turnips,' and Fanny felt much the same.

The next port of call, when the *Equator* returned, was to be Apia, on the island of Samoa. On the way, they were hit by a hurricane. The excitement of the heavy seas and violent squalls of wind exhilarated Louis but Fanny, though courageous, found it hard to endure. She was glad her mother-in-law wasn't there to suffer the discomfort of being drenched, as the cabins let in water under the strain of the torrential rain and the whole ship was awash. It was a relief to reach Samoa in the Navigator Islands and get land under her feet, though Apia didn't attract them at first. They themselves were not exactly attractive to the inhabitants either, looking, as one of the local missionaries described them, like a troupe of down-at-heel entertainers. Fanny, dressed in a decidedly crumpled 'holoku', wore a huge, battered straw hat and carrier her guitar; Louis had a calico shirt on, and wore a pair of thin, baggy cotton trousers; Lloyd's earrings were large and golden ones and he wore dark glasses (only because his eyes were weak), and Joe as ever looked the macho artist with his moustachios.

They stayed with a white trader called Moors, who had a Samoan wife, and here Fanny sat on his verandah facing the sea and tried to take stock. Louis would roam the ocean for ever if she let him, but it would not do, not just for herself but for the family as a whole, and even more importantly, for Louis's work. He couldn't write comfortably or in any regular, settled fashion on board ship, and she wanted to see him write. But she also wanted a home again, a proper home, with a garden she could plan and cultivate with a long-term future in mind. Louis still imagined he would return to England when he was completely better. Though she doubted if such a return would ever be wise, she could not say so, since it would imply that she thought he would never be healthy enough to withstand the cold winters of his homeland. The thing to do, surely, was to go along with her husband's fantasy and at the same time encourage his other ambition also, to have a residence of some sort in the South Seas. Samoa would do very nicely, not just because the island was more beautiful than it had at first appeared, but because communications with England were, relatively speaking, good.

There were three ships calling each month which could take and bring mail, on a regular route between San Francisco and Sydney.

The search began. Moors took them away from Apia up into the hills, where immediately they noticed the difference in the air. This was the place to be, just a couple of miles from the town and yet remote enough to provide perfect seclusion. They bought 314½ acres (127.5 hectares) of what was really only bush, wild land without any dwelling on it. Moors would have the land cleared and a temporary cottage erected while a house was built to their own specifications; it would be large enough to accommodate Joe and Belle and Austin and Lloyd and Aunt Maggie whenever they wished to live with them. Louis wrote excitedly to Baxter that this little estate, christened Vailima (meaning five waters), had everything – stunning views, lush vegetation, complete privacy. Funnily enough, Fanny was not so enthusiastic. She was the one who wanted to put roots down and have a real home, but going along with Louis's passion for Vailima was, in her own mind at least, a form of compromise. She had to go with the tide – Samoa was where her husband showed himself more than willing to buy a property and if she hummed and hawed with reservations he might never be brought to the point of decision again. Samoa, and Vailima, it would have to be, or they would wander around the South Seas for ever and she'd be doomed to a life of seasickness. She tried to be as excited as Louis, but could not get over her instinctive dislike of the Samoans (whereas she had loved the Tahitians) or her dread of the vast amount of work needed to turn Vailima into a self-supporting unit. She would have to do everything herself and felt exhausted and alarmed at the prospect. But she was determined to put a brave face on it. She didn't want people to think she was sacrificing herself for the sake of her husband as a 'good wife' should. 'In fact,' she wrote, 'I *can't* make a sacrifice for him; the very fact that I can do the thing in a way makes a pleasure to do it, and it is no longer a sacrifice, though if I did it for another person it would be.'

The building of even makeshift accommodation was going to take time, so while it was being done, and the ground cleared for the larger enterprise, Louis decided to pay his long-promised visit to England, going via Sydney. His health was just about the best it had ever been – '[in] his present state of almost rude health', wrote Fanny – and he was anxious to see his friends and visit his publishers as well as enjoy 'civilisation' for a little while. Lloyd had gone ahead, joining Belle and Austin, who had been waiting in Sydney, as instructed, for the last six months. Their party arrived at the Hotel Victoria in February, once more inviting comment at their extraordinary appearance. If Apia found Fanny's 'holoku' strange, Sydney found this weird dress even more so, though it was her best grey silk, and Louis's 'good' suit was so creased after months in a packing-case that it looked shabby beyond belief. The grand Hotel Victoria received the couple snobbishly, unaware that they had a famous author in their lobby, and so the Stevensons removed themselves to another, less impressive hotel. Neither of them could tolerate judgements about people made on the basis of their attire.

They were both looking forward to what Sydney had to offer – bookshops, restaurants, educated company. In fact, almost two years of roughing it, whether on board ship or on small islands, had given them a taste for the sort of social life they normally professed not to need. In spite of a warm welcome, Sydney proved a disappointment. In no time at all, they were both sick of journalists wanting to interview them and the adulation of Louis's fans soon palled. But worse than that, he caught a cold, the first for ages. The doctor moved Louis to the Union Club, saying this was where he could be properly cared for, but the club was an all-male one and his removal there meant Fanny could not be with him night and day. Their plans to go on to England went ahead, but had to be scrapped when Louis did not recover. Instead, he developed a fever and then, to Fanny's despair and his own anguish, he had a haemorrhage. The only thing to do was to get him back to the warm South Seas as quickly as possible. But the maritime unions were on strike and the quays full of ships at anchor – no one was sailing anywhere.

Fanny's resourcefulness in this crisis was greater than ever before. She showed an absolute determination to surmount all obstacles and get her very sick husband back to a climate where he could survive. She herself went to every single shipping office, searching for a ship, any ship, that would take them back to the South Seas. She would not take no for an answer, feeling sure that someone somewhere would be flouting the unions, or that there must be some essential traffic the unions would have to allow, or even that in this vast harbour there would be a ship crewed by non-union sailors. So it proved. She found that the *Janet Nicholl*, a steamer belonging to a Scots firm – how appropriate – and crewed by Melanesians was about to sail. She went to see the captain, who turned her down flat, so then she contacted the owners, threatening them that her husband, her *famous* husband, would die on their hands if they did not grant him a passage. Belle, who had heard one owner tell her mother very firmly that such a thing was out of the question, was astonished, on returning to the room, to hear him giving instructions as to how to reach the *Janet Nicholl* and board her. Fanny's powers of persuasion owed nothing to feminine wiles but instead to sheer toughness – when she had to, she could intimidate others, a trait of hers in which her husband revelled.

Getting Louis on board was an anxious business. The tension of manoeuvring the board-like stretcher to which he was strapped, wrapped up in blankets, over the high bulwarks was not helped by drizzle, or by the rolling of the ship. There was an atmosphere of doom, with Fanny sitting silently in the rowing boat, eyeing the ship's blackened hull (black-painted sides covered in coal dust). She and Louis had never been on a ship as sinister-looking as this one. Belle had no confidence in the 'half-naked black men' who carried the sick man to his cabin, and was frightened by the sound of a drunk lurching around on deck. But Fanny, who kept a diary on that trip, found the old *Janet Nicholl* much more comfortable than the *Equator* had been. For a start, there were two bathrooms, and a wide deck to walk on once calm seas were reached, as well as a large airy saloon. Even the food was good. There was only one other passenger, a Mr Buckland, known as Tin Jack, a trader, and he fascinated Louis. By the time the ship reached Auckland, Louis was beginning to recover and Fanny felt she could go shopping. So did Tin Jack, unfortunately. He bought, among other things, some fireworks to amuse his native retainers when he got back to his trading post. These exploded one night and the flames set light to the baggage. Everything blazing was hurled over the side in a panic, but just in time Fanny spotted that a trunk about to go the same way contained Louis's manuscripts. She managed to persuade the sailors to extinguish the flames on deck and keep the scarred trunk.

In spite of this fright, Fanny reckoned afterwards that the cruise on the dour-looking *Janet Nicholl* was 'perhaps the happiest period of my life'. It was a statement as strange as Louis's own, that he had only ever been happy in Hyères. What was there to make Fanny so happy on that voyage? Louis was still ill, if regaining strength daily as soon as they reached warm seas; she was not as seasick as she had been on other ships but she still preferred dry land; and she records that she had rheumatism. But on the other hand, she had her husband to herself and she was keeping a journal to supplement his diary and so had the feeling of working with him, which she liked. She felt mentally as well as emotionally intimate with him, a feeling she treasured. Louis, she wrote in her journal, was 'a man of few intimate friends and even with these he was reticent to a degree'. Baxter, Henley, Colvin, Gosse and even Mrs Sitwell might have contested that last phrase, but Fanny was supremely confident of her closeness to her husband. She was proud of it, and rejoiced, on board the *Janet Nicholl* as it ploughed its way towards Samoa, that the bond between them had strengthened with time.

But still she longed to have a home to return to and fretted during the cruise about what kind of progress would have been made at Vailima. Apia was one of the *Janet Nicholl*'s ports of call, so she and Louis had the chance to inspect their new property. They were relieved to find the estate had been cleared, ready for building to start, and that a small wooden house had already been knocked together for their temporary occupation when they returned. Neither of them was quite sure when that would be – they were going to cruise for three months. The strange thing was that Fanny, anxious though she was to have a home, did not seem to regard Vailima as their absolutely final destination. She seemed to imagine that a place which would appeal more to her might be found and wrote that she hankered after an island like Nassau, not far from Samoa. The

Janet Nicholl sailed past it and she longed to go and inspect it, but the surf was too rough for her to attempt going ashore in the boat. Louis went with the sailors and came back enthusiastic. He was well again, looking tanned and fit, obviously well able to jump in and out of boats. Fanny, on the other hand, was not (however much she later vowed how happy she had been). Apart from her rheumatism, she had other troubles: once more, she was convinced she was pregnant – which, at her age (fifty exactly) would have been remarkable. She was surely not pregnant but menopausal. She was well read in medical lore and well acquainted with her own body, so for her to tell a friend years later that she had thought herself pregnant seems odd. It sounds almost as if she were trying to make clear that her marriage was flourishing in all respects, including the sexual, however ill her husband may have been.

In fact, towards the end of the *Janet Nicholl* cruise, he had another relapse, bitterly disappointing himself as well as Fanny. He blamed it on the heat in his cabin where he had been hard at work. The thought of returning to Sydney, where he had been so very ill, did not appeal to him while he was still so weak, so instead he stayed at Nouema, the ship's last stop before Australia, while Fanny and Lloyd went on alone. She was reluctant to leave him, but thought that it might be better if she went ahead to prepare for his reception so that he could slip in as quietly as possible once he was well enough to join her. This he did, quite quickly, but almost immediately caught another cold and was prostrate. It was terribly depressing. Illusions of returning to England were smashed – even a visit would be fatal for Louis's health. He was obliged to write and tell his friends so. When they heard the news, instead of being sympathetic and understanding they were disbelieving and angry. And they blamed Fanny. She, not ill-health, was keeping Louis from them. Reading their letters, Fanny cried all night. She was cast as the possessive wife, endlessly manipulating her husband to his disadvantage. They had never seen him in the South Seas, mostly healthy and well, living an outdoor life and revelling in his ability to walk and ride and do all the things a man of forty ought to be able to do. In England, he'd spent more than half his time in bed, coughing or wheezing, whereas in the tropics, if he was ill, he recovered quickly and was hardly prostrate at all. The lesson was glaringly obvious to Fanny, but his friends refused to believe it. She was cutting Louis off from them and – or so they were convinced – from the source of his work, from its inspiration. What, after all, had he written since he left England? Nothing whatsoever to compare with *Kidnapped*, *Treasure Island*, *Dr Jekyll and Mr Hyde*. And very nearly nothing at all. Fanny was ruining his work, robbing him of his genius by keeping him in an unstimulating environment.

Fanny was made to feel like some kind of criminal, and nothing Louis could say could soften the impact of his friends' hostility. But she knew she was right – Louis could *not* risk going back to England – and so she just had to accept the criticisms. Even Sydney was not good for him. It was the start of the Australian winter and the sooner they were back in Samoa the better. She organised their return passage on a German steamer, but first she sent Lloyd back to England on an important mission. Skerryvore, her Bournemouth house, given to her by her father-in-law, would have to be sold. The money was needed to build and decorate the Vailima house and since it was her family who were draining Louis of his money (principally Belle and Joe Strong), it was time for her to contribute her share. 'But this money is yours,' Louis protested. True. It was. It was her only money, her valuable bit of economic independence, but since what was Louis's had always been hers, she thought that what she had should be his. They shared money as well as everything else, and she was extremely conscious she had had very little to share.

There were other important decisions to be made before she and Louis left Sydney. If he was never again to go to England, what should be done about his mother? They could not leave her in Edinburgh alone. Lloyd was instructed to bring Aunt Maggie back with him. Then there was Belle. Belle assumed that she and Austin would be staying in Sydney, supported by Louis if Joe could not make a living. She'd never wanted to leave Honolulu, and having given way on that one because she had no choice, she was reluctant to give way again. Why should she move on a second time, when she had made friends in Sydney and grown to like it? The answer was: because her stepfather said so. He wanted his family together. Joe Strong was draining him of money and he wanted him away from temptation and under his eye. But it was more than that. He told her that she and Lloyd were all the family he had and he didn't want them far away. He wanted his family to be a unit, with himself its head.

What Fanny thought is not known. Having Belle and company resident in Sydney might well have seemed to her preferable. But whatever her feelings, it was agreed that the Strongs would follow on when Vailima was ready. Meanwhile, she and Louis would go and camp there.

V

As soon as she got back to Samoa, Fanny had to start working harder than she had done in her whole life, apart from her Reese River days (when she had been young, strong and healthy). By the summer of 1890, she was fifty years of age and for the previous decade had been plagued by a variety of ailments which made her physically much weaker and mentally not nearly as resolute and steady. Her husband needed to be looked after with ever-increasing care and she could not look to him for the kind of practical help she needed. Finding help was one of her major problems. Previously, in the houses they'd rented throughout their married life, she had had to find household maids, but maids were not top priority at Vailima. What was called for was a good deal of brute strength to put the estate into proper shape. She needed labourers to work under her supervision in the garden and to finish the interior of the house. She didn't speak any Samoan and with her famous inability (and unwillingness) to learn foreign languages she was not likely to pick it up easily.

And yet this exhausting period had its satisfactions and pleasures. She and Louis lived in the temporary wooden cottage, which Moors had erected. It had only two rooms, but Fanny's home-making instincts soon had them looking attractive, the walls hung with 'tapa' (the local cloth made from bark and decorated with patterns), the floors covered with woven straw mats, the windows hung with pink and maroon cotton curtains which she'd quickly run up and Louis's books carefully arranged on six shelves. It was cosy and colourful, and both of them enjoyed the intimacy of their quarters. But Fanny wasn't in the cottage much – she was out from dawn to dusk struggling to make a garden out of the cleared area of bush. She had grand ideas of making it not simply beautiful, full of all the flowers and shrubs she could persuade to grow, but also valuable, producing all the fruit and vegetables they would need to live on. Louis admired her efforts tremendously; writing to friends, he described how 'rain or shine, a little blue indefatigable figure is to be observed howking about certain patches of the garden. She comes in heated and bemired up to the eyebrows.' But slowly, she made progress, directing her Samoan helpers with emphatic gestures to make them do what she wanted and to plant everything the right way up. Almost every plant she tried flourished, and flourished rapidly. The pigs were harder. She was determined to keep pigs (as well as hens) much to Louis's amusement. He wrote that she fought endless battles with her 'wild swine' and would not let the big black sow outwit her.

Naturally, all this outdoor work, a lot of it heavy, tired her, but to Louis she seemed finally in her element. She was, he teased her, a peasant through and through – he saw her as glorying in battling with the land which she owned, and loved as much as any human being; he, on the other hand, was an artist and could not get excited by ownership. If he meant this as a joke, or thought his wife would be complimented by being told she had the soul of a peasant, he miscalculated. Fanny was hurt. It depressed her to be so labelled and then she was annoyed that it depressed her. She wanted to be an artist too, if a feeble one compared with Louis. He'd made her feel suddenly inferior in a way he never had done before and she brooded over the slight. 'My vanity', she commented, 'lies prone and bleeding.' But it was more than her vanity which suffered. She was not, in fact, a vain woman but she did cherish certain dreams of achieving some measure of literary or artistic merit and did not like to have them exposed as illusions. If she was indeed a peasant there was the implication that she should stick to peasant-like tasks and she did not want to be condemned to such a fate, however inspired she was by transforming the estate into something productive and lovely.

Meanwhile, the main house was being built and in this Louis was as involved as Fanny. He might not be able to do the field work, though he had a go at slashing the undergrowth (a sign of how much better he was), but he could pore over plans and make decisions about rooms and features. Each of them drew and redrew the plans, trying desperately to keep the price of building, and of fitting the interior, down. Every single bit of the materials – glass, wood, nails, pipes, paint – had to be imported from Sydney or America. The cost was prodigious, however hard they tried to effect economies. Some everyday things they fixed on turned out to be appalling luxuries, such as a chimney so that they could have a fire. Who in the South Seas had chimneys? No one. Building it was extravagant, costing thousands (and thought mad). It was Fanny who did battle with the builders, standing over them and trying to make herself plain through the sheer force of her personality. It was even more exhausting than working on the land, and gave her terrible headaches, but after six months of this it was Louis who went to Sydney for a break, not Fanny. But for once she seemed almost relieved to be on her own, though also a little nervous. Lying in the cottage at night, it would suddenly strike her how isolated she was, dependent on one servant, a German called Paul, for her safety if anything should go wrong. There had already been a taste, though a mild one, of what a hurricane could be like, and she had felt the tremor of an earthquake once. Her bedroom was not the most reassuring place to be, either – it was crammed with tobacco tins and wine bottles, for which there was no room downstairs, as well as all their clothes, and her easel and paints (though little painting had been done since Paris), as unlike a woman's bedroom as it was possible to imagine. In the dark, it was quite sinister and claustrophobic.

Louis was away longer than she expected because he fell ill, and had to be nursed in Sydney by his mother who had just arrived from England. She was coming to live with them, or rather to see if she thought she could. Fanny had misgivings too. Aunt Maggie, for all her spirit, was a most proper Victorian lady who had very set ideas about behaviour. Fanny had not been fooled by the readiness of her mother-in-law to adapt during their voyages together – those were adventures; living in Samoa would be something much more challenging.

For a start, there was the problem of a lady's maid. Fanny didn't have one. She did everything for herself, and in the matter of clothing and adornment, the chief concerns of a lady's-maid, 'everything' amounted to very little. Maggie would expect a maid and there was none available. 'The bush is no place for fine lady companions,' Fanny wrote in her diary, and expressed the hope that her mother-in-law would manage with help from herself. She was a little alarmed to find that when Louis arrived with his mother she had brought her own sofa with her. Life in Samoa was not one of lying on sofas, and in any case there was nowhere to put it in their crowded cottage. Quite how Aunt Maggie was going to fit in was far from clear.

In her letters home to her sister, Aunt Maggie's own doubts emerged, though carefully glossed over with apparent delight at what she found. Louis, now recovered again, looked tanned and well, if even thinner than usual, and Fanny she thought blooming, in spite of all her hard work. She was amazed at the triumph of Fanny's garden, describing all the onions, turnips, parsley, tomatoes, green peppers and bananas growing in abundance – she had never seen anything like it. But the hours her son and daughter-in-law kept did not please her. Breakfast was at the heathenish hour of six a.m., lunch at eleven a.m., dinner at five p.m., and then bed at nine p.m. She realised this routine was in response to the climate, but all the same she found it hard to get used to. The weather was poor, with days and days of heavy rain, and finally Aunt Maggie could stand this strange existence no longer. She did the sensible thing, returning to Sydney, to wait there in comfort until the big house was ready. It was a relief all round. There was perhaps also a little smugness in Fanny's diary entry that her mother-in-law had not been able to tolerate the discomfort that she herself had tolerated for months without respite.

By April (1891), the main house was ready for occupation, though far from finished. From the outside, it looked striking, with its peacock-blue painted walls and bright red roof and verandahs, but inside it was less impressive, reminding some visitors of an empty barn. Fanny had wanted the house to be airy, partly for reasons of health and partly for aesthetic reasons, and every effort had been made to give a feeling of space, with sliding glass doors opening on to verandahs so that the rooms seemed to project outside. Colour was important. She hung a yellowish-terracotta 'tapa' in the dining-room and had the ceiling painted cream; the large windows had curtains of cream and silver gauze lined with orange silk; and the doors were painted the same peacock-blue as the outside. She and Louis were to have separate rooms, for the first time. No reasons were given for this decision, except for the fact that each liked a different colour scheme. Fanny wrote that she liked 'a soft jewelled look', pinks and reds and dark green, while Louis preferred black, white and light blue. She took a lot of trouble preparing her mother-in-law's room, anxious to make her as comfortable now as she had been *un*comfortable before. She gave her a sea view, put white mats on the floor, and painted the walls pale green. Aunt Maggie, returning in mid-May, was pleased with it and everyone relaxed. But this time she had not come alone. She had brought with her from Sydney a young woman, called Mary, to be her maid, deciding after her previous brief experience that she could not be doing without one. Right from the start, Mary's presence created tension. All the other servants were Samoan and Mary could understand neither their language nor their ways – she was isolated and inclined to be aloof, with no intention of trying to integrate herself fully into the household. She tried Fanny's patience sorely – asked to do the slightest thing, Mary would say it was not her job. She was Mrs Margaret Stevenson's maid and companion, and hers alone.

To add to the tension, the Strongs had arrived at Vailima, completing the family unit. At least the presence of eight-year-old Austin gave Aunt Maggie something to do – she became his teacher, though all she taught him was poetry and prayers. But it gave some structure to her day which Fanny felt she needed. Aunt Maggie spent a great deal of time in her room writing letters, and otherwise, apart from reciting poetry with Austin, had nothing more interesting to do than varnish all the books in the house (to preserve them) with her maid Mary. She admired Fanny's diligence in the garden, telling her sister in letters how amazing her daughter-in-law was and how ferociously hard she worked, but nevertheless there crept into her praise a hint of disapproval. In her opinion, Fanny worked *too* hard, and no good would come of it. She noted in August of that first year that 'Fanny has not been very well lately – I fancy the result of a long course of overwork . . . she has really laboured prodigiously . . . and I have often predicted a breakdown'. It was no part of being a good wife to turn herself into a full-time estate manager: in her mother-in-law's opinion, she had her priorities wrong.

But Fanny saw things differently. It was vital Vailima should be self-supporting and if she didn't run the estate nobody would. Louis was writing, Lloyd looked after the servants, Belle helped Louis (she was becoming his amanuensis) and looked after Austin, and Joe Strong was so unreliable that he disappeared down to Apia most of the time. Far from helping Fanny, he infuriated her by drinking heavily and taking a Samoan mistress. Joe, she decided, would have to go, and that meant a divorce from Belle. Fanny seethed over the situation, which grew worse all the time. Not only was her son-in-law a drunkard and womaniser, he was also discovered to be a thief, 'robbing the cellar and storeroom at night with false keys'. Louis could keep fairly calm about all this, but Fanny couldn't. She found it hard to keep calm about anything. Her rages, and the way she worked herself up into them, quite alarmed her mother-in-law, who believed that Louis should live in an atmosphere of peace and tranquillity and it was his wife's duty to create this. But the effect on Louis of her fury with Joe Strong was not nearly so upsetting as people imagined. In fact, it was Fanny's volatile nature which went on attracting him – he loved her obvious passion about everything. One thing about his wife: she was never boring.

On the other hand, once the second full year at Vailima was nearly over, she was becoming increasingly difficult. Louis reckoned the trouble began round about the beginning of 1892. Even before that, Fanny had suffered spells of ill-health – headaches, dizziness – but a short holiday on her own in Fiji had seemed to put her right. Her mother-in-law noted that on her return she looked 'very well and thoroughly set up by the change of air'. But the improvement hadn't lasted. She seemed to lose her temper more frequently and often it was with Louis.

There was, wrote Louis to Colvin, obviously 'something wrong', but what? Was it physical or mental? He was 'miserably anxious' and at a loss over what to do. Sometimes the scenes Fanny created were ridiculous and petty, such as when she voiced her hatred for someone Louis liked, and refused to have them in her house; but sometimes they seemed truly hysterical and based on nothing. According to Louis, she 'passes from death-bed scenes to states of stupor', lying for days without moving. At least that was better than having her ranting and raving. This was not the wife he had known for the last twelve years, but some other creature. He called in the doctor who announced there was no danger to life. 'Is there any danger to mind?' Louis asked, and was told that this was not excluded. After the doctor's visit, there was a scene worse than any before, so awful, Louis wrote to Colvin, that he couldn't 'harrow' him with it. It was 'a kind of set against *me*; she made every talk an argument, then a quarrel; till I fled her and lived in a kind of isolation in my own room'. Every time he came out of it, there was another attack – 'a hell of a scene, which lasted all night – I will never tell anyone about it, it could not be believed and was so unlike herself . . . Belle and I held her for about two hours; she wanted to run away.'

It was the worst thing that had ever happened in their marriage, worse than any of Louis's haemorrhages. Those had brought them closer together, sustaining each other through the horror. But now, Fanny's mental state threatened to drive them apart and that was terrifying. She had nursed Louis expertly and devotedly, but he didn't know how to deal with this complete and inexplicable change of character. His mother, thankfully, had gone back to Scotland by the time Fanny was at her worst. The word 'mad' was never used by Louis, but the fear that Fanny was in some way mad never left him. It seemed to him that medical help of a sort superior to that available in Apia had to be sought, so he and Belle took her to Sydney. The change alone seemed to work a transformation – 'the first few weeks were delightful: her voice quiet again – no more of that anxious shrillness about nothing that had so long echoed in my ears.' But once back in Samoa, though taking the medicine prescribed – presumably some kind of tranquilliser – she 'got bad again'. This time the 'badness' took the form of a melancholy that could not be breached. 'I am broken on the wheel, or feel like it', Louis wrote. If it had not been for Belle and Lloyd – 'both as good as gold' – he did not know how he could have managed.

But manage he did, hoping the new medicine would eventually take effect, and ever optimistic that the old Fanny would be restored to him. He wrote to his mother that, though his wife had been 'devilishly ill', she had improved vastly. But Belle, to whom he was dictating the letter, broke in with a protest, telling Aunt Maggie that her mother was *not* improving but instead lying in bed, not eating, not speaking, not smoking. She was like a zombie, taking no interest in anything or anybody. But at least she was calm, and for that Louis was grateful. Just as, when he was so very ill, Fanny would develop illnesses of her own once the crisis was over, so he became ill now that she appeared to be recovering. Again and again they would each write in the terms Louis now used to his mother: 'half my illness was the dreadful bother about Fanny's.' When a photograph taken of his wife in Sydney arrived, he thought, looking at it, that he should have realised how ill she was when she sat for it, whereas, in fact, he had thought her better. Her appearance in it was strange – she was, he wrote 'pale, penetratin' and interestin'', but definitely not herself, not the beautiful Fanny he loved.

Nobody else ever thought Fanny beautiful. At various times, she was described by Louis's male friends as fiery, startling, and – a strange word for the times – sexy. Those were the compliments. The insults, of course, were far more numerous, insults about her weight, her hair, her skin and her clothes, the sort of insults hurled at Mary Livingstone so frequently. Women had been equally dismissive, failing entirely to recognise what Louis saw in her. What he saw was a kind of beauty, even then, in 1893, when she was fifty-three. Playing a family party game called 'Truth' one evening at the beginning of the worst period of her illness, Louis gave Fanny the maximum ten points for 'Beauty'. She was annoyed with him, telling him not to be so silly but to play the game properly – she was quite happy to be awarded ten points for 'Work' and would hope to score them for 'Intelligence' but felt it was making fun of her to give her ten for 'Beauty'. But Louis was solemn. He would not budge. 'I am honest,' he said, looking at her steadily. 'I think you are the most beautiful woman in the world.' It was a tribute any wife would be proud of and reassured by, and yet Fanny appears to have remained dubious, seeing little beauty in herself. She'd never traded on her looks – she was all personality. And she had enough self-awareness and common sense to know that it was her daughter Belle who was the beautiful one. But this judgement of her husband's – that she was beautiful – mattered. It was only one of many indications that sexually their relationship was far from dead, in spite of repeated illness and the other strains their marriage had been subject to. Louis desired his wife, never anyone else. He delighted in her physically, even if everyone else saw a plump, grey-haired, middle-aged matron. Hints of this creep into his correspondence all the time, even to his mother, to whom he described Fanny coming to him with a pair of corsets she'd made, 'in despair' because she couldn't get the laces to fit the holes (which he saw she'd plugged in on one side upside-down) and he took great pleasure in fixing them and then admiring her in the corsets. Then there was the time they were out in a boat and Fanny wanted to change her dress. She asked Louis to hold up a shawl so that she could do it discreetly and the boatman wouldn't see, but when her head emerged from her gown she found him trailing the shawl and not using it as a screen at all – 'he said he couldn't countenance prudery.' He loved to look at her, seeming to take extra pride in her voluptuous figure. Describing to his mother Fanny wearing a black velvet gown he'd bought her, he wrote: 'You should have seen Fanny . . . she looked immense!' Immense was how he seemed to like her.

Aunt Maggie, arriving back in Samoa after her year in Scotland, thought her daughter-in-law was 'much more nearly herself than I expected, which is a comfort', but a couple of months later she was reporting that Fanny wasn't well and that she had gone with her to stay in the Tivoli Hotel in Apia to give her a rest. Fortunately, this was all Fanny needed, she was not suffering from anything more sinister; but Aunt Maggie was critical of Fanny having 'dozens of schemes on hand'. Some of these were to do, as usual, with the estate – making a perfect, level lawn, for one – but others were social. Fanny was doing some entertaining, which Maggie relished, especially as it showed off the Heriot Row furniture she'd had brought out – she loved to see guests seated round her old dining-table. Fanny proved a good hostess too. Never in any of her previous homes had she been called upon to do any formal entertaining, but now that Vailima was finished and furnished, it provided the perfect backdrop for dinners and parties and she rose splendidly to the occasion. All the produce they served was from the estate, giving an added glory to the dinners. Louis boasted to Colvin of the abundance of raw materials – 'salad, beans, cabbages, tomatoes, asparagus, oranges, limes, pineapples – galore; pints of milk and cream; fresh meat five days a week'. Everything was fresh, nothing tinned. Indeed, if a tin had to be opened 'the gnashing of teeth when it has to be done is dreadful . . . no one . . . knows what the Hatred of the Tin is'.

There were many descriptions of festivities at Vailima, all of them attesting to the warmth and generosity of the hospitality and painting a seductive picture of the great house glittering with lights from scores of candles, high above Apia whence the guests came, riding up the recently improved track and tying their horses to the posts outside. Some were regular visitors, but others were from the ships docked temporarily in the harbour – often the entire crew was invited up for the evening. Louis wrote that he was swollen with pride at how magnificent his house looked. But there was also another kind of entertaining initiated by Fanny even before the house was properly finished and not on the same scale as these later lavish parties. She started a club, with Louis's encouragement, consisting entirely of Samoans and what Aunt Maggie described as 'half-castes, the Stevenson family being the only white people to be admitted'. Twenty-five people had been invited on Fanny's fifty-first birthday and received on the front verandah, prettily decorated with Chinese lanterns and decked with flowers. Here they all sat and chose a name for their club (the Royal Vine-ula Club – vine-ula being the name of a flower), while sandwiches and cakes and lemonade were served. Fanny was chosen as president, and an entrance fee fixed for the future, and then they all sang songs. The purpose of the club was meant to be cultural more than anything, but ended up social, with everyone eagerly meeting once a month and enjoying simply coming together.

Louis liked this. As Fanny had realised years ago, her husband was a much more gregarious character than he would ever admit. He might say he preferred to be alone with her but she saw his need for other company and how he drew stimulation from people gathered round him, having quite a taste for being the genial presiding host. If things had been otherwise, if they had lived in England, then those rowdy evenings with his male friends, which she had thought so injurious to his health, might have satisfied this side of him, but as it was it had been up to her to create a substitute, which she did. The dinners and parties were not events she needed for herself – much more than Louis, she truly had no need of outside company. They diverted him, not her. For her, they were extra work when she always had too much work, and drained her of the energy she would much rather have spent on the garden. She rarely had the time any more to write letters – Louis claimed she'd stopped writing them altogether – and could only with difficulty keep adding to the articles she hoped would be published in book form. It was really, according to Louis, a cookery book, but Fanny herself referred to it as the 'Diary of a Mad Housewife' in which she would distil the accumulated wisdom of over thirty years of running very different households in very different circumstances.

But the purpose of the proposed book was really to earn some money. Fanny, like so very many wives, longed to have money of her own, however well her husband provided for her, however generous he was. The money from Skerryvore, which could have been her own personal nest-egg, had gone into Vailima, though she had squirrelled a small amount away. 'I thought', she wrote in her diary for 1893, 'sometime I might wish a few shillings for a private charity and hid it away.' But she would have liked not a few shillings secreted but instead a regular means of earning far more than that – and she thought she was capable of it. 'I would work very hard to earn a couple of pounds a month,' she confessed, but what held her back was 'my position as Louis's wife'. It would not do. If she took gainful employment of any sort it would be seen as humiliating for her husband. But Fanny wanted to earn money for the same reason certain women have always wanted to do so: it would have meant power, power to do with it what she wished without need for consultation, or feelings of guilt or of being beholden. In her case, there was also the burden of knowing it was her family who drained Louis of his earnings. He never once threw this in her face, always regarding Belle and Lloyd and Austin as his children as much as Fanny's; luckily, she never knew that Louis had written to his cousin Bob, just at the point when she was struggling to complete her collection of articles, 'I sometimes feel harassed. I have a great family here about me: a great anxiety.' He meant more than his immediate family members, of course – he meant the entire household of servants – but the point was the same. Money was always a worry, and Fanny would have liked some of her own.

What she wanted her own money for at that time, in 1894, was to help Mataafa, the Samoan chief whose candidature to administer the laws she and Louis supported. But another chief had been preferred by the joint rulers of Samoa (Great Britain, Germany and USA) and Mataafa, who defied the decision, was imprisoned. Fanny was roused to a great fury over this – as indeed was Louis, but he preached caution, not wishing to be ordered off the island for flouting the government. Each of them, on various occasions during their marriage, had taken great stands of principle, glorying in righteous indignation of one sort or another and appearing excited at the prospect of some measure of martyrdom, but usually it had been Louis who was inspired to champion some cause, and Fanny the one to back him and egg him on, proud to see him (as she thought) fearless. Now it was she who, of the two, was the more vehement and she despised him for holding back – 'I intend to do everything in my power to save Mataafa,' she wrote in her diary, '. . . and if Louis turns his face from him by the fraction of an inch I shall wear black in public . . . if he is brought in to Apia a prisoner I shall go down alone and kiss his hand as my King. Louis says this is arrant, mad quixotism.' In fact, she didn't go alone when she went to the prison – Louis went with

her – and she didn't kiss Mataafa's hand. Their visit, nevertheless, was very public, rather more so than Louis wished, and all
the fault of a defiant Fanny, daring him not to match her. 'He
called me an "idiotic enthusiast". Well, he's another.'

She was right. They both had in them a fanatical streak, they
both indulged in manic behaviour when roused, and each
recognised in the other this reckless trait. It was like answering
like, part of their passion for each other, the spice that
prevented their relationship from ever becoming bland. Sometimes, it made them seem antagonistic towards each other and
misled people into thinking all was not well between them – the
very 'bite' in their marriage could sound so fierce and
frightening. They sometimes seemed to tremble on the brink of
a violent public row, the tension palpable between them, their
words sounding barbed and meant to wound. Once, at a dinner
to which most of Apia had been invited, Louis made some
remarks which were far from respectful towards America and
something in his manner was interpreted by others as a slight to
Fanny. And she, for her part, could address Louis in tones of
what sounded to others like contempt – this was no way for a
'good wife' to speak to her husband. She didn't care. 'What sort
of devil from hell is the British matron and why should I, of all
people in the world, take her for my pattern of conduct? It is
like being a sham paralytic.' But she was no paralytic, sham or
real. She never dissembled. She was always 'straight and true',
saying what she thought, never deferring to any superior
authority Louis was supposed to possess by virtue of being her
husband, and never fearing him. Her confidence in their
partnership was complete – there was no need for remorse, for
begging forgiveness. She expected him to understand, and he
did, even if during her mental breakdown he was tested to the
limit.

Others did not. Louis was seen as the victim of an hysterical,
possessive, domineering wife, as far from 'good' as it was
possible to be. Only Lloyd, Belle and Aunt Maggie knew
Fanny's true worth, knew how for all her faults she was loved
so completely by Louis and thought by him to be the perfect
wife. He said it again and again in his correspondence to all his

relations and friends, letter after letter over the years proclaiming his pride and immense satisfaction in his wife. But it made no difference. Outsiders looking in on the marriage were determined to see misery and pain, and to hold the wife responsible for it. It was she who had removed him to a god-forsaken South Sea island to keep him to herself and in doing so she had ruined him as a writer. It was she who had saddled him with *her* family, draining him of money long after finance should have ceased to be a problem. They – Henley, Colvin and, in particular, Gosse – could not forgive him for preferring Fanny to them and so they maintained he was her prisoner. She was never the right wife, not the right age, the right nationality, the right class, the right type. She fitted none of their preconceived notions of what their young lad's wife should have been. None of them had either the sense or sensitivity of Louis's parents, who recognised with such speed and relief that their son's marriage was like their own, a match between lovers, and that therefore nothing else mattered.

Perhaps because Louis was so acutely aware of how Fanny suffered at the hands of his friends he frequently went out of his way to pay extravagant public tributes to her, and never more so than at the Thanksgiving Dinner Fanny had organised at the end of November 1894. It was one of the most spectacular occasions Vailima had ever seen, with all the Americans then in Apia invited and seated at the long table in the great hall. Belle described afterwards the huge, swinging lamps hanging over the table, throwing the highly polished Heriot Row silver into glittering relief and sparking off the crystal goblets and bowls. The food was superb (and all as usual provided by the estate, even the 'pumpkins' for the pies, which were really a brand of sweet potato Fanny had found growing in the woods) and the drink abundant – sherry, Bordeaux, Madeira and port with champagne afterwards. After dessert, Louis made a speech. He always enjoyed standing at the head of his own table in front of his family and friends, but this was a special speech, couched gracefully in language which rang with sincerity. He spoke clearly and carefully, saying how thankful he was for his wife, to whom he owed not only his happiest years but, through her devoted care, his very life. He had reason, he told them, to be grateful to America for much that was brightest in his life, and that brightness was Fanny. His mother, listening, was moved as much by this tribute to her daughter-in-law as she was by the tribute her son went on to pay to her – it seemed right to her that Fanny's worth should be so plainly acknowledged.

It was as well that it was. The next few days, even though the sun shone and Vailima looked beautiful, Fanny was depressed, full of premonitions that something awful was going to happen. It was not unknown for her to experience such forebodings – like most emotional, highly strung people she swung between highs and lows and her imagination did the rest – but this time they were intense. She confessed them to Louis and her children and her mother-in-law, and they all did what people usually do in such situations – tried to reassure her, to remind her of other instances when she had felt the same and nothing had happened. Louis tried to tease her out of her gloom, telling her she was childish and riddled with superstition, but she could not be shaken in her conviction of impending doom. On 2 December, a Sunday, Louis read a new prayer he had written specially which sounded like another attempt to banish Fanny's demons – 'Go with each of us to rest . . . call us up . . . eager to labour, happy, if happiness shall be our portion – and if the day be marked for sorrow, strong to endure it.' It seemed to help everyone relax and the day ended with a game of boisterous charades. The next day, Fanny heard him read to her the beginning of Chapter IX of his new novel (*Weir of Hermiston*) which she thought good, but still she was low, though containing her strange fears better. In a further attempt to distract her, Louis talked of future plans – maybe they would visit the USA the following year. He played patience with her, and then said he'd make his special mayonnaise for supper. Together, they mixed oil and lime juice – and then he suddenly paused, put his hand to his head, said, 'What's that?' and then 'Oh, what a pain!' and 'Do I look strange?' 'No,' lied Fanny, for once not straight and true, but terrified into pretence.

He died that evening and was buried on the top of Mount Veia above Vailima, the next afternoon. To say Fanny was distraught was a grotesque understatement. She was over-whelmed with grief. Now no longer a wife but a widow (though she never, ever, used that word), ahead of her she had another eighteen years of life during which, after the first year of recovery, she travelled, made a new relationship (though never married again), and did many interesting things, but as far as she was concerned her real life was over. That had been with Louis. Her feelings about her own identity seemed to change. She was far too strong a personality to feel she was now nothing, that only being Louis's partner had given life meaning – that was nonsense – but on the other hand she lost her focus. For fourteen years everything had revolved round Louis and now there was no centre. It is a feeling that all wives of Fanny's dedication are bound to feel, the price, perhaps, of an intensely passionate marriage, the sense of loss proportionate to the weight of love and intimacy that had been there. She still felt herself to be his wife, went on defining herself by reference to him, initially finding some comfort, but only a slim one, in guarding his memory and in trying to protect it from the attacks which came.

To Fanny, being a wife never ended, but then she did not wish it to.

Reflections

I admire Fanny Stevenson as much as I pity Mary Livingstone, and, while I could never have been a wife like her either, her life doesn't fill me with such dismay. In her marriage to Louis, she was less constrained than Mary not just because he was very different from David Livingstone, but because her own expectations were different. By the time she met her second husband she had rejected the notion of abject submission – she had travelled, she had been in contact with bohemian people who allowed that women were creative too and did not relegate wives entirely to the domestic sphere. Fanny could, and did, fight her corner and was Louis's equal in a sense that Mary was never David's.

But nevertheless, she fulfilled many of the conventional roles of wife just as surely as Mary did. Those words in the marriage service, 'in sickness and in health', were ominous for Fanny. There was a great deal of sickness in her marriage to Louis. Sometimes, it seemed her prime function was to be a nurse, and of all the jobs a wife is called upon to do nursing must be quite the worst. It scared me, remembering how my own mother-in-law's life had been dominated by the need to nurse a husband suffering from multiple sclerosis. Unlike Fanny, who knew when she married Louis that she was marrying a sick man, my mother-in-law had had no inkling of how her major role as a wife would be as nurse. Her husband had been a particularly fit and healthy man when she made those vows promising to look after him in sickness and in health. But once he became ill, within seven years of their marriage, her days were spent washing and feeding him and pushing him around in his wheelchair, until he became bedridden. She had four young children to look after and no nursing help whatsoever. Once a year, she was given a rest when he was taken into a convalescent home for two weeks. Even then, she felt she should visit him, and when she did she told me how he would tell her to come close and then whisper in her ear, 'Get me out of here!' She always did, cutting short her own brief respite from nursing, her compassion far outweighing her need to rest.

I used to try to imagine myself in this situation. Would I be able to do what she did? I doubted it (and still do). But my sister-in-law does it, as do thousands of other women. Her husband also has MS. All that has changed is, mercifully, the amount of help available to her, in contrast to the lack of it for her mother. Yet, in essence, she is just as bound by that vow to look after her husband 'in sickness' and 'for worse'. The MS Society, as well as many other such societies, records how the demands of needing to nurse wreck marriages. The level of commitment necessary imposes the most stringent of tests and it is hardly surprising many fail it. My sister-in-law doesn't. It is not simply that she is as kind and caring as her mother but that she sees herself as having no choice. Marriage, to her, was a commitment for life, whatever happened. The bad luck which befell both her and her husband could not be predicted nor could it be prepared for, though the church service tries to cover all eventualities. Would she have made the same vows if she had known what the future held? Would anyone? Is it right to ask them to? Shouldn't there be some let-out clause? But then if there were to be such an escape route, what would be the point of marriage, of commiting oneself in the first place?

At any rate, it was something I worried about greatly. I certainly never saw myself as having any potential to nurse – I didn't have the temperament for it, never mind the skills. My unsuitability to be wife-as-nurse was demonstrated very quickly and clearly on our honeymoon. We went to Sardinia and a few days after we arrived my dear husband developed a boil on his bottom. He was in agony, the hideous thing growing bigger and redder by the hour, and a doctor was called to our hotel. She was a large, powerfully built woman who, it quickly emerged, did not believe in antibiotics to treat boils (though the boil was probably too far on anyway to do anything but lance it). What she did was squeeze it with her hands. She spoke no English and we spoke no Italian, but we each had some French. I'd thought I could leave her to it – God, I didn't want to see a boil burst – but no she instructed me to stand beside the bed, upon which he, the suffering patient, lay face down, and hold a bowl, filled with boiling water, which had been brought to the room. I was to be *'une bonne femme'* and help. To keep the bowl steady, I had to look at it, and so could not avoid having in my field of vision the sight of her broad, strong fingers pushing and pummelling the boil. Groans of pain came from the recumbent figure on the bed and a thick yellow, disgusting pus began to come out of the boil. The bowl of water began to wobble in my hands as she dipped some gauze in it, the room swam mistily before my eyes, and the last words I heard before I hit the floor were, *'Un peu de courage, madame!'*

Quite. No courage at all, from a wife merely watching a husband in pain and in no pain herself except in her imagination. The doctor's contempt was fully justified. How on earth was I going to cope? What kind of wife would I be if called upon to nurse? When we got home, back to the Vale of Health in London's Hampstead, there was another test. I'd always known he had asthma but I'd never seen him have an attack. His line was that he'd had it as a child and was now clear of it. What a lie. That was how he dealt with it, by denying it, and usually it worked very well as a technique. But one night, a foggy night in November, when the pond over which our flat looked was blanked out with thick mist, he started wheezing. It got worse and worse and I didn't know what to do. He couldn't speak and I thought he was going to choke. He had no Ventolin inhaler at the time, only some medication in tablet form and this didn't work. I rang the doctor. She came and gave him an injection, and he recovered. Soon afterwards, she prescribed the inhaler, and since then, and since we moved from the (in his case) misnamed Vale of Health, he has never had such a severe attack. When he has a mild attack, he knows how to handle it and so do I. The name of the game (some game) is distraction, taking his mind off it, and I can do that.

But what if he had had to have dreadful operations and I had been called upon, as his wife, to dress his wounds? What if he'd succumbed to horrible diseases which required me to clean sores? I'd have been useless, crashing about and fainting all the time. I've always been a fainter, from a very early age. I could faint just entering a hospital or, never mind entering one, seeing one in a film – crash, that would be me in the middle of a row in a cinema. Definitely a bad bargain as a wife, not a Florence Nightingale bone in my body. But, as that great woman so famously said in her *Notes on Nursing,* there is more to the task than the practical business of bandaging wounds. There is the psychological aspect, and maybe, once I'd come round from the faint, I could handle that.

Surprisingly (well, I was very surprised) I found I could. Invalids like to feel someone is looking after their needs competently, without fuss and yet firmly. That I can do. I even like doing it. I can wash fevered brows, provide tempting food, plump up pillows, change sheets and pyjamas – full marks there, I think. And I can deal with the 'I'm-never-going-to-get-better' moans and the 'I'm-so-bored-talk-to-me' entreaties very well. I can parry fear with common sense, soothe by pointing out minuscule signs of recovery, cheer by stressing that this will not go on for ever (whatever it is). I am not patient or calm by nature, but I can be both when I am the wife-as-nurse. And yet I wonder if I could find the reserves of strength over long periods which Fanny had to find. I've never had to look after a sick husband for more than a few weeks – an attack of jaundice, two cartilage operations, that kind of thing. It's been more of a test dealing with the trivial complaints – then, I feel irritated to be regarded as a nurse just because I am a wife.

Most wives will be familiar with what I mean – the so-called 'flu' (which is only an ordinary cold), the agonising, sinister stomach pains (merely the result of greed), the dreadful earache (two hours at a football match on a freezing day without a hat). All of these demand attention, from wives who are expected to offer unlimited tender loving care. I can only manage so much. He likes to detail his symptoms in a way that amazes me, mainly because I never do the same. Wives, on the whole, I think, don't. They simply don't say, 'I've got a terrible sore throat and I feel hot and sweaty, what shall I do?' What they do, what I do, is dose myself with aspirin and go to bed. I don't want to share my illness and I don't want to be told what I should do when it is so obvious. I don't want to be nursed, but he does.

But in a long marriage, as both partners age, the nursing bit is bound to loom more seriously even if nothing dramatic and tragic happens. Fanny never got to that stage (and neither of course did Mary). Louis was dead before he was old and in the fourteen years they were married Fanny nursed specific illnesses and not general frailty. It's when couples hit sixty that the marriage service promise (not that I ever made it) to look after each other, that 'in sickness and in health' part, takes on a whole new dimension. I've had a chilling glimpse of what it can be like. In the last decade, rheumatoid arthritis has come to call and when it was first diagnosed I had intimations of what it was going to be like nursing a husband virtually crippled. Walking was painful for him, typing agony, his whole very active life distorted, and with it the threat that his personality would be too. He has always been a madly active person, ever restless, never walking if he could run and dash. To see him obliged to use a stick, forcing himself to walk a mere hundred yards, was frightening, and even worse was watching him struggle with massively swollen hands to use his word processor. No walking? No working? He'd go mad, and so would I. But true sympathy was easy to find when the need for it was so acute. The nursing wasn't a matter of obligation, it had nothing to do with duty as a wife, but was a natural response.

All the same, a future in which wife-as-nurse seemed destined to obliterate all other roles was unbearable to think about. What would it do to us? I know enough wives who've had to find out and I didn't want to be one of them, fearing I'd fail to sustain the sympathy over a long period of time. One half of my head said there could be no escape if this fate befell me – 'for better for worse' even if I'd never actually said those words – but the other said I'd have to, I'd have to find some measure of escape, devise ways of escaping a role I didn't want (though who does?). In fact, a drug was found to which the arthritis responded and, miraculously, his limbs straightened, the pain subsided and within a year he was back to normal, within another he was off the drug and still well. During the time he was on it, and had to take it without fail, he would have liked me to be in charge of the tablets, doling them out as required, but I refused. It was his responsibility. I didn't want to be pushed into being the one who in effect controlled his medication. I can't bear to see wives saying, 'Here, dear, here's your pills, now take them like a good boy.' What on earth does that do to a marriage?

About his other problems I will show merciful restraint and say little, though they are all relevant to the wife-as-nurse role. There is, for example, the stomach problem. He has not got an ulcer but something like an ulcer, some tendency for the stomach lining to become inflamed, resulting in searing pains during the night. Always in the night. I wake up, hear the crinkle of tinfoil as he opens and takes a tablet. I lie there, sleep ruined, remembering what he drank in the evening: white wine, red wine, whisky (because Spurs won/lost, it makes no difference, celebration or consolation both call for whisky). Sometimes, he has the effrontery to say, 'You shouldn't have let me have all that wine' or whisky or whatever, and I am furious. I don't intend to 'let' him do or not do anything. Being his wife does *not* mean I have to.

This is deeply, deeply boring and has nothing to do with me as his wife. Real need, yes; self-created need, no. I think wives should be tough. They should refuse to become surrogate mothers.

Fanny proved a good hostess once she was settled in Samoa, but her attitude to entertaining and being sociable while she was living in Bournemouth struck many chords with me. Louis wanted company, she didn't. A good wife even today is expected to welcome her husband's friends and be hospitable and, just as it did between Fanny and Louis, this can cause trouble.

My mother was staying with us, soon after we were married, and we went for short, sedate walks in the evening. It was August, during a spell of hot weather, and we were taking a rest, sitting on a bench, when two men stopped in front of us and said hello to Hunter. They were both journalists and there was some animated chat about newspapers. They asked where he was living and he told them, said we lived in a flat five minutes away. Then I heard him say, 'Why don't you –' and I knew what would follow, so I cleared my throat and he got my (mean) message and finished '– drop in sometime.' When, of course, he had been going to say 'come back with us and have some coffee or a drink'. My mother was appalled. As we walked home, she told me I'd behaved badly, that my husband had wanted to invite his friends round and it was my duty as his wife to welcome them. I said it wasn't. I said there was no such duty. I didn't feel like having these two strangers home and if he wanted to he could have a drink, or whatever, with them somewhere else. She tried to get Hunter to agree with her, and to be annoyed with me, but he said he didn't really care. But in spite of what I'd said, about having no obligations socially as a wife, I felt guilty. He knew how antisocial I was, he'd always known and accepted this, but perhaps now I was a wife I should try harder.

The late Nicholas Tomalin, his immediate superior on the *Sunday Times* where he was soon working, certainly thought so. Nick was a very successful journalist, an amusing and charming man, clever and well liked, with a huge circle of friends whom he was in the habit of entertaining regularly and generously at his Camden Town home where he lived with his wife Claire and three daughters. We'd been to dinner there. Twelve of us sat round a big kitchen table and ate a delicious meal. It must have seemed that I was thoroughly enjoying myself but I wasn't, though I felt ashamed that I wasn't. For God's sake, *why* wasn't I? I just don't like dinner-parties, that's all. It's silly, I know, but I would always rather be somewhere else, preferably at home.

Anyway, one day Nick rang, asking if he could pop round and see me that afternoon. He knew Hunter was out of town because he himself had sent him to interview someone, so I couldn't imagine why he was coming at all. Why would he want to see me? But he came, and we sat in the garden drinking tea and he was very pleasant, as he always was, and then he put his cup down down very carefully and said there was something he wanted to say which he hoped would not offend me. He didn't mean in any way to upset me, he was speaking as a friend, but he wondered if I'd realised how much my dislike of any kind of socialising was going to hinder Hunter's career. He said a journalist had to have contacts of every variety, that it was essential to mix with as many people as possible and move in as many different circles as he could. He had to entertain and be entertained and the co-operation of a wife was important. It was doing him no good at all to have a wife reluctant to participate in the social round.

I was stunned. I can't remember what I said in reply, if I said anything (I usually do). I know I didn't laugh, as I should have done, and I know I wasn't angry, which would have been justified, but probably not a good idea. I think I was too shaken at this image of myself as a wife-who-was-a-career-wrecker to be able to respond at all. Nick had touched my fear that I was a bad wife, he'd voiced my own dread. I liked him, and believed absolutely that he was indeed, as he had said, telling me this for my own good. We chatted some more, and then he left, and if I didn't exactly cry with mortification I was absurdly near doing so. Then Hunter came home and was treated to this saga, accompanied by wails of misery. First he said Nick had a cheek, then he said that to believe what he'd said was stupid. He rhymed off a list of journalists whom he admired and knew for a fact had wives who never went anywhere. He said it was just that Nick operated in the way we knew he did but that didn't mean everyone else had to. I should ignore him, and what's for supper?

But I didn't ignore him. I thought a lot about what he had said, and worried. What worried me most wasn't even the career bit but more that I was denying this husband of mine a side of life he enjoyed. He liked parties, he was gregarious. I was making him suppress part of his personality. I fretted over how to resolve this difference between us – couldn't he go to parties on his own and I stay at home? But apparently not. Invitations were for couples, for both of us. If I didn't accept, he couldn't, it wasn't done, it would be thought odd and upset the balance of the dinner-party. This insistence on joint acceptance seemed mad to me, but that's the way it was.

The solution was, of course, to compromise, and for at least two decades we did. If he really, really wanted to accept some invitation which required me as his wife to accept too, then I agreed. I went with him and tried to go with good grace. And we had dinner-parties ourselves, and even big-thrash-type parties. Not many, but some. Organising these events was no bother. I like cooking and enjoyed preparing the food, and I like making the house look attractive – oh, I could do him credit as a good wife when I tried and for a while I tried very hard indeed. But I couldn't be doing with these performances, everyone doing their turn and nobody really ever getting to know each other. It wasn't the sort of entertaining I liked. I liked having real friends with their children for lunch and then a walk on the heath.

My mother approved of that kind of entertaining, whereas of course dinner-parties were middle-class inventions to which she had no wish to aspire. When I was growing up, hospitality was extended almost exclusively to family, and it meant mostly the giving of big teas involving a massive amount of baking, so that the table groaned with scones and cakes. The preparations for these teas were lengthy and included not only the baking but the starching of a white tablecloth and the ironing of a smaller, embroidered one to go over it diagonally, and the polishing of her only bits of silver (a tea-pot and sugar-bowl). If it was her sister Jean who was coming from Motherwell, with her husband and two boys, then the entertaining went on for days and my mother was driven to distraction trying to work out how we would all sleep. My father had to be persuaded to let Jean and Dave have his double bed while he and my mother slept on the couch in the living-room. My cousins slept with my brother in the other bedroom and when we were very small my sister and I slept end-to-end with them in the same double bed. It was all very exciting, this 'entertaining', but there was an air of almighty relief when it was over. I thought about my mother often during my dinner-party phase, especially afterwards when I too felt such relief.

Eventually, I stopped trying to be a good wife in that particular way. Times changed, and it was no longer quite as impossible for a husband to accept an invitation and say his wife didn't want to come too, thank you. He does now go places on his own and we are both happy. But once more, my behaviour brought a warning, from a woman this time. She'd seen Hunter at some party or other on his own and told me that if I let this go on I was 'heading for trouble'. I asked with false politeness what on earth she meant, and she said, 'He will forget he has a wife and it'll be your fault.' This time, I did laugh. I said I wouldn't mind being forgotten 'as a wife' but was quite sure I wouldn't be forgotten by him as a person, so that was all right, wasn't it?

I think that as marriages lengthen it is reasonable for husband and wife to take some of their social pleasures separately, especially if, like us, tastes are different. I love it when he goes to parties – though very rarely, and usually work-related – and comes back and tells me about them – it's so much more enjoyable than actually being there myself. In fact, sometimes these days I *urge* him to go when he isn't really keen just so I can have the pleasure of hearing his account afterwards. I tell him it will do him good, he'll have fun, oh go on *do* go . . .

Holidays are another matter. Fanny benefited enormously from having her own holidays – being a wife didn't mean she always had to have Louis as a companion to enjoy herself. Mostly these breaks were described not as holidays but as 'rests' for health reasons, sometimes involving treatment of some kind, but it came to the same thing. The urge to get away on her own became strong and so she went.

It is an urge, surely, felt by almost every wife at some point in a marriage – to get away, to think of oneself for a change, to escape all the domestic routines, and, indeed, to escape the husband however much he is loved, not to mention the children. All completely understandable and yet somehow thought not quite the thing for a *good* wife to want to do even today.

I approve of wives holidaying alone but I've never actually done it. The times I went away on my own in the first twenty years of marriage were not for holidays. I went to Carlisle to visit and look after sick parents and there was nothing remotely holiday-like about it. It was more like a punishment and I came back exhausted. Then, in the next two decades, I went away, very occasionally, for work, weeks in Cornwall researching a book about Daphne du Maurier, that kind of thing. When I did leave, for these two reasons, the preparation before I left was daunting. Being, in this respect at least, what I imagined to be a good wife (before I saw I was being a foolish one) I felt obliged to leave my husband all his meals. I shopped for him (and, in the days when they were young, the children) and I left detailed instructions for him, insultingly simple ones but he wasn't insulted, he pleaded for them – 'Put casserole in oven, Regulo 4, to reheat for one hour. Test hot enough before eating.' I pandered to his feebleness in the kitchen because I thought it was my job to. In time, it drove my growing daughters mad and, shamed, I stopped. It had taken me something like thirty years to see that it was not a wifely duty to allow a husband to be so pretend-helpless. When he asked, 'What shall I eat?' as I was about to go away, at long last I replied, 'Whatever you like, it's up to you.' Did he therefore shop and cook? No. He went to local cafés or existed on toast and cheese, hating it. More fool him. I've been a bad wife letting him get to this state.

But the fact remains that mercy-dashes north and research trips (few) aside, I have never left him to go on holiday. I wouldn't say, though, that I never had any yearning to. A week in the sun on my own, with him at home looking after the children, often seemed a deeply attractive idea. I feel annoyed with myself, looking back, that I never did do it. Wives should, mothers should if they can. It was not the organising which held me back, but more the sheer boldness of the thing and a slight guilt that I wanted to do it at all. He didn't, apparently. He says he has never had the slightest desire to go off on his own or with anyone else other than me. Now, isn't that extraordinary? When he does go away, it's always work-related, though considering that lately this has meant going round West Indian islands, it hasn't felt so much like 'work'. He would like me to go with him. I could go, no ties now, no babysitting worries, nothing to hold me back, but apart from once a year, our real holiday, I never do. I'd rather stay at home and write.

And that's how I have my holiday on my own, by staying at home. I love it. I love him to go off and leave me in our house.

There is nothing I do while he is gone that I cannot do while he is there – it is just that somehow I savour the solitude. It is very confusing, at least to me. The days proceed precisely as they do when he is there – I write, I read, I walk – but they feel different. It makes me wonder if more energy goes into being a wife than I've ever calculated, yet when he returns there's a rightness about it which in turn makes that thought seem nonsense. I think about war-wives, those women who suddenly had husbands again after gaps of months or years. We've never been apart more than two weeks, not nearly long enough to be put to any kind of real test. Gaps for us, for me at any rate, have been refreshing not destructive. I think they are necessary, especially if, like us, a couple works at home (or are both retired).

I've never wanted to go on holiday with friends, so that's not arisen – there's no attraction to be with another group, it's on my own or with him. And the truth is that we're very compatible on holiday. We like the same kind of things – the sea and swimming, long exploratory walks, islands, the quieter the better – and we both relish sun. Holidays are good times, as they should be. They are better with him than they would be on my own. The same doesn't apply to holiday days in London. Saturday is my holiday day, my weekly day off and I don't want him with me at all, I don't want to be a wife with her husband tagging along. I want to be a single woman. 'I'll come with you,' he sometimes says on Saturday mornings when he's bored, because there is no football and no junk sales he can ferret around for his many collections. 'No,' I say, 'you will not,' and off I go, selfish woman that I am. I want to wander as a free spirit, changing directions as I change my mind, without having to discuss where I'm going and especially without having to think about eating. I want to sit on my own in parks and observe others, I want to go to plays and films and feel isolated among the audience, I want to walk miles and miles along the river, over the bridges, through the squares, an oldish invisible woman. I emphatically do not want to be part of a couple, a wife. No one notices me and that's exhilarating. I don't speak for the whole eight hours or so that I'm out, except to ask for tickets and so forth, whereas, together, we never stop talking.

All this, obviously, is about independence. I don't think it makes me a bad wife. A wife needs to remember that she is not just part of a couple but an individual too with a separate identity.

In 1881, a year after his marriage, Robert Louis Stevenson expressed the opinion that 'Marriage is one long conversation, chequered by disputes'. Hearing the disputes between him and Fanny, Adelaide Boodle was only half-joking when she remarked, in her memoir of the Stevensons, that the sound of the two of them arguing as she approached their house might have made a stranger wonder if she should call the police. She had been genuinely alarmed, when first she knew Fanny and Louis, by their ferocious-sounding rows. It was Fanny's participation which alarmed people most: wives were not supposed to argue with husbands and certainly not meant to *shout* at them. Mary Livingstone never in her entire life shouted at David – wept, sighed, yes, but shouted, no. Fanny shouted a lot, both at Sam and at Louis. She didn't see it was any part of being a good wife to control her anger or stifle her opinions, and she didn't expect Louis to behave any differently. She thought arguments between husband and wife in a loving marriage were healthy.

So do I. We have argued our way through forty years, though rarely about anything that could be described as serious. I have to think very hard indeed to remember what our arguments have been about and even then I find it difficult. I know we used to argue about the children a lot, about what should be done with respect to some aspect of their behaviour, especially when they were teenagers. He was never a disciplinarian and yet he wanted them to be disciplined. By me. When we lay awake in the early hours of the morning, waiting for one of them to come home, the anxiety made us argue. He'd say they should have been told to be home by a certain time or they wouldn't be allowed out again, and I'd say they had been told, of course they had, and something must have gone wrong and it wouldn't be their fault, and he'd say why did I always defend them and I'd say I didn't . . . then, blessedly, we'd hear the key in the lock and relax. But we might still argue about it in the morning.

'Have you said that's it, no more staying out after midnight?'
he'd ask, and I'd say why didn't he say it and he'd say they'd
take more notice of me, and I'd say whose fault is that – and
we'd be off again.

We argued, too, and more seriously – Adelaide Boodle would
definitely have heard us – about the children's happiness. If one
of them was clearly unhappy I'd become utterly miserable
because of it and this would exasperate him. He'd say I
exaggerated their wretchedness and was being ridiculous,
letting it cloud my whole life. And I'd say he didn't really care,
he didn't take their distress seriously, he just ignored it and
assumed everything would work out in the end and meanwhile
there was no point in letting their state of mind interfere with
his. But we never argued over the things so many parents seem
to argue heatedly over. We never argued about their education,
for example. They'd go locally to state schools, no discussion
necessary. There have been no great matters of principle that
have divided us. I'm forced to conclude that most of our
arguments have been over essentially trivial things. Like Fanny,
I shout loudest, and I'm the more powerful in arguments,
mostly because I enjoy them. I like to argue. He doesn't. He
hates arguing, and quickly retreats into a defensive silence. He
knows that often enough he is right, but he struggles to prove it,
complaining that I can talk my way out of anything. A husband
with a different temperament faced with a wife like me would
have been driven to blows, but he manages to stay calm. All he
wants is that the verbal fight be over. He forgives and forgets
with astonishing ease. Nothing ever festers – these eruptions
are, if not meaningless, not in the least dangerous.

But to other people they must seem so. A wife overheard
screaming at her husband has always been thought to be a
harridan, a virago. Witnesses inevitably misinterpret in terms of
stereotype what they hear – they hear (as people heard Fanny)
what sounds like contempt, and they judge accordingly.
Whenever I hear couples shouting at each other, especially if the
wife is the more vociferous, I too feel the alarm and unease
people must experience when they hear me. It is ugly, this
marital arguing, unseemly, and one turns away from it
horrified. But no chance witness can possibly set this kind of

thing in its proper context – they can't know what has gone before or what comes afterwards and this knowledge can change everything. Louis usually knew why Fanny was moved to argue with him, he knew her state of mind, and health, and the pressures which caused her to be so volatile, and all this put their arguments into a different perspective. He rather relished Fanny's fury (except towards the end of his life when she really was mentally ill) seeing it as part of her passionate nature, which he loved. A married pair who claim *never* to argue but always to be in harmony puzzle me. To exist together, ever in agreement, suggests either a stultifying blandness about their relationship, or boredom. If you're bored, you don't argue, you just endure. And many a wife considers it worth doing that – she sees it as her duty, part of being a 'good' wife. I never have, any more than Fanny did, but unlike Fanny, I've had time to find the shouting fades out. When we argue now, as we still do, it is in a much more controlled way, quite dull really. It's more like having an over-animated discussion, both of us getting irritated but nowhere near upset.

Anyone who imagines that a wife who argues is somehow the dominant partner, as many people did in Fanny's case, is mistaken. Henley finally realised that, though all his circle assumed Fanny to be the stronger partner, because of her vocal dominance in so many instances, she was not. Louis was. In our case, in some ways Hunter is, and in others the balance is equal. What often happens is that we argue, he concedes – and then he does exactly what I have proved to him with my splendidly convincing arguments that he should not do. He does what he wants, which is what I do not want. When I tell him this, and wail that he agreed that I was right, he shrugs and says, 'I know.' So he goes ahead and carries out some plan which obviously (to me) will end in trouble; and then he groans and it is he who says I told him so, not me. 'Stop me next time,' he says. Sometimes, when he invites argument, when he begs me to tell him what I think about a project, I tell him that I know he's going to go ahead whatever I say, so I won't waste my breath putting the arguments against it. But he knows I will, because I can't resist it, and that's what he counts on.

We are a couple who argue. I am a wife who thrives on

argument and however much I want to be a so-called 'good' wife I won't give it up.

Fanny's success as a daughter-in-law was twofold: not only did she woo the Stevenson parents, but tried to make her husband a better son. She saw it as part of her duty to make Louis more responsive to his parents' needs. Often enough, before Fanny came on the scene, he had admitted to himself that he was selfish and that he didn't consider his parents' feelings nearly enough, but he had never tried to change his attitude. Fanny made him do so.

It worried me from the start that my husband didn't do enough for his mother, though he thought he did – didn't he let her do his washing every week when he was away at Durham University? So thoughtful of him, to go to all the trouble of parcelling it up and posting it, not easy when you're a busy undergraduate. And didn't he let her send him her delicious gingerbread with the clean clothes? When he was home, he allowed her to nag him into cutting the grass and clipping the hedges. He also let her lend him money. Did she have any to spare? Of course she didn't – she hadn't even enough for herself, but she always managed to scrape together a few pounds for him.

The truth was, he didn't need to be a better son because his mother had his sisters and his younger brother to depend on, but once they had all also left home, which was some years after we were married, the situation was different. His mother was living on her own, a widow like Margaret Stevenson, and she didn't like it. She was a woman who liked company (as he himself does). She enjoyed being at the centre of a busy household, and preferably one with children around. Unlike Fanny, I never urged her to come and live with us, though I've often thought I should have done. But trying to make her son into that kind of good son would never have worked, and I wasn't a good enough wife to suggest that it might. Much though he cared for his mother, and much though I admired and liked her, we were not compatible. She smoked and that in itself would've caused trouble, because her son can't tolerate it. So it was in other practical, financial ways that I tried to nudge him towards making his mother's life easier and more pleasurable. He was easily enough persuaded. But when Marion, one of his sisters, gave me the credit rather than him, I argued about it with her. She was firmly of the opinion that a man's wife was responsible for his assuming this kind of family responsibility. Men, she alleged, needed to be shown the way since they are not naturally sensitive to their duties nor do they have much imagination in this respect. She saw it as a wife's job to enlighten her husband. More alarmingly, she went so far as to *blame* the wife if her husband failed to come up to scratch. Feminist that I am, that attitude seemed to me decidedly *un*feminist. If Fanny's suggestion that Louis's mother should join them had been turned down why would this have been her fault? And if, when I'd pointed out to Hunter ways in which he could help his mother, how could it have been a failure on my part if he hadn't? As in so many other instances, too much seems still to be expected of wives.

Fanny was given a hard time by most of her husband's male friends. She tried for a while to win them over, but never had the success she had with her in-laws – converting the lads proved far tougher, and ultimately impossible. Once she and Louis had left England, the poor relationship she had with his old mates did not trouble her as much, but nevertheless, as his wife, she had wanted to be liked and approved of by them. Her difficulties highlight those of many wives: what are they to do about their husband's chums? Freeze them out? Compete with them? Relegate them to a separate compartment in his life? Make them their friends too? Or await events, see if they will just wither away of their own accord?

We had many shared friends at the beginning, coming as we did from the same small city and attending the neighbouring boys' and girls' grammar schools, but then, while I was still at school, he went to Durham University and naturally made friends I didn't know. Going to meet them wasn't something I recall enjoying, but it didn't seem too important to be liked by them when they were all going to go their different ways after university anyway. By the time we were married, only two of them had endured as friends and one of those had gone to live in America. That connection was, and is, maintained and kept alive with letters and photographs and the rare visit, but there has never been the slightest doubt so far as friendship goes that my husband is faithless. He doesn't yearn for his old buddies, and when he went to a college reunion (and he loved his college days) he couldn't seem to pick up where he left off. Sometimes I wish he had more friends of his own. Have I, as his wife, discouraged him from making and keeping them? Have I been a bad *wife* in becoming his only truly close *friend*? I don't think so. Fanny might even have found that, if they had indeed stayed in England, Louis's longing to carouse with his male friends would have faded (though it is true it had shown little sign of doing so). But when people marry young, as we did, the marriage can become almost a barrier to outside friendships – separate friendships aren't needed in the same way, and those that have existed before are rarely strongly rooted enough to survive. And yet women seem more inclined to make other close friendships which exclude the husband and give them a degree of intimacy the men don't achieve or necessarily want to achieve. I am no different from him in agreeing that he is my best friend as I am his, but nevertheless I do have women friends with whom I feel very involved and who give me something he cannot. This 'something' may not be important or significant, but it's fun: those hours spent with each other droning on about what are often purely feminine concerns. Sometimes he can even get close to being a little jealous. 'Where on earth have you been?' he'll ask. 'You've been *hours*.' 'Just chatting to Susie,' I'll say. 'What about?' 'Oh, nothing, it would bore you.' 'Tell me,' he says, 'tell me what you were talking about.' And I can't exactly. Two hours of what Elizabeth Barrett Browning used to call 'the slip-slop' of gossip can't be summed up. When I try to recollect what's been said between me and my friend all I come up with are a few banalities. He knows perfectly well that what I've said is true, I really have been talking about nothing, but it's the implied cosiness he feels excluded from. And he has no counterpart with a male friend.

This reminds me of how, when I was young, and one of my mother's women friends was in our kitchen talking to her, and my father came home, the friend would automatically leave –

the appearance of husbands was the signal to depart. A wife at all times gave precedence to her husband. That is no longer the unwritten rule, but I notice that if I am in a friend's kitchen, or she is in mine, and our respective husbands come in, we stop. We stop and wait for them to go, or if we don't precisely stop we talk differently till they've gone – and yet nothing whatsoever is being said which they could not hear. It's all about atmosphere, but also about just a snatch of minor independence, keeping something to ourselves however trivial. I wish Fanny had had a woman friend to provide that kind of harmless intimacy when she so badly needed it. She had Louis, but at times she needed another ear, apart from Belle's. It seems a pity she never had one.

Fanny seems to me to have been a happy wife but not as fulfilled as she might have been. Her interpretation of the role of wife permitted her more independence than Mary Livingstone ever had, but not enough. That little job Fanny yearned for in Samoa (not that one was ever offered to her) would have made all the difference, as would the publication of what she called her 'Diary of a Mad Housewife'. She felt too keenly her inferiority to Louis as the breadwinner and it sometimes made her bitter. She never for one moment deluded herself into imagining she had even a modicum of her husband's talent – she knew he was a genius – but nevertheless she hankered after a more equal intellectual relationship. In daily conversation with Louis, she never felt any great distance between them, but his achievements were far superior to hers. And Louis could shut himself away and write, whereas she couldn't. She had far too much to attend to, most of it in the interests of his comfort and well-being. A wife had to put the care of her husband first, before her own ambitions. She was financially dependent on him and if he wasn't well looked after, how could he work? And it was his work, his career, which was important. Nobody could dispute that.

But soon they could, and would.

PART THREE

Jennie Lee
1904–88

I

Mary Livingstone and Fanny Stevenson grew up in the full expectation of becoming wives. If they didn't marry, it would have seemed that something had gone wrong in the general scheme of things. But Jennie Lee, born in different times, grew up absolutely determined never to become a wife. The very word was hateful to her, symbolising as it did 'inferior', as well as a great many other words synonymous with humiliation. Women, by the turn of the century, and more especially after the First World War, no longer thought of marriage as the *only* passport to security. They had access to others, and some women had in any case realised that this so-called security had its disadvantages. The changes in the status of women were happening fast as higher education was opened to them. Few women were like Jennie, deciding as a result that marriage was no longer worth the candle, but she was by no means on her own in regarding wifehood as a calling to be avoided.

Towards the end of the previous century the Fabian and socialist Beatrice Webb had agonised over the meaning of marriage, for a woman intent on having a career. She came to the conclusion (aged twenty-six) that 'marriage is to me a form of suicide'. Her work (investigating working-class social conditions and trying to improve them) was what mattered. She did not want to have to give it up when she became a wife and therefore some man's slave – 'I hate every form of despotism,' she declared, and marriage she was sure was another name for it. Even after she'd met Sidney Webb (whom of course she did marry, and who never required her to sacrifice her career) she was writing in her diary: 'I am fearful lest my work should be

ended.' It was what Jennie Lee was fearful of, but unlike
Beatrice Webb she thought there was an alternative to marriage. She didn't need the respectability it gave or the status. She
planned to have lovers and enjoy all the advantages of the
married state without the disadvantages.

But she was not against marriage for all women, only for
some, only for women like herself, unsuited to the domestic
sphere and unwilling to obey a man. To Jennie, it was simple:
some women, women like her mother for whom she had the
greatest respect, were entirely suited to becoming wives and
found true self-fulfilment in marriage. Both types of women had
a place in society, and both roles – the wife and the career
woman – should be honoured. But the place she assigned to
herself bore no resemblance to the narrow niche accorded to
the unmarried women of the previous century. Then, the
worthy spinsters who consciously chose a career over marriage
gave up a great deal. They had to. If you were not going to be a
wife you were obliged to renounce sex, unless you were going
to become a mistress and be disgraced, and with it all thoughts
of having children. Jennie had no intention of denying herself
anything. Vowing never to become a wife did not mean vowing
to have nothing to do with men. On the contrary, she envisaged
entering into 'free' relationships within which she would enjoy
sexual union as well as companionship without losing a
modicum of her independence. She would have lovers, not one
miserable husband. She would change her mind as often as she
liked about whom she wanted to sleep with and never have to
suffer the inconvenience of a divorce. Children would be no
problem. She had no wish to have them, and would take steps
to prevent the conceiving of them. It was all quite clear to her,
growing up, but remarkably her determination never to become
anything as ordinary and implicitly submissive as a mere wife
was also accepted as gospel by her family. They didn't laugh
and say she would grow out of despising marriage and end up
dancing down the aisle.

And yet Jennie's mother, just like the mothers of Mary
Livingstone and Fanny Stevenson, had set a firm example of
what a wife should be and had tried to train her daughter to
follow suit – it was just that the training was rejected together

with the example. Euphemia Lee was described as 'a being without an ego', 'a dear Scottish dumpling, chuckling, resilient, selfless, alert, uniquely uncompetitive and unacquisitive', the sort of wife who made it her life's work to care for her husband and children, providing warmth and security and requiring little in return. Jennie herself paid endless tribute to what a good wife her mother was, commenting that she was a ferocious hard worker, ever up at dawn, cooking and cleaning without an hour's rest the whole day. She'd been born one of thirteen children and had before marriage helped her mother run a hotel, doing the cooking for its dining-room. After she married James Lee, in 1900 at the age of twenty-two, she worked even harder, not only running her own home but still cooking at the hotel and helping to do its laundry. There was nothing anyone could teach her about housewifely arts and she excelled at them all.

None of her skills was passed on to her only daughter. Jennie simply refused to learn. The extraordinary thing about this refusal was not that she would not copy her mother – there have always been plenty of rebel daughters in this respect – but that she was allowed to get away with it. Daughters in working-class families then were usually forced to help. The luxury of refusal was denied them when daily life was so hard for their mothers, with all the sheer physical labour involved in running a household. Wives exhausted themselves, and daughters were obliged to relieve them by learning as soon as possible to cook and clean and do the washing with all the hard work this involved. But not Jennie. No one whipped her into line. She got away with doing the minimum and did it badly. On Saturday mornings, her mother insisted that at least she should do the dusting in the house, one in a row of four-roomed cottages in Cowdenbeath (Fifeshire), but her attitude to this simplest of tasks was, in her own words, 'negative'. Her mother dusted by clearing the surface to be cleaned, then wiping and replacing each object, but Jennie merely swiped the duster in and out of plates and ornaments with no interest in, or intention of, being thorough. Halfway through any household job she would stop and read a book. An attempt was made to instruct her in the important art of shopping, but she messed that up too. Saturday afternoons would find her down at the Co-op with a list of what to buy, but she invariably mixed up the order, broke the precious eggs and bought sweets without permission. She was a disaster as a trainee wife, and, moreover, proud of it.

So, rather curiously, was her mother. Jennie exasperated her, but her scoldings were perfunctory – 'She had not the slightest idea how to be stern,' commented Jennie, scornfully – and her efforts to make her daughter knuckle down were half-hearted. She seems, very early on, to have decided that Jennie had the right to reject her own values – here was a girl, a very clever and wilful girl, who was determined to be something other than a wife. There seemed no point in trying to force her to do what she not only did not want to do, but did incompetently. Example hadn't inspired her, and chastisement would never work, not with Jennie's character. It was best to let her concentrate on what she *was* good at, even if some people thought such tolerance amounted to spoiling her. And what Jennie was good at had nothing to do with dusting and shopping: she was good at talking and arguing, talents fostered by her father, not her mother.

James Lee was a much tougher character than his wife. Jennie regarded him as 'the all-wise infallible one', the parent whose word she did obey and by whose opinions she was most influenced. It was her father she wanted to be like, not her mother, however much she loved her – what *he* said made sense to her, his critical socialist ideas finding an instant response in her heart as well as her mind. James Lee saw a revolution coming, one necessary to make the world a fairer place, and Jennie wanted to be ready to do her bit. Her father, for all his dedication to the socialist cause, was 'only' a miner, if one who chaired local labour union meetings, as his father and grandfather had done before him. He expected both his daughter and her younger brother Tommy to share his idealism, and they duly did, though Jennie was by far the more enthusiastic. 'I was not fair and gentle like my brother. I was dark and stubborn' – stubborn enough to believe that against all the odds she could make something more out of her life.

The odds undoubtedly were against her but, as she was well aware, not as hopelessly as they were against other working-class girls of her era. To start with, the Lees were not as desperately poor as most of the families among whom they lived. During Jennie's childhood her father was never out of work and, because there were only two children, his wages made some treats possible. 'I was one of the plutocrats,' observed Jennie, recalling the overflowing Christmas stockings, and the presents of books and a double-jointed doll quite beyond the reach of other families. She had no experience of true deprivation, never had to endure hunger or cold, never lacked any basic necessity as many of her contemporaries did. She was an indulged, protected, much loved child who came home from school each day to a blazing fire in the hearth, a kettle boiling for tea in the kitchen, a tray of scones just coming out of the oven, and a white cloth on the table ready for her to sit down at. Even more impressive than all this material care and comfort were the time and patience bestowed on her by her parents. She was positively encouraged to air her half-formed views, and when socialist propagandists came to talk to her father she was not banished but invited to listen and learn. Never once was she told she was only a girl and that she should stick to girlish things.

Yet there were some girlish things which did appeal to Jennie – she was not so much a bookworm that she scoffed at pretty clothes or being thought attractive. Her Aunt Meg, her father's sister, was a decided influence, both in appearance and in how she conducted herself, and Jennie took note. As a young woman Aunt Meg had gone to America but she came back to Scotland on visits every second year. Her niece loved how she looked, so stylish in a fur coat and the most beautiful hats. Jennie's mother was pretty but certainly not stylish and never looked like Aunt Meg who had about her an aura quite different from the other women around Jennie. And it wasn't just a matter of clothes and make-up – Aunt Meg was stylish in everything. She had become a cook in America, where she'd done very well, and earned enough money to seem rich to the Lee family. There was never any air of domestic drudgery about this female relative, and when she eventually went off at the end of each visit she took a touch of glamour with her, leaving Jennie determined to have some of it herself one day. She wanted to fight the socialist fight but look glamorous and live artistically while she did it.

Her mother, to her credit, was only too willing to help her. It was she, the housewife, who proved Jennie's biggest champion when it came to education. Most girls left school at fourteen, but Jennie, who'd always shone academically, wanted to stay on and then go to college. Her father hesitated, proud though he was of her ability. The expense of keeping a girl at school scared him. She should be out at work and contributing to the family purse. But 'mother was determined I should go on. Blindly determined . . . she would carry me on as far as she could. She was game.' It was the ultimate proof, if Jennie had needed it, that though her mother excelled at being a wife she did not expect her daughter to follow exactly in her footsteps and learn to be what she herself was. Nor was it a case of Mrs Lee's own ambitions having been thwarted by the lack of education Jennie was now receiving – on the contrary, she was content with her role in life and never expressed any yearning for a career. Her true worth was her recognition that all girls are not made for the same future and that they should be allowed an autonomy denied to her own and previous generations.

It was a point of view Jennie put forward in a series of essays written in school exercise books. Women, she wrote, were obviously all different, so 'why try to fit the infinite varieties into a rigid mould . . . [you] might as well force all women to wear size four shoes.' In another essay, grandly entitled 'Do Women Lack Initiative?', she fretted about the part love played in the lives of both men and women – 'How is it that the same emotion influences the life and work of the two sexes so differently?' She lambasted 'the dependence nature' which she saw as having been imposed on women by men, and the way they had been 'encouraged to acquiesce in their economic inferiority'. The trouble was caused, she deduced, by the institution of marriage, this desperation to become wives. 'Marriage', she wrote, 'is no longer the sole future responsibility.' Women's emotional life needed to be 'ennobled and enlarged' and not repressed or stultified by marriage.

At the time of writing, Jennie had little experience of any

romantic love. It wasn't that she hadn't been interested in boys (she had become so distracted by them at the age of fifteen, when she was still at Cowdenbeath's large mixed secondary school, that for the first time she wasn't first in the class) but that she hadn't found a like-minded one. Not until she progressed to Edinburgh University did love of this sort enter her life and begin to show her how complicated were the emotions, as well as the physical sensations, it gave rise to. She was extremely attractive, exuded vitality and sexual energy, and had indeed developed a certain style, dressing well, though with little money to do it on. She was ready, and more than prepared to defy convention, to enter into sexual liaisons which would see her living according to her own ideals and scorning marriage.

Here it was her father, not her mother, who went a long way towards helping her to be prepared. Before she left for Edinburgh, he put on the bookshelves, where she could not fail to notice it, Marie Stopes's *Married Love* (published four years before and giving extremely basic, but revolutionary for the times, information on birth control). In fact, it was so vague about the details of contraception that Jennie soon wanted much more precise knowledge. Edinburgh was the place to acquire it. She got to know a woman medical student who told her all about the various methods of birth control, and also about the 'bad and indifferent methods of abortion . . . better to enjoy and suffer than sit around with folded arms . . . please God, lead me into temptation.' He did. Dan Gillies, aged twenty-three to her nineteen, attracted her greatly. She met him during the course of her political activities, when he spoke at one of the socialist party meetings she attended. He was a brilliant orator, full of the kind of idealistic passion she shared, and he was a genuine working man, a rivet-heater from Glasgow, not a callow student. She was ready to have a full-blooded affair with him, but it never happened. 'I intended to have a plaything,' she wrote to her best friend Suse, 'instead, I am up against a man who is stronger and cleverer than myself in every way.' Her response was to declare: 'This love business leaves me perfectly indifferent.'

This was hardly true. She was battling to separate strong

feelings of physical attraction from those of emotional and intellectual commitment. She'd always promised herself that sex and love should, and would, not be confused – she wouldn't have to *love* someone to have sex with him. She wasn't even sure love existed in its own right – maybe, or so she suspected, love was *only* sex. It confused her, sitting on a train, to meet an Indian who was 'exceedingly handsome and intelligent . . . I made no definite promise but he expects to see something of me . . .' So did Dan, but her initial interest in him was waning quickly. He was not the man she had thought he was from his speeches. She had unusual ideas as to the sort of man she did in fact want. She was drawn to 'big, simple people, free from affectation'. All the men she had admired, those socialist propagandists invited home by her father, had had what she thought of as a purity, an innocence about them, a naïvety about everyday matters in striking contrast to the sophistication of their intellects. That was what she was looking for in a man, what she thought she'd found in Dan. She was soon disillusioned, writing to Suse that he wasn't after all 'an unsophisticated child of nature' but instead that he sounded 'an ominously modern and familiar note'. Fortunately, at this point, before any real sexual adventure took place, Dan was sent to prison for his political activism during the 1926 General Strike. The ruthless Jennie was vastly relieved. He was sentenced to four months – 'Thank goodness for all concerned that I had cooled towards him before this occurred.'

Nobody else ever came nearer to becoming her lover during her student days, though she was highly aware of her own attractiveness and the power she had. 'I have been told,' she commented to Suse, '. . . that I have eyes like the cinema!' In other words, that she was sexy. She knew that. She despised herself for it, but she loved making herself look good, spending more time than she thought a serious-minded woman should on her appearance. She wanted to work for a socialist revolution, but she also wanted to see herself in 'a deep crimson silk chiffon velvet dress, made almost sleeveless, and with that long loose tie in the front . . . the tie . . . in heavy black *crêpe-de-chine* or satin'. She would look gorgeous in it, and she craved looking gorgeous. Too much of her time, she felt, went into mooning about clothes when it should have gone into some honest work and continuous thinking and not such frivolities.

But she was too hard on herself. She was doing plenty of thinking and had worked extremely hard both at her studies and for the socialist cause during her university days. It was not just that she wanted to do well for her own sake, but that she felt a deep obligation to justify her mother's faith in her. Financially, she was dependent for half her class fees on her family and, though her mother never mentioned the struggle it was to find this money, she was well aware of it and tried to relieve the situation by winning prizes which would provide money. Even so, money went on being a worry and hampered her from being able to attend some of the socialist conferences she wanted to go to. When the organisers of one such conference wrote to invite her, her father told her to reply that she was already a burden to her people through educational expenditure. Considering she had just started teaching that summer, the moment she had taken her degree and was qualified, and had earned enough to contribute £124 already to the family exchequer, she felt this was unfair and that her father 'should be made to feel that arithmetic of the situation'.

Teaching was not something she had really wanted to do, but it was the only job that presented itself. It was 1926, the year of the General Strike and, though her brother had emigrated to Australia, meaning there was one less mouth to feed, money was tighter then it had ever been. She was living at home and had to have a job, and teaching was the only professional one available. Even getting a job as a teacher hadn't been easy – she'd had to wait for the local education authority to appoint her to a school – and the teaching itself made her 'feel like hell'. She exhausted herself trying to teach according to her own ideals, without brutality, and bringing to it an understanding of the impoverished backgrounds of most of her pupils. But it was tough and, though coming home to be looked after, as ever, by her devoted mother, was a comfort, there were strains there too. Her father, as a result of his own part in political agitation, had been demoted from a 'fireman' (meaning a deputy, or inspector) to an ordinary miner. The return to such hard physical work shattered him. Jennie came home each day to witness her mother, the perfect wife, trying to anticipate her father's every wish, making him special dishes – 'a light milk pudding with the white of an egg whisked on top' – because he couldn't digest anything else. He was almost at the end of his strength and had decided to join Tommy in Australia. Both parents, wrote Jennie to Suse, had definitely made up their minds that this was their only way out.

Jennie wanted a quite different way out. Emigration, she told Suse, was not for her 'until I have investigated London, Paris, and maybe New York, and see definitely what shape I am making towards Westminster'. One step towards it was to start attending the conferences she hadn't been able to afford as a student, the kind of gatherings where she would be noted by influential people within the Labour Party. Her first trip abroad was to Brussels, to the Socialist International Conference in the summer of 1927. The letters she wrote from there to Suse had nothing to do with politics. They were all about her first real love affair, her first sexual experience. T'ang Liang-Li was a young Chinese intellectual who had become the London correspondent for a London newspaper. His personality, according to Jennie, was 'infinitely cleverer, subtler and more understanding' than her own. He was passionate and devoted, and though she responded to, and welcomed, the passion, she was troubled by the devotion. At first, she'd been relieved that T'ang already had a girlfriend. Another woman might have resented this and set herself to usurp the existing girl, but believing that T'ang was already committed and wanted only an affair made Jennie feel secure. But he broke with this girlfriend – 'I advised him not to . . .' – and told Jennie he wanted their union to be perfect. He also wanted to marry her, at once. This sounded the loudest warning signal of all to Jennie, and she felt obliged to spell out to T'ang that, though he pronounced himself finished with experimentation and ready to commit himself only and entirely to her, she did not feel the same. She was 'just at the beginning' and might some day desert him in the same way he had ditched his previous girlfriend. 'This business has a lot of pain in it', she told Suse, 'as well as pleasure.' T'ang wanted her to come to London and live with him, on his money until she could support herself through freelance journalism, which he was confident she would be able to do, but he could not persuade her.

During what turned out to be a fairly brief, if intense, affair with T'ang, Jennie never once thought of herself as being 'in love'. Indeed, she was as doubtful as ever that, so far as she was concerned, this condition could exist. The sex had been terrific, but what did it have to do with love? As for marriage, she assured Suse it had never been even a remote possibility. All her energy was going into trying to get out of teaching (though she worked hard at it and did her considerable best to be a good teacher) and into politics. That's what she wanted to be, a politician. A year later, in 1928, at the age of twenty-three, she was chosen by the Independent Labour Party (ILP) to be their parliamentary candidate for North Lanark in the approaching by-election. She was wildly excited and put everything she had into canvassing to great effect – those who had thought her youth, her sex and her looks would be fatal handicaps were proved wrong. Her passionate commitment to socialism, her absolute identification with the problems of the constituents, and her fiery speeches won people over. She won the by-election.

She was on her way, in love not with T'ang but with politics, married to the cause she cared so much about. On the overnight-sleeper she caught from Glasgow to London she was as euphoric as any bride. Nothing intimidated her. 'I will have London at my feet,' she had boasted to Suse, and in no time she did, or political London anyway. The entire male House of Commons appeared mesmerised by this lovely, sexy, stylish young Scottish woman, who looked so radiant and bore herself with such staggering self-confidence. There had been few women in the House before – Lady Astor had taken her seat in 1919, and she had been joined by three more women in 1923, but none of them had looked like Jennie. Lady Astor had kept to a sort of severe uniform of her own invention, and the other women, except Lady Terrington, had had no interest in clothes. Jennie stood out and all eyes were upon her, which suited her fine. A few weeks after her first appearance in the Commons, when the General Election had seen her seat confirmed, everyone waited to see how she would make her mark. That

1929 election had been called the 'Flapper' election, because sixty-nine women candidates had stood and fourteen had been elected, all of whom were anxious to show they could be just as capable as the men, but the Labour Party was in office with only a tiny majority and could hardly take risks. Jennie was at something of a disadvantage anyway. She was expected to abide by ILP policies which, unfortunately for her ambition, often clashed with mainline government policies. (At that time, there were several parties-within-the-party and the most maverick of them was Jennie's, the ILP.) Her chances of being noticed and marked down for future responsibility were not good if she spouted ILP views too loudly. But, in fact, it was hard for her to make any kind of impression in the chamber, because she was so overwhelmed with the detail of what being an MP turned out to be. She badly needed guidance, and more than any other new colleague the one who provided it was Frank Wise, another, but very experienced, ILP member. Frank, however, did more than put her straight on policy matters – he fell in love with her, and she with him.

Frank Wise was forty-five years old to her twenty-five. He came into the 1929 Parliament as MP for Leicester, after an already distinguished career as an economist. A Cambridge graduate, Frank had been called to the Bar but then joined the civil service, becoming economic adviser on the Soviet Union. He was not only clever but also physically dynamic, an athlete who climbed, played football and was an accomplished rider. And he was married, with four children. This deterred Jennie not one bit – as with T'ang's existing girlfriend, it only made her feel safe in a love affair with Frank. He couldn't try to persuade her to become a wife. She had no scruples about Dorothy, Frank's wife of twenty years, either. Dorothy had a first-class degree, was a teacher and a JP – but Jennie didn't fear her wrath. As far as she was concerned, Dorothy could stay Frank's wife and welcome to the role. She didn't even want to live with Frank all the time, but was perfectly content to have her own flat. She'd started off in Dean Street, Soho, but during her affair with Frank she moved to Guilford Street in Bloomsbury, round the corner from his London base in John

Street. She liked her own space and didn't mind the coming and going all the time between the two flats.

But Frank did. He was completely bewitched by Jennie and desperate not just to be with her all the time but to make her his wife. Very soon he wanted to divorce Dorothy and marry Jennie as quickly as possible. Writing to a friend, he described Jennie as 'very clear-headed' and said 'she achieves an amazing combination of cool detached judgement with warm personal feelings which at once bewilders and delights a mere Englishman'. But it was this very clear-headedness and cool detached judgement which worked against him. Jennie didn't want Frank to divorce Dorothy and she had no desire to become his wife. The word, the role, was still taboo. She did love him, but not to that extent. Times spent with him, usually abroad when Frank was on some kind of business trip and she joined him, during the parliamentary recesses, were wonderful but they did not change her mind. She was aghast when he told Dorothy he wanted a divorce, and relieved when Dorothy refused to give him one. Then, two years later, as Frank grew more and more restless with a situation he found agonising, Jennie and Frank both lost their seats in Parliament in the General Election of October 1931.

This put their affair to a hard test. They had not the same easy access to each other that belonging to the House of Commons had given them. Worse than that, Jennie had to earn a living, mostly as a journalist. She was certainly not going to crawl back to Scotland and teaching, and snatched at the opportunity which arose for her to go on a lecture tour, expounding the socialist cause, to America. From there, her letters to Frank confirmed that she still loved him but was no nearer to wanting him to divorce Dorothy and marry her. She assured him: 'Darling, you would be surprised if you knew how dull and virtuous I am these days . . . [there is] no one I want to flirt with.' Yet at the same time she left him in no doubt that she would not guarantee her fidelity to him: if there *were* someone worth flirting with, she might flirt, and more. It wouldn't mean much, but if she was apart a long time she might indulge in sexual comfort if it came her way. Early on in their relationship, she'd warned him that men reached the stage very quickly of wanting to sleep with her and it wasn't her fault. If he 'left a gap' it would be easy for her to succumb and fill it.

Her resistance to the idea of Frank's divorcing Dorothy was not, however, only because she didn't want to marry him herself and become that hateful thing 'a wife', but because she didn't want either of their careers damaged. While they were both MPs, the damage caused by a divorce would, judged Jennie, be 'calamitous', and once both had lost their seats, getting re-elected as, respectively, the guilty party in a divorce, and the woman cited as the offender, would be impossible. Again and again she dinned it into Frank that divorce would be disastrous for their ambitions and that those ambitions were far, far more important than their personal happiness, which he imagined he'd only find if she could, and would, become his wife. Marriage was an impediment to ambition. Furthermore, it would actually wreck their relationship.

In December 1931, when Frank was becoming more insistent than ever, Jennie wrote a letter in which she tried harder than ever to make him understand what becoming his wife would do to her. They had just had one of their many partings and when he saw her off at the station he'd absent-mindedly called her Dorrie (his wife's pet name). She wrote that 'a kind of alarm bell rang': he'd called her that because she'd *sounded like a nagging wife*. She told him that, though she had indeed come close to the 'stupid boorish nagging' wives were famous for, he had to appreciate that it was marriage which made women nags. And as for men, it made them jealous. She couldn't bear the thought of Frank regarding her as his property and therefore thinking he had a right to be jealous. She was, she said 'a rather overvital animal with the temptation to love others as well as you' and even though she loved him 'more completely than any other man' this did not 'still my curiosity and even temporary infatuation for others'.

She seemed to think that Frank would see nothing contradictory in her statement on the one hand that she loved only him and on the other that she was capable of 'temporary infatuation' with others, an infatuation invariably leading to a sexual relationship, however brief and, to her at least, meaningless. When Frank was around she had eyes for no one else, but when he wasn't she had other companions. One of them was Aneurin Bevan, MP for Ebbw Vale, an ex-miner and a passionate socialist like herself, though he was not a lover. She liked his company immensely and admired the way he enjoyed himself with women without getting trapped into marriage. He regarded marriage as something to be avoided at all costs, just as she did. They acknowledged each other's sensual natures and for both of them, as Jennie put it, 'celibacy was no part of our creed'. They gloried in 'free' relationships which, so long as they were discreet, would not in any way threaten their political ambitions.

What did begin to threaten Jennie's by 1932 was a change in the attitude (to a divorce) of Frank's wife. She had finally, and reluctantly, yielded to her husband's desperate desire that his relationship with Jennie should be put on a more regular basis and that they should separate. She still wasn't ready for a proper divorce, but she agreed that some sort of settlement should be made soon. By the next year, the details of that settlement were being worked out, and Dorothy had acknowledged the inevitable. On the twenty-first anniversary of her marriage to Frank, 2 November 1933, they had dinner together after the theatre, Dorothy struggling hard to be civilised and conceal her bitterness. She could see that Frank was very, very tired and felt sorry for him in spite of her own anguish and need for comfort. He saw her off on her train at Baker Street before he went home, and then the next morning, Jennie's twenty-ninth birthday, he rushed round to her flat to wish her happy birthday. It was a Friday and they longed to spend a weekend together, but Frank was committed to going north to speak at various political meetings. He fitted in a day with his old friend Charles Trevelyan, who lived near Morpeth. There, walking in the woods on the Sunday afternoon, he collapsed while climbing a stile. He died with brutal suddenness of a brain haemorrhage, before help could be summoned.

For Jennie, it was an appalling shock. Frank was a fit, healthy man in the prime of life and, in spite of his tiredness, there had been no signs whatsoever of anything being physically wrong. Trevelyan hoped to get to Jennie before the news could reach her and break it to her himself, but he was too late. She heard the news from a journalist, by telephone, which added to her trauma. She was alone in her flat, and lay all night trying to comprehend what had happened. She didn't sleep and she didn't weep – it was all, as she later wrote to Suse, 'too fantastically unbelievable'. Very early next morning, when Trevelyan arrived, reality broke through. Then, she wept passionately, but even this open grief did not last long. She knew she had to steady herself quickly or go under completely and there was only one way to do that: work. That was all life held for her now: work, the work she and Frank had cared so much about. With considerable courage, she forced herself to go to Newcastle to attend two political meetings. She did not go to the funeral but she did write to Dorothy, the widow who could at least grieve publicly and openly.

Dorothy wrote back, a letter quite startling in its compassion and generosity, saying she fully understood the agony Jennie was going through, and blaming herself for her love not being 'big enough' to let Frank go so that he and Jennie could have been together. She saw clearly that Jennie had given him 'youth and inspiration' and that she herself had been 'middle-aged and nervy and often on edge and too much preoccupied with the children' which had contributed to what happened. She was devastatingly honest, admitting that though, of course, she would never have wanted Frank dead, his death, his parting from her through death, was in some awful way easier to bear than losing him entirely to Jennie. She ended by inviting Jennie to go to Frank's flat and take away anything of hers, and hoped that in the future they could perhaps be friends.

But the future was a place Jennie did not want to be. Without Frank, she felt vulnerable and hopeless. Nothing seemed to have any point any more, not even work. She thought of suicide only to lecture herself on cowardice. Life was 'just hell'. Her mood was black and she felt it affecting everyone around her and tainting everything she did.

But Aneurin Bevan refused to let it affect him. He was kind, considerate, ever ready to squire her about and was in general what Jennie called 'a good pal'. For her, that was enough. For him, very quickly, it was not. He wanted a pal who was also a lover and, given the situation he and Jennie found themselves in, with both of them in the public eye and their ambitions still intact, that meant making her his wife. From marriage being no part of his life-plan it became essential. The struggle was to get Jennie to agree to marry him.

II

Jennie had far more in common with Nye Bevan than she had had with Frank Wise so far as background and personality went. Jennie's comment that they could have been brother and sister, and Nye's response that if so it would have been with a tendency to incest, were fair enough. Both were from mining families (and of course Nye himself had been a miner), both had been brought up in mining communities, and both had had their political vision influenced, if not entirely created, by the hardship and poverty they had seen around them. But there the similarity ended. Jennie always knew she, in comparison with Nye, had had it easy. Nye was one of ten children, eight of whom survived infancy, with all that meant in terms of resources; he'd left school at the age of twelve to go down the mine, and after that educated himself; it was through his own efforts that at twenty-two he finally got a scholarship to the Central Labour College in London.

His father, like Jennie's father, was a loyal union man and treasurer of his local lodge, but he was neither a political activist like James Lee, nor the dominant partner in his marriage. Phoebe Bevan was the more forceful. Nye got his physique from her and also his determination. Nye, after he came back to Tredegar when he finished college, was unemployed and for a while suffered the humiliation of being virtually supported by one of his sisters, Arianwen, who had a good job as a typist. It wasn't until 1929, when he was thirty-two, that he escaped to London again and could support himself once he was elected as MP for Ebbw Vale. There, in the House of Commons, he saw and met Jennie Lee who, at the beginning of that parliament, made a far greater impact than he did. Everyone marvelled at this golden girl who had risen so rapidly through the party ranks and now prepared to dazzle Westminster.

It was a while before Nye attained anything like the same prominence, but when he did he eclipsed Jennie as a speaker. Whereas in the Commons the fire and passion which had made her hustings speeches rousing were diluted, Nye's were increased. He was aggressive and fearless, quite impossible to intimidate. His style of speaking displayed all the skill of an experienced actor and yet his sincerity was evident. Outside the House his growing reputation as a *bon viveur* (today he'd have been labelled a champagne socialist) confused people – here was a die-hard socialist, ever scathing about the privileged, idle lives of his Tory opponents, wining and dining with the best of them and enjoying great success with women. He made friends across party boundaries, seeing nothing wrong with associating in his leisure life with those he attacked in his political life. There was something wild about him as well as something solid, and this appealed greatly to Jennie – he reflected what she felt about herself. But whether she was as physically and emotionally attracted to him as she was to Frank was at first doubtful. Nye's attraction for her all lay in his powerful personality and intellect, and even then it was more a relationship of equals rather than recognition of a superior mind, which, so far as Jennie was concerned, was what she felt she looked for in a man. Nye, though seven years older, was by no means the potent older man she had once told Suse she was looking for.

But he was good fun and she relished their clashes of opinion. Nye scorned her devotion to the ILP – he himself would have nothing to do with any of those parties within the main Labour Party – and Jennie had reported with some sense of embarrassment how he had told her to get into a nunnery and be done with it if she was virtuously going to stick with her principles and remain with the ILP. He accused her of being nothing but 'a Salvation Army lassie', more interested in being a social worker than a real politician determined to bring about change. But she admired his vigorous denunciation of her stand, and thought he was the only one of the younger MPs who could be depended on to think for himself and be at all times what she called 'anti-inertia'. After Frank died, Nye became more attentive than ever, and she was grateful to him for being so solicitous. But the truth was, Nye was not Frank, and her grief for Frank did not seem to lessen.

All the same, Nye's company did help her to rise above her wretchedness and get through the days – so much so that she made no objection when he suggested he should move in and be there during the nights too, when it was hardest of all for her to be brave. A little before Christmas 1933, six weeks after Frank's death, Nye did move in to her Guilford Street flat. She knew, though, that this would only be a temporary arrangement – she was going off to America on another lecture tour in January, so there was no question of Nye's becoming permanently installed. She told him that when she returned she was going to rent a country cottage near London. Nye replied he would share it with her. Jennie demurred. Living together in such an obvious way would give rise to gossip, and that sort of gossip would damage both their careers. Precisely, said Nye, and that was why they must marry. Marriage, from being an impediment, had become a practical necessity. It still need not mean anything – it was a mere piece of paper, a sop to convention enabling them both to continue in their work without fear of scandal.

Nye's arguments were all logical and rational, and it was the right way to appeal to Jennie, but they could not conceal what was really driving him: he was genuinely in love with Jennie. Marriage, for all his previous determination to avoid it, signified more than a legal arrangement. He had no desire to make her, within marriage, the kind of wife she had always dreaded becoming, so she need have no fear of being required to become a domestic drudge. It cannot have escaped his notice after even the most brief experience of living with Jennie that she was utterly hopeless as a housewife and cook. There would be none of that sort of marital comfort. Nor can he have deluded himself into thinking Jennie, as a wife, would be sexually faithful. She hadn't, in this respect, always been faithful to Frank, whom she had loved so passionately. She'd always made it plain that she didn't believe in monogamy. But Nye's love for her was so great that he had absolute confidence their marriage would work. It would just be an unusual marriage, that was all, one in which Jennie would redefine the role of wife. And he would be proud to have the sort of wife she would make instead of some submissive little *hausfrau*.

He was persuasive, and he was strong. More than anything, strength was what Jennie needed at that time. Masterful men were not creatures before whom she had ever bowed – she was masterful herself and used to defying them – but there was undoubtedly, in her then vulnerable state, something comforting in Nye trying to take charge and tell her what to do for her own sake as well as his. Frank had always made her feel secure – she once told him she felt he had thrown 'a warm cloak' round her – and so indeed had her parents, and now here was Nye, attempting to do the same. She doubted if he could succeed in giving her that feeling of being utterly protected, but suddenly it seemed worth a try. He seemed to understand that Frank had been the love of her life, and to accept this. But there was the future to face, and he would help her face it.

Nye took her for a splendid dinner at the Café Royal in May 1934 and finally persuaded her to marry him. He then went off to America, and when he returned in September, announced their engagement. On 25 October, they were duly married at Holborn Register Office, to the intense interest of the press. Two friends were witnesses, and the only family member, from either side, was uninvited: Billy, Nye's brother. Jennie said he was 'dressed to kill and in an awkward mood'. None of the Bevan family approved of Jennie and, unlike Fanny Stevenson, she had done nothing whatsoever to endear herself to them. She was furious with Billy for coming, of his own volition, to represent the family and when, at the wedding lunch at The Ivy afterwards, he demanded beer instead of champagne, she said she wanted to strangle him. Meanwhile, the reporters and photographers were noting all the unconventionalities: Jennie didn't wear a hat, or gloves; she didn't accept a ring; and she let it be known from the very beginning that she would never allow anyone to call her Mrs Bevan. She was Miss Jennie Lee, married or not. Nye beamed approval.

The honeymoon was delayed until January. They went to Spain, to Torremolinos, where Jennie saw Nye at his most flamboyant. He was utterly at home there, wearing a magnificent Spanish cloak, a sombrero and a scarlet *facha* round his solid waist. They both loved the sun and the way of life, the antithesis of what they had known as children. It was a carefree time, probably the most carefree they were ever to have, and Jennie came back to London feeling more cheerful than she had done since Frank died. This was fortunate, since a difficult time politically was ahead for both of them. The Labour Party was beginning to concentrate more on its policies towards Europe, and what its reaction should be to what was happening there, than on domestic issues. Jennie, who was not an MP, was heavily involved in work for the International Women's Committee against war and fascism; Nye, who was an MP and whose constituency included a large number of unemployed men, was heavily involved in supporting hunger marches. Both of them were active and busy, Jennie as a journalist, Nye as a speaker at rallies as well as an MP. Rarely were a husband and wife more united in their aims and in the direction of all their efforts. For both of them work, political work came first, and this made of their marriage a partnership of equals of an extraordinary kind.

Yet there were problems, and these were in turn caused by their being equals, by Jennie's absolute refusal to take on what were assumed to be the roles of the wife. She'd said she wouldn't and she didn't. But a household had to be run, both of them had to be looked after. Nye could manage very well without too much cosseting – it was Jennie who couldn't. Right from the beginning of living on her own in London she had had to have a cleaner, the redoubtable Annie, 6 feet (1.8 m) tall and muscular, who polished floors superbly and generally made Jennie as comfortable as her mother always had done. Now more was needed. To Jennie, the solution was clear: as soon as they found a house, her mother should come (with her father) to look after them. Everyone would then be happy. She could see no obstacle to this neat plan. Nye adored her mother from the moment he met her (soon joking that he had had to marry the girl to get the mother) and she adored him. James Lee was not quite so bowled over initially, but that didn't worry Jennie. But first a house had to be found and that took until the summer of 1936, when they bought Lane End Cottage, near Reading, about 50 miles (80 km) from London.

Both of them were wildly excited with their first home, and now Jennie revealed a side of herself which did, at last, fit in with traditional notions of a wife's function. She might have no interest in housework but she knew how to create a home, and she approached the task eagerly with both great energy and taste. Jennie directed all the renovations and supervised all the decoration. Once the structural changes had been made, and the interior decorated, she spent days scouring antique shops and sales to find the right furniture. The end result was charming and admired by all who visited. Jennie, the Home-maker, was a new creature, a positive triumph as a wife.

Everything was now ready for her parents to come down from Scotland and for her mother to start looking after her and Nye. Jennie didn't see it as 'employing' her mother or as using her as an unpaid servant. She designed a two-bedroom cottage for her parents, which was built in the garden, so that they would feel independent, and then her father was persuaded to give up his job and accompany his wife to Lane End Cottage to live there permanently. Jennie regarded herself as having done her mother a favour because 'shopping and cooking and gardening all day long never seemed to tire or bore her'. She was by then fifty-six, but as energetic as ever and delighted to be useful to her daughter and the son-in-law she was so comfortable with. Not surprisingly, the general view of the Bevan family was that Jennie was not the sort of wife they would have wanted for Nye – fancy needing her own mother to run her household.

As usual, Jennie couldn't care less what they thought. Neither before nor after marrying Nye did she attempt to woo his family, never seeing it as any wife's duty to embrace her husband's relatives with affection. Nye had taken her to Wales, to show her all the places he loved, and she had of course been introduced to all his family, but she had no interest in really getting to know them. She went with Nye once to his constituency, Ebbw Vale, and that was it – it was his job to look after it, not hers, and she had no intention of adopting a supportive role as so many wives did. She had important work of her own to do, though since she still hadn't got back to parliament (she failed to win the North Lanark seat in 1935) this was still journalism and not the work she longed to be doing. She went to America again, to lecture, perfectly happy to leave Nye in her mother's excellent care. Interestingly, she did seem to agree it was her responsibility as a wife to see that her husband *was* looked after even if she was certainly not going to do it herself. Nye exhausted himself and she did worry about him. Weekends at Lane End Cottage were precious, used as they were for Nye to relax. They listened to music together and read poetry. This helped Nye's mood more than it helped hers – she felt frustrated, longing as she did to find a parliamentary seat again. She sensed that she was marking time and occasionally coming dangerously close to pretending she was the wife she did not want to be, the little woman waiting at home to soothe her hard-working husband.

The war changed everything. Within nine months of its declaration in September 1939, Churchill had become Prime Minister and Labour had been brought into a coalition government for its duration. Max Beaverbrook became Minister for Air Production, and it was he who offered Jennie a job. She leapt at the chance to be busy and active and toured the country persuading the workers in the aircraft factories to work even harder and to carry on through the air-raids. Now she needed periods of rest at Lane End Cottage just as much as Nye. But she wished she could be at Nye's side, in the centre of all the ongoing drama, and suddenly she was given her chance. Cecil King offered her a contract to write a column as the *Daily Mirror*'s political correspondent, which she accepted (resigning from the job Beaverbrook had given her). Now she was in the Press Gallery of the Commons, and if not at Nye's side, or on a par with him, involved properly, and quite importantly, in what was going on. But only four months into the new job, she was sacked (Churchill had begun to complain about the *Mirror*'s line and King was afraid his paper would be suppressed), and was again frustrated and impotent. This Nye could not bear. Jennie as a wife working at full pressure was an inspiration;

Jennie as a wife thrashing around looking for some meaningful contribution to make was a worry. If their marriage was to go on being one of equals, Jennie had either to get back into parliament or find some work of a more satisfying kind than she'd found so far.

In 1942, at the end of almost two years during which she'd toured America again, raising support for the war and trying to bring America into it, and had also written a pamphlet in support of Russia (*Russia, Our Ally*), she stood as a candidate in the Bristol Central by-election, though as an Independent and not on behalf of the ILP. The war, or rather the ILP's absolute opposition to it, gave Jennie the opportunity to leave the party she had stayed loyal to, against her own interests and against the advice of both Frank and Nye. In 1914, as a young girl, she had seen her parents campaigning against the First World War and had followed their lead, but in 1939 she agreed with Nye that the war against Hitler, the war against fascism, had to be fought. But standing as an Independent did her no favours. The label she ran under was Independent Labour, but with the Labour Party having decided to agree not to fight any by-election seat vacated by a Tory (so as not to rock the coalition government) Jennie got no support from its members. She canvassed energetically, as she did everything, holding daily meetings in all kinds of different venues, and all kinds of famous friends came to speak on her behalf. Everyone thought she would win since the Tory majority at the last general election had only been 1,500.

She lost. It was one of the most surprising by-election results of the war, with a swing *to* the Tories when everywhere else there were swings against them. Jennie blamed her old party, the ILP, who had run a candidate against her, but it was obvious that the main Labour Party's attitude had had a great influence – she had needed their backing. If she wanted to get back into parliament, as she so desperately did, then she would have to seek re-entry to the Labour Party proper. Conveniently, it was by then possible for her to convince herself that the reasons why she had belonged to the ILP and not the main Labour Party no longer obtained, and also to make some token apology for criticising Labour policy in articles she had written.

She promised 'full and generous' support in future for 'the broad policy of the party'. She was readmitted and five months later was adopted by Cannock as its candidate in the coming General Election.

By then the war was over. For Jennie, it had been an easy, if frustrating, period. She'd toured America, done a lot of journalism and helped with propaganda. But for Nye, it had been hard, devoted as he had been to harrying the Prime Minister, whom most of the country hailed as a hero. He'd attracted great opprobrium and been criticised from every quarter, and yet he had held firm, pushing for the conduct of the war to be governed by the need to eliminate fascism and spearhead a socialist revolution. Jennie admired him tremendously. The more outrageously outspoken he became, the more he grew in stature in her eyes. Far from being a wife who counselled caution, she backed him completely and encouraged his daring excesses. No husband could have had more understanding and enthusiastic support from a wife. He was a confident man anyway, but given Jennie's agreement with everything he said and did his confidence grew and grew – she made him feel he could do anything, and that he could endure any amount of hate mail and vilification. They were together in what they believed and what they wanted to achieve and the exhilaration of this unity of purpose added a whole new dimension to their marriage.

But it was not quite one of equals any more. Nye had outstripped Jennie in fame. He was the coming man for Labour while she had lost her place. Slowly, by infinitely subtle degrees, she was beginning to see that Nye, not she, had a great future. He could lead the Labour Party. He could become Prime Minister and put into operation all their idealistic plans. This prospect excited her, but not for any wifely longings to share the glory. She wanted to work *with* Nye, not stand on the sidelines, and to do that fully she had to win the Cannock seat. It was a good constituency for her to try to win. Cannock, in a coal-mining area, was already a Labour-held seat, and she had only one opponent, a Tory who was a Sussex accountant. It was a large constituency, though, and took some covering, but as ever, Jennie coped admirably with all the travelling and speaking. Now that the election was open, Nye could, and did, come to speak at her biggest meetings and between them they wooed the electorate triumphantly. He was dynamic, she was explosive – the combination was irresistible. And the two of them were in their element, relishing the fight, inspiring audiences with their vision of a future under Labour. Jennie duly won the seat with almost 50,000 votes to her rival's 29,225. Nye, of course, held Ebbw Vale, and the Labour government came triumphantly into office.

For Jennie, the satisfaction (and the relief) was immense. Now at last she was, theoretically at least, on a par with her husband, an MP like him and with high expectations of being called upon to fulfil some useful function in government. There were twenty-one women in the new Labour intake, some of them already experienced parliamentarians (Ellen Wilkinson, Eleanor Rathbone), but Jennie had high hopes and feared none of them as rivals. She herself wasn't new to parliament, as so many of the women were, and she was not only in excellent health but also had no children and a husband who far from perhaps resenting her time being taken up by parliamentary business would welcome her contribution. She was, or so she believed, not ambitious for her own advancement so much as for the implementation of Labour policies. She wanted to work with her fellow party members to get things done, particularly in housing, as quickly as possible to fulfil her election pledges. But it was Nye she expected to see given some important job, not herself. She knew she wasn't completely trusted yet, and how could she expect to be when for so long she'd stayed loyal to the ILP and had been regarded by prominent Labour Party members as a troublesome rebel? She would have to earn her stripes first. What she wanted was to see Nye offered an important job; a minor one would be an insult and she was adamant that he should refuse. When he was given the immensely important dual Ministry of Health & Housing honour was more than satisfied. He would be the youngest Cabinet Minister in Attlee's government and charged with working miracles.

His new prominence and the enormous responsibilities that came with it presented Jennie with another test as a wife. Nye would now be under great strain and need looking after more than ever. Luckily, towards the end of the war, Jennie had realised, sooner than Nye did, that it was not going to be practical to live at Lane End Cottage, however much they loved it. Going backwards and forwards 50 miles (80 km) each way when both of them would need to be in London all week would be gruelling, and the idea of having a small London flat as well as Lane End was not only a dismal prospect – neither of them wanted to go back to flat-dwelling, and the essential Ma Lee would not fit in – but financially difficult. They would have to move back into central London, into a house large enough to absorb her parents in such a way as to give them the same illusion of independence they had enjoyed at Lane End. Jennie had set herself to find such a place. Because of the war and the bombing, many people had left London and put their houses up for sale. So in 1944 Jennie had bought 23 Cliveden Place, a street running off Sloane Square in Chelsea. It was a Georgian terrace house with plenty of space within its four storeys to accommodate her parents. Once more, Jennie had had a house to renovate and plan and turn into a home and she had enjoyed every minute of organising the transformation, though not the last phase of the bombing: 1944's VI and V2 rocket-bombs. But by the time Nye was made a Cabinet Minister, everything was in place.

Now it was Jennie's turn to entertain as befitted being the wife of a Cabinet Minister. Nye had never had any inhibitions about spending money on the good things in life – wine, food, books – and he had a highly developed aesthetic sense, appreciating beautiful furniture and paintings and artefacts, so Jennie had a free rein, within their financial means (not great) to do what she liked in Cliveden Place. What she liked was what Nye liked too: a slightly bohemian life-style, but comfortably so, colourful and spacious and lacking rigid formality. Excellent meals were provided for the friends and colleagues who came there (though none cooked by Jennie) and Ma Lee, once installed, was in her element. The social life in No. 23 was thought of as lavish by many people and not in keeping with the beliefs of the host and hostess, but neither Nye nor Jennie listened to such criticisms. Nye, in Jennie's opinion, worked ferociously hard and deserved all the material comforts he could get. She was never going to be ashamed of providing an attractive and even luxuriously comfortable home for her husband.

Harder for her to manage was being entertained *outside* their home. Nye had official functions to attend and as his wife she was expected to accompany him. For a start, she never liked evening engagements – she was a lark, at her best in the morning and always sleepy in the evening. Nor was she good at hiding her boredom, and most of these functions were painfully boring. Not for Jennie the permanent charming smile as she sat at her husband's side – she was far more likely to have a fixed scowl or to yawn. She hated the embassy dinner parties and what she called 'the frozen cod' type of entertainment when politeness was all. And she absolutely refused to retire with the ladies, as wives were still required to do in those circles. She couldn't, and wouldn't, obey this absurd convention, and Nye luckily didn't expect her to. When she left a dinner on one such occasion, at the Yugoslavian Embassy, Nye followed her. He agreed that it was absurd for her to be banished with the other wives – 'What am I supposed to do, talk about babies?' – and cheerfully flouted convention with her.

Babies were another source of possible contention. Nye loved babies. He was brilliant with all children and it was naturally assumed by his family that he would have several of his own and would make a wonderful father. In 1945, Jennie was forty-one and childless. She and Nye had been married eleven years, more than long enough for family and friends to fear that there would never be a baby. Nye was to be denied children by a wife who had gone far enough in marrying at all and was not going to go even further against her own nature and become a mother. She said she had made this plain from the beginning: no children to get in the way of her work, to which she was dedicated. She had practised birth control successfully since her student days, but should there be any accidental pregnancy she had no doubts about what she would do. She would have an abortion, in Holland. Married to Nye, she never did need to resort to this so far as is known, but she did once become pregnant. Nye's reaction is not recorded, but Jennie had a miscarriage, so there was no moral dilemma. Nye's acceptance of his wife's decision not to have children seems to have been without resentment – if Jennie didn't want them then it was her right, as the woman who would have to bear them, to say no.

But he knew Jennie very well and because he did he knew how hard it was for her ever to change her mind. She would see it as weak, signifying some loss of control in herself. Perhaps because he knew this, he tried to make things easier for her by, she said, asking her very gently 'with his unfailing love' if maybe she should think about the whole question of children again before she was too old for having any to be an option. Jennie wavered. She thought maybe after all she would like one child – though Nye had always been adamant that he wanted a brood or none – and consulted a doctor who, in fact, advised her against trying in view of her age. The risk of some abnormality was too great. But there is evidence that Jennie did try at this period, though perhaps only in the sense of not being scrupulous about birth control. She thought herself pregnant once, and was excited about it, but it turned out to be a false alarm and after that there were no others. The marriage remained childless, and if there were regrets they were not openly expressed. Jennie certainly didn't feel any sense of failure as a wife simply because she had not produced children – there were far more important functions for her to fulfil.

Protecting Nye became the greatest of them. As Minister of Health and Housing he was a target of abuse for the many enemies he made and some of them specialised in dirty tricks of a type still wearyingly familiar today. He had to be permanently on guard against being framed in what would look like compromising situations. A favourite trick of the tabloid press was to try to photograph him with a prostitute. He was in the habit of going for late-night walks, to clear his head before bed, and it was easy enough to hire a prostitute to accost him and make it look as though he were accosting her. After one such attempt, Nye came home in a fury, insisting that Jennie should in future accompany him – he needed his walks to relax and he was determined not to give them up. Jennie, always of course sleepy at that time and hating the thought of being dragged out into the cold, dark streets, nevertheless complied. She saw it as her duty to be a kind of bodyguard. In other ways, too, she tried to protect her husband, seeing him as far more vulnerable and sensitive than his image suggested. There was the hate mail, for example – it flooded in and was indescribably vitriolic and foul. Jennie made it her job to censor all their post and deal with its contents appropriately.

She worried most of all about his health. Nye looked incredibly strong but he wasn't, and she constantly kept a close eye on his health, both physical and mental. Early in their marriage, Nye had had to have an operation on his back and ever after she monitored his back pain, writing to Suse that it 'dragged at his strength'. Once he was a Cabinet Minister she saw him as 'strained to the limits of his considerable physical and mental powers' and fretted over the way he drove himself, working twenty-hour days and more, and hardly ever taking so much as a day off unless she insisted. Once, she had been happy to leave her mother in charge of his comforts, but by the mid-1940s, at the time of the greatest stress for Nye, she felt she had to be there for him as much as possible. 'He was', she wrote, 'so lost and woebegone when left to come home to a house with no me . . . he did not like to be on his own.' She was essential to him, the only person to whom he could talk absolutely freely and who thought like him. Her influence in this respect was enormous and recognised as such by everyone. Many political colleagues did not approve of Jennie's role. They thought she encouraged Nye to be reckless (she did) when she should have counselled caution, and that she never presented to him the other side of an argument but allowed him to think his (and hers) was the only one. She bolstered Nye's ego in a way that was not so much supportive, in the manner of a good wife, but inflammatory.

Jennie would not have denied any of these charges. She was proud of them. People were quite right, she did push her husband to be bold and stick to his beliefs. But she was no longer, as some people thought, seeking power for herself. Nothing was for herself. By the time Nye was a Cabinet Minister and in the throes of a violent upheaval in the Health Service, the balance in the marriage had changed. They were nothing like equals now in ambition – Jennie's was on hold, and she knew it.

III

Back in the Commons after the Labour landslide of the 1945 General Election, Jennie soon felt herself, to her own surprise, to be ill at ease. Though she had never been an outstanding orator there, as she was on the hustings, she had never felt nervous or apprehensive, and now she did, especially if Nye was in the House, on the front bench listening to her. Nye himself hated these occasions and tried not to be there. His agitation on her behalf was all due to what Jennie later called 'his old chauvinist pig showing through his rational self'. He was deeply protective of her and couldn't bear the thought of his wife being jeered at and given a rough ride, or of having to witness her flounder and lose her way.

Jennie, by this stage of her marriage, saw this protectiveness as both a blessing and a handicap. She reflected that though before she had married Nye she had rejected the absurd notion that she needed protection – she could fight her own battles, thank you, and was famous for doing so – she found that marriage had indeed given her a protective cover which, she was obliged to realise, in retrospect, she had after all needed. She felt the benefit of it. It 'shielded me from gossip', and gave her a security quite different from that she had felt with her parents as a child or with Frank Wise as her lover. Nye's devotion wrapped itself tightly round her and far from suffocating her made her feel strong, ready to face anything.

One of the downsides, however, was that right from the beginning of the 1945 parliament the suspicion began that with Nye Bevan so powerful his wife would receive unfair advancement – he was nicely placed to push her forward. When he appointed her to the Central Housing Advisory Committee, as soon as he took on the dual ministries of Housing and Health, this was seen as evidence that the husband would back the wife over others who were just as well qualified for the job – Jennie would benefit simply through being his wife and without making her own way. Naturally, this was anathema to her, but she knew the charge was not true. Nye appointed her because he thought she would do a good job. She applied herself diligently to the work of the committee, chaired by Nye himself, and presented its only report competently (on rural housing). In the Commons, she harried the Minister of Supply for refusing to grant early release from the forces to the building workers needed to put Nye's ambitious housing programme into operation. But that only convinced people that she was merely a mouthpiece for her husband, his stooge, his blindly loyal wife.

It was galling for Jennie and made her furious, but it was the price she paid for being Nye's wife, part of what enemies insisted on presenting as a double-act. One reporter (American) actually asked her if Nye wrote her speeches, so great was the conviction that he was speaking through her and using her to say things which as a Cabinet Minister he wasn't free to say himself. She was closely watched in the Commons every time there was a division, how she voted being read as an indication of how Nye was thinking, especially if her vote went against official Cabinet policy. Whatever she said or did, she could not escape the unfairness of being judged hardly to have a mind or will of her own. But though she raged against the injustice of this false image, she nevertheless accepted the underlying premise that Nye was superior to her. He was. He was in a position she now knew she could never be in. It was no good speculating on whether as a single woman, MP for Cannock, she could have soared to his heights and been made a Cabinet Minister. A strong part of her still yearned to be at the forefront of the Labour Party's efforts to transform the conditions in which the majority of people lived, but she was sensible and honest enough to acknowledge that, for whatever reason, that kind of promotion was lost to her. Nye was the man, Nye had the potential to become leader of the party in the future, Nye was a future prime minister who could put into effect their joint dreams.

Nye was also 'her' man. If Jennie was suspected of being his mouthpiece, he in turn was suspected of being far too heavily influenced by her, and Jennie's influence was feared. Everyone knew that in this marriage it was not a case of the husband leaving his work behind as he went through the front door of his home at night. On the contrary, he walked into a continuation of all the discussions and consultations he had been involved in during each day. Jennie was placed, as few wives ever are, to understand all the issues at stake and furthermore to have strong views on them. It was not a question of Nye's not knowing his own mind and needing Jennie to know it for him – that idea was ridiculous – but rather of Jennie *because* she knew his mind so well effortlessly being able to match his thinking. She may have been, as so many alleged, disastrous as a mate for Nye, but from his point of view she was invaluable. Never once did he need to feel his wife was unaware of the problems he faced, or that it was beyond her to understand their complexities. Jennie understood perfectly and that was a huge relief for a man under enormous stress.

The greatest period of stress was, of course, during Nye's years as Minister of Health and Housing when he was fighting to establish the National Health Service. The worst year was 1947, when the pressures resisting this were at their most extreme and Nye was coming home, if he came at all, exhausted. Health, unlike Housing, was not Jennie's field. She was on no committee to do with it and took no part in the many health debates. But that was not to say that she didn't care as much as Nye about getting this great Bill through – she did, every bit as passionately – or that she in any way underestimated the difficulties he faced. She worried that he might have a nervous breakdown, writing to Suse during 1947 that he was being 'eaten into' and that no one but she could understand how near the edge he was. She had 'to keep the balance for him', her prime function by then, she thought. One of the ways she tried to do this was by controlling access to him in his scarce leisure time. Real friends, and family, yes (though she limited even their access), 'but the great thing is to keep up one's guard with strangers'. She acted as a guard-dog herself, and was greatly resented for doing so as well as heartily disliked.

This dislike of her was in striking contrast to Nye's own popularity. Almost everyone who knew him liked Nye, even his political enemies. He was 'a character' but the warmth of his personality offset his more aggressive side and his robust sense of humour endeared him to people. Jennie was 'a character' too, but she was too sharp, too arrogant, for her aggressive side ever to be overlooked. People feared her tongue and resented how she dealt with them, which was often rudely, without charm, and with none of Nye's wit. She scored no points at all as a wife for easing her husband's way socially. Even many of their joint friends found Jennie hard to take and at one time or another she fell out with most of them. Women especially were wary of her. She said she had always had good women friends but if so they are difficult to identify in any number – only Suse stood the test of time as a friend of Jennie's and even she was pushed to the limit. Those who did like her fell more into the category of hero-worshipper than friend – women like Joan Loverock, first smitten in 1945 when she heard Jennie speak during the election campaign at Cannock, and who worked for her in that constituency for the rest of her life. Joan was awe-struck by Jennie's star quality – 'with her black hair, beautiful clothes' and 'a proud arrogant look' she thought Jennie was like a film star. Other women fell under her spell and adored her so much they could put up with any amount of high-handedness but they were in the minority.

Not that Jennie appeared either to notice or to care about her own general unpopularity. She had always despised those who tried to curry favour and to whom being liked was more important than speaking their mind. She was not going to alter her ways just because her husband was now so important, and it bothered her not a jot if people found her too abrasive. She acknowledged that 'in some ways I am wholly unsuited to public life' but that was just too bad. She had a job to do and she did it to the best of her ability. Nye came with her to open the 1,000th council house to be built in Cannock since the war, but otherwise each dealt with their own areas separately. They were not, said Jennie, a double-act like Oswald and Diana Mosley, 'dragging round the country in double harness'. She was on her own there, looking after herself, though typically, just as she had her mother at home, she had Mollie Rowley, a Labour councillor, waiting on her hand and foot in Cannock. Mollie brought her breakfast in bed, picked up her clothes from the floor and generally spoiled her. Mollie saw only her good side.

It was a side her in-laws still failed to see. Very early on, they seem to have hoped the marriage wouldn't last, and when it did they were disappointed. In their opinion, Jennie was not a proper wife. Proper wives, good wives, looked after their husbands themselves without passing the job to their own mothers; proper wives nursed their husbands tenderly, while Jennie, though concerned about Nye's health, hated sickness and was bad at coping with what it involved in the way of caring in a practical way; proper wives gave their husbands children; proper wives did not have careers; proper wives did not, ever, put their own wishes first; and in Wales proper wives slept with their husbands in double beds, whereas Jennie and Nye soon had not only separate beds but separate bedrooms. It was a puzzle to the Bevans that, though Jennie scored nil on any list of what a good and proper wife should do or be, Nye was utterly devoted to her – that, they could not deny. At first, they concluded he was sexually in thrall to her; they hoped that this attraction would wear out or else that Jennie would have affairs and Nye reject her. But the separate bedrooms situation, which they could not help being aware of, and the failure to link Jennie's name with any sexual scandal, rather knocked that idea on the head. Proper wife or not, they were stuck with Jennie and had to accept it – but that did not mean they had to like her, and they never did.

Jennie didn't like them either. She was devoted to her own parents but this was because she saw herself as having been truly loved and cherished and brought up in the very best way possible. But she saw Nye's experience as being quite different and therefore leading to a very different relationship. His young years, or so she alleged, had not been as happy as hers – 'So much was denied him', she reflected, 'or made furtive, and furtiveness was a quality wholly alien to his nature.' It left the adult Nye with a strong sense of duty to his family but as far as Jennie was concerned duty should not bind him to them the way love bound her to her own family. If she had felt Nye's family rivalled her in his affections, then she might have tried to form a better relationship with them, but she knew it was no contest: Nye loved her far more and would always put her first. Secure in this knowledge, Jennie went on regarding the Bevans, as always, with indifference. When she stayed (not very often) in Tredegar, she treated their homes as she treated everyone's, as hotels where she expected service; and when they stayed with her, she often excluded them from Nye's company, claiming he needed privacy, even from them.

The worst rows were with Arianwen, the sister who had once supported Nye when she worked as a secretary and he was unemployed. Arianwen disliked Jennie from the moment she saw her and never changed her opinion. In 1938, Nye had helped his mother buy a house in Tredegar. He and Jennie had been married only four years and didn't have much money, so Nye's contribution made quite a hole in their modest bank balance, and Jennie rather resented his generosity, so much so that she suggested a council house would do for his mother. This caused outrage in the family and luckily Nye overrode Jennie and went ahead with buying the rather imposing stone house in Queens Square. When his mother died, the house passed to Arianwen, who was by then married and had a son. It seemed sensible that when Nye visited his constituency he should use the Tredegar house and so it was decided, apparently amicably, that the house would be shared. The house had four bedrooms. Jennie insisted three should belong to her and Nye for their occasional use, which left one for the permanent use of Arianwen, husband and son. The son had to sleep downstairs. It was hardly a fair arrangement, but Arianwen was obliged to accept it. What she could not accept was Jennie's idea of sharing which, in short, meant Arianwen should do all the cleaning. Jennie expected to arrive and find her rooms immaculate. When they were not, she complained. In Arianwen's eyes she was not only a bad wife but the worst possible sister-in-law. What she failed to understand was that

Jennie had no interest whatsoever in being that awful thing, a wife. She was Nye's friend, his lover, his inspiration, but never his wife.

Her attitude to Nye's family was all the more puzzling when she needed the Bevans' support, needed to close the joint Bevan/ Lee ranks to face a threat potentially damaging to Nye as a Cabinet Minister. Her brother Tommy was becoming more of a problem than ever during Nye's period as Minister of Health and Housing. The tabloid press, then as now, ever on the look-out for scandal to do with prominent politicians, would have loved knowing about the black sheep of his wife's family and Jennie was acutely aware of this. Tommy had not fared well in Australia. Far from making his fortune, he had not even obtained a steady job for himself, and after the war (during which he was slightly injured) he became an alcoholic. By that time, he had married and had three children (including a daughter named after Jennie). In 1947, his wife Rose wrote a pathetic letter to Jennie, describing Tommy's drunken rages and how he had started to beat Jim, their fourteen-year-old son. She begged her not to tell her parents, but said she needed some sort of help, preferably the sharp removal of her husband to his native country.

Jennie was appalled at the idea. How the journalists would love the sight of her bedraggled, drunken brother staggering in and out of 23 Cliveden Place, the house of the Minister of Health. Her contempt for Tommy was total – how could he, brought up as he had been with such love by such good parents, sink to this degrading level? It was beyond her comprehension. All the love she had felt for her brother evaporated and she wrote to him letters of such blistering scorn that he said he'd stopped reading them, so she need send him no more, though if she enclosed £10 he would stop pestering her. But worse than a drunken brother would be a criminal brother, and Tommy feared he was going to be done for embezzlement – 'I look like bringing disgrace on my folks', he wrote to his wife. In 1949, to Jennie's horror, she heard that Tommy was on board ship on his way home. He was supposed to be off the drink but on the drugs (which had been used in his 'cure'). Once back, he was soon on the booze once more, and borrowing shamelessly from his bewildered parents. Jennie was livid at his exploiting them, but she knew they would never close their door to him – he was their son, and would endlessly be forgiven. He was always promising to reform and always he defaulted. Jennie had none of the compassion her parents showed and refused to get involved with him. She wanted him to return to Australia as soon as possible. Back he duly sailed, to a wife who didn't want him, only to decide he had made a mistake, and started looking for a way of working his passage home yet again. Jennie dreaded this happening, and wrote to him that if he couldn't give their poor mother love and support then 'at least be man enough not to lean on her . . . I am contemptuous of words offered in place of decent behaviour.'

Nye, of course, knew about Tommy, but Jennie tried to shield him from her very real worry that her brother would become a serious liability – he was her problem and she tried to deal with it as efficiently (and as ruthlessly) as possible. In 1949, the National Health Service Bill had gone through but the problems of implementing it were only just beginning. Nye was obliged to go on begging for more money and arguing his case in a Cabinet reluctant to give it. Increasingly, the necessity of bringing in prescription charges was mooted, to which he was violently opposed. Such charges would go against the whole spirit of the new NHS and it would cease to be the truly socialist measure of which he was so proud. Jennie, of course, encouraged him to stand up to those in the Cabinet who claimed that either prescription charges, or charges for false teeth and spectacles, would have to be made. She thought he should resign rather than back down on his promise that charges would not be brought in – resign, and go on to glory, she was sure, as a future leader of the party. But Nye didn't resign. Instead, he accepted that at some future, undetermined date the proposed flat rate of one shilling (1/-) per prescription *might* be imposed, on condition that if it were, old age pensioners would be exempt, and on the understanding that the charge should be acknowledged as a necessary measure to stop exploitation of the new free health service and not to raise money. Personally, he hoped that, though the amending clause to the NHS Bill went through, sanctioning the right to impose the prescription charges *if needed*, it would never come into being. Jennie was reassured enough by his confidence to be able to vote for it.

But everyone knew that the problem of financing the NHS would not disappear. The more the costs escalated, the greater would the strain be on Nye to resist bringing in other charges already discussed but not included in the amending clause. Jennie saw him becoming more and more exhausted and made it her business to get him right away from all the stress. In post-war England, not many people had the opportunity or the means (with travel allowances strictly limited) to visit all the European countries so freely accessible before the war, and of course much of Europe had been badly damaged by war, occupation and invasion, but Nye as Minister of Health and Housing could go on semi-official trips and turn them into holidays. This Jennie was all in favour of – the more Nye got away from London, the easier it would be for him to relax and the easier for her to distract him. Distraction, as well as rest, was what she felt he very much needed. Nye, she acknowledged, did need company, and so did she – they were not a couple who wanted to retreat and see nobody but each other on holiday. Both were convivial, delighting in having long, lively meals with like-minded friends who could tell, and appreciate, entertaining tales and understand the spirit in which they were told – she didn't want Nye's often outrageous-sounding remarks to be misunderstood. So Jennie tried, with considerable success, to vet anyone wanting to come close to Nye and filter out the risks.

One holiday, a journey from Rome to Naples and then over to the Isle of Capri, was very successful – sun, at last. They were guests of the Italian Minister of Health and along the way they received official hospitality from local dignitaries. Best of all, everywhere they went they were invited to sample local vintages. It was, commented Jennie 'quite a survival test'. Nye, who had a strong head, survived better than Jennie, but both enjoyed themselves hugely. They alternated between riding in the chauffeur-driven car provided and joining the Italian officials on the accompanying bus. Jennie seems to have been better liked on these sort of trips than she was at home – her natural ebullience was more attractive to Europeans (and perhaps her sharpest retorts were not understood). She'd also liked to think of herself as easily assimilated in other countries ever since, on her first visit abroad, someone had told her she had 'a face for travel', meaning she could easily be taken for a Russian, an Italian, or a Spaniard, because of the shape of her face and her colouring – and this pleased her. She was quite good at foreign languages too, though never exactly fluent, and always tried to pick up some of the language of any country she visited.

Nearly always, the official trips would be combined with private visits, giving Nye an opportunity really to relax. It was what Jennie liked to see – Nye thousands of miles away from those who were making his job difficult, if not impossible, sitting basking in the sun in the company of congenial people. Going back to London was hard, and there were those who resented the holiday they had had. Socialists were not supposed to swan off to Italy and enjoy the good things in life when those others whom they professed to care about were suffering at home. Jennie (and Nye) had no patience with this point of view. What did they want Nye to do, collapse, have a breakdown? To go on doing his job he absolutely had to have these breaks. In making sure that he did, Jennie had become an excellent wife, scheming and organising and, if necessary, bullying her way to finding escape for herself and Nye.

She felt very strongly, and never more than during this period when he was Minister of Health and Housing, that no one really understood Nye as she did. There were aspects of his character hidden from all but her. He had a sensitive side rarely seen – nobody realised, she felt, how deeply Nye could feel things, how he could be moved to tears and needed so much comfort. She gave as an example his reaction to the death of a friend, when he took the glass he had toasted him with and threw it into the fire they were sitting beside. His grief was open and awful, and she thought his gesture, which would have seemed melodramatic and false in another man, was deeply moving in Nye. People knew he was sensuous, that he loved life, but they were not so aware of his more depressive side – they didn't see him low and full of doubt and anxiety as she did, nor did he want them to. She and Nye, she said, had 'the most private relationship any man or woman could have' and she was proud of it. Because of the confidence she had in this being so, she simply wasn't interested in the image other people had of her, or the gossip that circulated to the effect that her marriage was not all it seemed. She herself, by 1945, had stopped having those 'passing affairs' she had been so tempted by (or so she said): 'the days were over when he could not be sure of me.' If they were not over for Nye, she didn't think it mattered. Whatever else she was, Jennie was not a jealous wife.

Whether Nye was jealous is more debatable. He didn't like his wife flaunting her sexuality (as he felt she did when she wore dresses showing too much cleavage) and though he believed her when, well into their marriage, she said there was nothing in various friendships she had with certain men, she realised he couldn't help exercising that 'tom-cat protectiveness' which slightly annoyed her. By 1945 she was not sleeping around any more, but she reserved the right to do so if she wished, in keeping with her belief that sexual encounters meant nothing except a bit of momentary pleasure. There were rumours constantly afloat about both her and Nye, but she ignored them. If Nye *was* having sex with someone else, good luck to him but she didn't need to know about it. Her tolerance of what other wives might consider a fatal weakness was generous, though it was perhaps never seriously put to the test – not all the attentions of the tabloid press ever unearthed any affairs of Nye's after his marriage, which is not to say he didn't have any, but which does support Jennie's view that if he did no other woman was ever important to him. That was always her point: their marriage, their partnership, was much more than sex. Why wives fussed so much over sexual fidelity Jennie could never understand.

There were far more important matters to worry about, especially with another General Election approaching in 1950. For two years before that Nye had been on the defensive (over the battle to delay the bringing in of NHS charges) and now he was on the attack over the question of nationalising steel. The proposal to do so had been included in Labour's programme before the 1945 election but it had not been implemented. The genuine explanation was that there had been far too many other plans to put into operation, but nevertheless Nye (and Jennie) saw nationalisation of steel as the real indication that their party was serious about truly socialist measures. He threatened to resign in 1947 if a Nationalisation Bill was not prepared for the next session. He'd threatened to resign before, of course, and had been supported, even urged to do so, by Jennie; she loved seeing him as a rebel who stood up for his principles. In fact, yet again he did not resign, accepting a compromise in the form of another postponement. But the general opinion was that Nye was getting too big for his boots and challenging Attlee's leadership. Jennie longed for him to do so, but Nye himself was not interested in what he called 'palace revolutions'. He went on fighting his corner, trying to persuade the rest of the Cabinet to agree with him rather than try to get what he wanted by forming some kind of splinter group within the party. Steel, in the end, was won: a Nationalisation Bill was passed in the 1948–9 parliament.

Then came the 1950 General Election. Nye had wanted it earlier, so that the socialist programme could receive the endorsement it needed from the country and be carried on with a new momentum. He was confident, as were all his colleagues, that Labour would be returned with a healthy majority. He was wrong. He and Jennie were both re-elected, but the overall Labour majority was a shockingly small six seats. Nye was blamed by many members of his own party for the poor result, to Jennie's fury. The argument was that he had scared the middle classes with his speeches denigrating the Tories, especially his famous declaration in Manchester that they were 'lower than vermin'. Jennie now had to support a husband who was not only loathed by the opposition and used by them as a bogeyman to frighten the electorate, but who was seen as dangerous by his own party. Nobody agreed with his reading the result as showing that the Labour Party had not gone far enough in its promise of socialist measures – on the contrary, his colleagues believed the electorate had been scared off. The nationalisation of steel had gone too far to cancel, but once that was through, the government simply marked time.

This maddened Nye – rightly, in Jennie's opinion. She didn't attempt to soothe or placate him when he came home but, on the contrary, wanted to see his restlessness and sense of frustration result in his seizing the opportunity to challenge Attlee's by now lack-lustre leadership. Nye would have none of it, but he did want promotion within the Cabinet. The post he wanted was Foreign Secretary, but he was offered Minister of Labour: a disappointment, but he was prepared to accept if he could be assured that he would be involved in deciding economic policy. Attlee duly promised and he became Minister of Labour. He was not exactly happy about this, and once he'd begun his new job even less so since the prime function of his department seemed to be imposing wage restraint, a negative sort of policy alien to Nye's entire way of thinking. Further-more, the old battle over health charges was starting again with Gaitskell as Chancellor of the Exchequer insisting the time had come to bring the previously agreed charges in. This made Nye furious. He disliked Gaitskell and despised him – he was 'nothing, nothing, nothing'. Jennie, always a good hater, did not restrain him or to try to make him see that far from being 'nothing' Gaitskell was as dedicated to the fight against inequality as he was but wished to go about it in a different way. She reported that Nye came home 'white with fury' after his arguments in Cabinet with Gaitskell but this rage of his did not frighten her. She thought it a good sign, a sign that at last her husband was working himself up to push himself forward and no longer be hampered by misguided notions of party loyalty. When he walked out of a dinner where Gaitskell was present, loudly proclaiming he would not sit down with a man 'whose aim was to destroy the NHS', Jennie loved it. This time, she was sure that if Gaitskell did indeed finally impose NHS charges, Nye would resign.

The running drama came to a head on Budget Day, 10 April 1951. Nye and Jennie stood together behind the Speaker's chair, ready for a quick exit. The tension was palpable. For days before, people had been asking Jennie to stop Nye resigning, an action seen as incredibly damaging for an insecure government. Her response had been to turn on them with contempt – did they not realise that her husband was the only one brave enough to defend the socialist principles which their party was supposed to be founded on? To George Thomas, for example, she had shouted, 'You yellow-livered cur . . . get away from me!' Nye was going to be a hero and her sole purpose she saw as stiffening his resolution at the crucial moment. It had now come. The moment Gaitskell announced the long-deferred charges, the very charges Nye had agreed *might* have to be made but which he had been confident never would be imposed, she and Nye left the chamber, Jennie the one who called out 'Shame!' But it took two weeks for Nye actually to resign, though the decision had been made then and there. A note survives from his wife urging him to do it at once and not to wait, as he had apparently considered, until after the party meeting. Meanwhile, others tried to effect a compromise yet again, with Gaitskell willing to accept that the new charges need not be permanent, which would give Nye a loophole, a way of saving face. Nye didn't want one and Jennie certainly didn't want him to back down. There is no doubt at all that those close to them were right to say his wife was Nye's 'dark angel'.

On 23 April, Nye finally made his resignation speech in the Commons. Not a good speech, it was full of an all too obvious bitterness. Only Jennie was excited and optimistic: her husband would now come into his own.

IV

There were many people, on both sides of the House, who thought Nye Bevan's resignation amounted to a political tragedy. What would he do now? What would the Labour Party do without him as a minister? What would they do about him wreaking havoc (which is what everyone thought he would cause) on the back-benches? His future role was indistinct and the omens for his success ominous.

For Jennie, the test was extreme. Since first she had met Nye in 1929 he had always been the rising star, clearly destined for great things. Their marriage in 1934 made her the wife of a most successful husband; now, seventeen years later, she was suddenly the wife of a man who was generally reckoned to have ruined his own career, for the moment at least. He was deeply troubled, an unhappy man, embittered and anxious, and he needed all the reassurance she could give him that he had done the right thing. Encouraging him, urging him on when he was a powerful minister was one thing, but supporting him now that he was displaced, was quite another. And Jennie knew that she was blamed for what others thought was Nye's downfall – she had tipped him over the edge and now it was her job to pull him back up. She rose to this challenge superbly, but it was not easy. To be with a man endlessly tormented by his own political situation was exhausting – the hours and hours of self-analysis, the endless going over of motives, the recriminations – all drained her energies and left her feeling whipped herself.

What made things worse was that her father was dying. He and her mother were still with them in Cliveden Place, with Nye very much part of their daily lives. Even now, when he was in such difficulties, it was Nye's practice to go straight down to see his father-in-law in his sitting-room (a bed had been put in it for him once he became too weak to climb any stairs). Nye talked to him while Jennie absented herself, glad to do so. The strain of her father's terminal illness, and her mother's distress at his approaching death, put her into such a state of agitation that she could hardly cope with giving the kind of support needed. Instead, Nye provided it, able to talk to her father as she could not, steadily, without becoming engulfed in grief. And in the background, to increase the stress still further, was the ever-present problem of her brother Tommy whom she had tried to banish from her life, but who lurked there, still threatening scandal. Everything seemed to be on top of her and all the time she was expected to fulfil her function as MP for Cannock and bolster her husband's confidence. It was in such circumstances, she reflected in a note she made, that women gave up their careers – husband and home had to come first in any serious clash. She pretended to address Nye in this note (though he never saw it) telling him that for all her strongly held, lifelong views on the right of women to truly independent careers she had come to the conclusion that 'it is the woman's part to give way' if both husband and wife are in a position of 'excessive strain'.

In fact, she did not give way in the sense of giving up her own career, but she certainly saw herself as consciously giving way so far as furthering her own ambitions went. In 1952, the year after Nye's resignation and when her father had just died, she would have liked to stand for the National Executive Committee's (NEC) constituency section, but she didn't. If she had stood, she thought she would have had a good chance of being elected, and had she been elected she saw this as robbing Nye of a male ally he needed. It was for her an act of personal sacrifice and it was not made without resentment. She felt rebellious, hating what she saw as the necessity of keeping herself in the background. Nye was still the best hope for keeping the Labour movement truly socialist and she must do everything she could to get him once more into a position of power. At home, there had to be harmony and there was no place for her own ambition – any grumbles of discontent with her lot must be suppressed.

Jennie was not, of course, good at suppression. Storming and raging were her forte, and the cost to her of trying almost to match her own mother in serenity was high, so high that she welcomed any temporary separation from Nye. His developing taste for foreign travel, a taste both of them had always had, but which had not been greatly indulged before the 1950s, suited her. She encouraged him to go without her to India, Burma and Pakistan in the spring of 1953 and felt immediately, and not at all guiltily, relieved to be without him. She wrote that she looked forward (when she knew he was going) to 'a few quiet weeks . . . in which I could relax at home and see to . . . things . . . neglected during the political storms'. These 'things' were not those that other wives might consider to have been neglected – Jennie didn't mean she was going to make new curtains or carry out any other domestic task. Her mother did all that. It was more the satisfaction of having no need to worry about Nye and therefore able to put herself first. This didn't take any dramatic form, it just meant allowing the pressure she had been under to lift. She had time to think and take stock and look to the future in a way that had nothing to do with what Nye was going to do politically. She saw one thing clearly: they both needed to get away from London. The decision in 1945 to give up Lane End Cottage had been made for what were then very good reasons, but now, though they were both still MPs and those reasons were theoretically as strong as ever, since they needed to be near the House, other more urgent ones seemed more valid. Nye was restless and disillusioned, and she was exhausted and often depressed: they both needed escape and diversion, something to distract them from the tensions of all the political in-fighting. The answer, she decided, was to move back into the country.

Nye had always wanted to have a home in the Welsh mountains, but wherever they went, it would have to be within tolerably easy reach of Central London, just as Lane End had been. Jennie asked various friends to keep a look-out for a suitably modest country property and one of them came up with the suggestion of a farm, Asheridge, 3 miles (4.8 km) from

Chesham in the Chilterns. A farm was the last thing Jennie had in mind, especially one with 50 acres (20 hectares) and numerous buildings, but it was going cheap, £9,000 for the lot, and was within the financial limits she had in mind. Thinking it would be a day out anyway, she took Nye to see it at the first opportunity and he fell in love with it, or rather with the possibilities it offered, at once. They bought it.

Nye was delighted at the prospect of becoming a farmer, promptly acquiring a small Jersey herd to graze the fifty acres and impatient to add pigs and poultry. The farmhouse was Jennie's problem, but one she relished – it was a return to the kind of restoration and renovation she had supervised and enjoyed at Lane End. She and her mother saw to the transformation while Nye went off again, to China and Japan this time (as a member of a NEC delegation), and when he returned he hurled himself with the sort of enthusiasm he hadn't shown for a long time into being a farmer. The exercise and fresh air were good for him and Jennie saw the psychological benefits clearly – Nye was back to being optimistic again, ready to consider standing for the party treasurership.

But just as Jennie was hoping things were taking a turn for the better, her mother was diagnosed with breast cancer. The shock was profound, so much so that when told the news by the doctor, she writes in her memoir that she 'screamed hysterical-ly', and Nye had the greatest difficulty in calming her down. Her grandmothr had died of cancer and Jennie knew her mother would remember the agony of that death. She was determined to protect her from knowing what was wrong and when Nye had soothed her sufficiently, she went in to her mother, who was in bed, under the impression she had flu, and told her not that she had advanced cancer but that she had a treatable abscess. She and Nye had agreed that this was the best solution. Her mother would not want them to be worried. Her whole life had been spent protecting her daughter from worry and now Jennie saw it as her responsibility to do the same for her mother. So she acted as though her mother's illness really was fairly trivial and Nye went along with the pretence. But this kind of dissimulation went entirely against Jennie's nature – being forthright was her way, and to have to lie and pretend and be convincing, while so very distressed, exhausted her when she was already worn out emotionally with supporting Nye.

There was also the matter of what would happen to her comfortable household, now that her mother would not be up to running it. They had always had extra help – cleaning ladies, kitchen help, and people to do the shopping – but Ma Lee had supervised and organised them all. Now there would have to be a proper housekeeper, and since her mother was not to know how ill she was, this person must pretend she was only helping and be careful *not* to seem to take over. The whole business was a nightmare and Jennie feared her smoothly functioning domestic life, so essential for Nye's well-being, would disintegrate. Inevitably, it did, though never quite as disastrously as she had envisaged, largely thanks to Nye himself. Jennie didn't suddenly turn to helping in the kitchen or taking over the provisioning, but Nye did. It was he who stood beside the daily help on occasions and provided the extra pair of hands needed to wash up, and he did it cheerfully, chatting easily with the different women employed in a way his wife could never manage. Jennie paid full tribute to his assistance, but she worried about what this extra strain was doing to his health. Home should be for resting and now, because of her mother's illness, it wasn't.

It didn't help that for much of the time Nye and herself were living in yet another place, and a comfortless one. Since neither she nor Nye could stand living in hotels, Jennie had rented what she herself described as 'an appallingly furnished two-roomed flat that did not even have a bath' in Gosfield Street (behind Broadcasting House), where they could sleep after late-night sittings in the Commons. It represented, she wrote, 'everything he loathed' – it was dingy, ugly, cramped, dark and altogether more than his fastidious and aesthetically sophisticated nature could tolerate, but tolerate it he had to. She maintained she had been unable to find anywhere else near enough to Westminster and within their means. Tired and distracted, she had no energy to try to beautify the place or at least to buy some different furniture (which, since the flat was rented, she didn't want to do anyway). But she felt considerable guilt about Gosfield Street, because she always acknowledged that home-making was part of her role. Asheridge was their real home but the time spent in London meant Gosfield Street should also have offered some homely comforts and it didn't.

When Nye was abroad she didn't have to worry about the dreariness of Gosfield Street. She liked to think of him having a good time, though one of these good times in 1957, just when things were so difficult at home for her, resulted in further stress, which she could have done without. Nye had gone with Dick Crossman and Morgan Phillips to the conference of the Italian Socialist Party in Venice, a trip paid for by what Jennie referred to as 'the hard-earned money of Party workers including his own people in South Wales'. He went looking very smart indeed, in a beautifully cut new suit, and thoroughly enjoyed himself tasting the Italian wines and discoursing on their merits. He was a great hit at the conference, speaking in support of the left-wing Socialist Party, and an even greater hit socially. But back in England, the *Spectator* published an article ('Death in Venice') in which it was suggested that all three of the British delegates were drunk. Nye was furious and demanded an apology, which was refused, the reporter sticking to the story, so all three men decided to sue for libel.

Jennie did nothing to restrain Nye from taking legal action, though the words of the reporter were mild enough – 'Messrs Bevan, Morgan Phillips and Richard Crossman . . . puzzled the Italians by their capacity to fill themselves up like tanks with whisky and coffee . . . the Italians were never sure if the British delegation was sober.' Perhaps another wife would have told her husband not to be so pompous, and that there was nothing very damning or disgusting in the description. But Nye, she reported, was 'blazingly angry' and furthermore 'his pride was hurt'. This appeared to be the clincher: hurt pride. Jennie could identify with that. She approved of pride, it was part of her own character to be proud of her own virtues and she made no attempt to mock Nye out of his pride on this occasion. Nye hated the Tory *Spectator* and was determined to extract damages from it. He, and the others, accordingly sued, and won their case, receiving £2,500 each (which, in 1957, was a very great deal of money).

The strain for Jennie was not so much in worrying about

clearing Nye's reputation – she had no worries about that – but in dreading having to pay legal costs if the case went against him. All of what she called 'our modest savings' were in her name for precisely this reason, in case Nye ever did get himself sued, or was involved in some legal battle. He was capable of saying the most outrageous things in public and it was always perfectly possible he would slander someone who would react by taking him to court. So Jennie, gifted with a good deal of financial acumen (a blessing in a wife for Nye, who had little), had taken over the management of their joint monies and had everything in her name. Jennie was scared. She didn't want any risky legal battles, so standing by Nye was brave of her (or foolish). It helped a bit that by then they were better off, not through their pay as MPs (this was still poor, with no allowances for office costs yet) but from their journalism. They also both received presents from wealthy friends, mostly in the form of contributing to election expenses by providing a car for their use, or treating them to holidays, but sometimes in straight cash gifts. With these windfalls, the astute Jennie opened a 'special' account, so special that she didn't declare it for tax purposes. Jennie saw nothing corrupt in this – it was not as though money was given for favours to be received – absolutely not. Neither she nor Nye could be bribed. She saw the special account as the means through which Nye could be pampered as he deserved, in a way which would ease the stress of working so incredibly hard. It paid, on occasion, for first-class accommodation when travelling, for taxis, and for staff. She saw it as her duty as a wife to provide for Nye in this luxurious way. He had had a taste for luxury before ever he met her, long before he had a wife at all, but she managed such indulgences for him once they were married.

She was a good manager, sometimes too good. Jennie was the one who dealt with tradesmen and, rather shockingly, she was mean. Both at Lane End and Asheridge extensive building work was done, and the tradesmen had to wait months for payment. Sometimes the work had been perfectly done and there was no excuse for delaying payment, and sometimes she would quibble over some detail and attempt to justify the delay. Whether Nye knew this is doubtful – the whole point was that Jennie dealt with such mundane matters so that he didn't need to be bothered – but he would hardly have been pleased with her. And yet in her own accounts she was meticulous, noting every penny she spent, so that it was never a case of not knowing the value of money and what it meant to people. She knew all right, she just couldn't bear to think she might be cheated, and she feared that everyone had the wrong idea and thought she and Nye were actually *rich*, anathema to her. If they were rich, they wouldn't have been renting a horrible flat in Gosfield Street, a continuing aggravation.

But she was busy, she had no more time to devote to flat-searching. Not quite as busy as Nye (who in 1956 did become Party Treasurer and then Shadow Foreign Secretary) but nevertheless fully preoccupied once she had allowed herself to be nominated for the Women's Section of the NEC, the section she had always despised but which, humiliatingly, she had come to see was her only way on to the main council. Her public life demanded more of her than it had ever done and, as ever, it had priority. She was not going to give up being Cannock's MP, or writing for *Tribune*, or working for the various committees she was involved with, most of them to do with international affairs. There were speeches to write – on coal, on housing, on colonial policy – and visits to Cannock to make, and these were more important than running a home. It struck her as absurd that not everyone thought so – she was outraged that anyone should imagine that the stress she was under in these years, the mid- to late-1950s, should be relieved by *giving up her work*. The idea was monstrous. Nothing, not even her very genuine love and concern for both Nye and her mother, would make her do it. Such an act would negate the whole of her life, make a nonsense of everything she had struggled to achieve. It would turn her into that creature she had always despised, a mere wife of the old sort, a martyr, a woman who saw marriage as servitude. She would not do it, however desperate she became, and whatever conclusion she had previously come to in that private note.

By 1958, she was desperate enough to be on the edge of a complete nervous breakdown. In her diary, she made a list of all the things she had to do one day in February and it was daunting. Her housekeeper at Asheridge was in hospital; her eighty-year-old mother was still battling on, surviving her cancer, but needing more and more help; Nye was very tired and regularly arriving at Gosfield Street to find no food; their farm manager was ill 'and useless'; and the emergency home help was also ill. Everything was on top of her. She needed support and though she knew Nye loved her, and worried about her as she did about him, she suddenly felt he was letting her down. Why should *he* get all the sympathy and encouragement? She needed it too. Earlier, the summer before, she had got to the point of writing him a furious letter, alleging that he gave her no self-confidence. He may well have thought this was something she had in abundance, but it was no longer true and if he hadn't been so wrapped up in his own troubles he would have seen it. She asked him, with marked bitterness and hostility: 'is it your real and unshakeable conviction that nothing I do matters a damn . . . ?' If so, he was saying all she was, and stood for, was totally ineffective. He was leaving her 'naked and lame'. She was, she wrote, not like him – 'I have to have something to sustain me.' But in the midst of her raging there was also a touching humility. She reaffirmed what she had believed for many years by then, that Nye was 'a thousand times' more important to their age than she was. He represented all she most passionately believed in. But nevertheless she needed some of his time for herself and she had been afraid to demand it. Even writing this letter felt selfish, when she knew he was under such pressure and had so many people making demands on him, but she had given in to her own need to write it. He had to know how things stood, how near she was to cracking.

But she never sent the letter. Later, she called it 'mad', but it was hardly that – impetuous, yes, but far too coherent to be mad. She was at the same point as so many wives in her situation (though there were few of them then) when everything becomes too much and they find in themselves a need they are almost ashamed to confess, the need to lean on someone stronger than themselves who will sort everything out as they believe themselves to have sorted things out for others, in particular their husbands. Jennie knew she had chosen to be what she was, a woman whose 'public duties', as she put it, were more important than personal happiness or ease of living, but that did not make the weight of her troubles any lighter. The solution of halving those duties, or reducing them considerably, was never for her an option and that was what she was protesting about. 'It would have made matters worse, not better, if I had given up my political work.' So strong was her conviction that this was true, she didn't bother querying it, and neither, fortunately, did Nye. Her 'mad' letter didn't need to be sent to him. He was well aware of the state his wife was in and wrote to her that summer, when he was in Scotland, that he realised she was depressed and that he was worried about her. He asked her to 'buck up and remember we have a whole summer together at the farm. We must hug the thought of our secret happiness and not let public duties weigh on you too heavily.'

There was more, though, weighing on Jennie than public duties and domestic problems. What had contributed to her sense of confusion and her feeling of intolerable strain was a fundamental and vital difference of opinion she had experienced in the months before with Nye. Always, they had agreed on everything that mattered – same socialist ideals, same determination to see them fulfilled. But slowly, throughout the previous year, a rift had opened between them over the H-bomb, and it had frightened her. She wanted to agree with Nye over something so important but she couldn't. She was all for nuclear disarmament, as was the left wing of the Labour Party, but Nye was not at all convinced that this, even if it could be achieved, would preserve peace. Once, he had urged that Britain should suspend nuclear testing immediately, but now he changed his mind, deciding that unilateral disarmament would be to declare Britain impotent, which would have disastrous consequences on the balance of power. At the Labour Party Conference in 1957, in Brighton, Nye had accordingly defended retaining the possession of the H-bomb. For Jennie, it had been absolute agony to be opposed to her husband at a time when she knew he would be vilified by all their political friends. 'He did not have even me on his side,' she was compelled to state, and she hated having to do so.

She had tried to change his mind. Always, they'd argued about things but never from such dramatically opposed positions. Usually, arguments were about interpretations, or about how something or other should be done, about the best way to bring about what they both wanted. This was different, and it was dangerous. It was not in Jennie's character to smile and agree to differ. She saw things in black and white, and never more so than over the H-bomb. But argue though she did, as forcefully as she knew how, Nye would not budge. He was quite happy to listen to her, as he always was, but she could not persuade him that her view was the right one. (So much for those who called Jennie an evil influence.) He was his own man, impervious to his wife's pleas, and her influence weighed no more heavily with him than that of others. For Jennie, this was torture. She thought he was wrong, but did not want to have to witness what his stand would do to his reputation. She dreaded the speech he proposed to make at the conference where the vociferous advocates of unilateral nuclear disarmament would attack him mercilessly. It was an appalling dilemma for any wife to be in, to be asked to watch the man she loved be abused knowing that, in essence, she was of the same opinion as the abusers. Which should come first, loyalty to husband or loyalty to principles?

The night before that conference she said that she stopped arguing with Nye, giving him the peace he needed to prepare for the traumatic day ahead (but others staying in the same hotel say they heard Nye and Jennie's raised voices well into the early hours). She could hardly bear to be in the hall, and the experience was every bit as terrible as she had anticipated. She had always been proud that, as she put it, 'we rally to the other's assistance in times of crisis', but rallying on that day was harder than it had ever been because she did not think he was right. She loathed the thought nevertheless of seeing Nye 'humbled and tamed' and passionately hoped he would, by some miracle, manage in his speech to effect some sort of acceptable compromise over the H-bomb. But he didn't. Twenty years later, she could still hardly bear to remember how he had made a complete and total uncharacteristic mess of his speech. His famous passion and fluency deserted him, and where once he had been expert at dealing with hecklers now, at first, they stopped him in his tracks. It was painful to listen to him as he tried to persuade the delegates to trust him. He was as much against the use of nuclear power as any of them, but at the same time he believed Britain should never be obliged to 'go naked' into the conference chamber. International diplomacy demanded that if other major powers had the bomb, so should Britain.

What Jennie saw that awful day was her husband slipping from being the idol and the hope of the left wing of the Labour Party into being, in their opinion, a traitor. It pained her more than anything ever had done, and the injustice of it made it easier for her to rush to Nye's defence whatever she thought of his stand. She hated to see him, scarlet in the face, hoarse from shouting to be heard above the din, trying so desperately to defend his point of view. Nobody understood him, nobody appreciated that his attitude arose from comprehending the international situation better than they did. She couldn't wait to get him off that platform, out of that hall, away from those either yelling in outrage or weeping tears of disappointment. She was afraid for his health, and so were other observers, one of them thinking he might be about to have a stroke, so evident was the strain he was under. Jennie acted then as a good wife should. She took him back to Asheridge as quickly as possible and once there shielded him from all callers. Then she sat down and defended him in an article she wrote for *Tribune* – though *Tribune* was furious with him – and in responses she blasted off to his public critics. The fact that she, as a left-wing Labour Party member, had agreed with those critics was now beside the point – she had no difficulty at all in putting being a wife first.

Nye, she clearly saw in the dismal weeks following that Brighton conference, was a deeply wounded man, and this altered their relationship. She was, she wrote, 'guarded' now, and so was he. They were no longer saying exactly what they thought to each other. It was too dangerous. Arguing about the H-bomb had always meant they were on thin ice, but now the ice itself had splintered and it was best to stand absolutely still until it was safe to proceed, with infinite caution, to firm ground. Poison pen letters kept arriving, accusing Nye in melodramatic terms of having 'ripped the heart out of social-ism', and she did not always succeed in keeping them from him. And on top of everything else, he had a heavy chest cold, which always alarmed her. The best thing to do was get him right away, as far as possible as quickly as possible, so she pushed him to take up an offer to lecture in America. There, he would not see the newspapers labelling him a 'Tory', or 'Gaitskell's poodle', nor the caricatures so cruelly lampooning him. And, most important of all, he could gather strength for the coming General Election when, if Labour won, he would become Foreign Secretary.

Jennie did not go with him. Even more than he did, she needed to be on her own to recover, to build up her own emotional strength without worrying about his. When he returned, she tried hard to make sure they both had more time at Asheridge on their own and in a way the Brighton Conference had made this easier – so many of their former close friends were now cool towards them (though only temporarily as it turned out). She concentrated on trying to do what Nye liked best, which was listening to music and reading and best of all pottering around the farm. There was always something of a practical nature to be attended to, and Nye loved getting his hands dirty. Occasionally, they walked to the Blue Ball, a pub half a mile from the farm, and had a drink. Nye liked to take a jug down with him and have it filled with draught beer, becoming very cross if Jennie bought bottles. He was not really a beer drinker – he preferred good wine – but it went with being in the country. The friends who did visit at this period noticed that Jennie was much more subdued than usual – quiet, almost wistful, lacking her normal ebullience. She appeared constantly anxious about Nye and her attitude to him was much more maternal. What he ate, what he wore, how he slept caused her great concern and she watched over him as her own mother had once watched over them both.

But all the time she was waiting not only to see him recover his old fighting spirit but to see the tide turn again in his favour, as she was sure it must. Nye still had within his reach the leadership of the Labour Party – not for one minute did Jennie concede that Gaitskell had it for keeps. He could still become leader of the opposition and when the next election was won, as it surely would be, eventually Prime Minister. She never lost sight of this goal, wanting, as she did, power for Nye not for its own sake but so that he could put into effect those socialist ideals which had guided their whole lives. Nye would come back into favour, he had to. She would have considered herself a failure if she had not believed this, if what had happened at the Brighton Conference had in any way weakened her faith in him. Her confidence was essential to him, and it was still there, even if they were both more 'guarded' with each other. She didn't beg him to spare himself and give up, she didn't say she couldn't stand the strain any more, but on the contrary, urged him at every turn to believe in himself and carry on trying to convince others that far from betraying socialism he thought only of bringing it to full fruition. No wife could have been more loyal, and if Jennie's influence was so often said to have been malign, or at the very least misguided, this was an example of it being exerted overwhelmingly for the good.

By the next party conference, at Scarborough in 1958, Jennie saw what she had hoped and believed would happen begin to take place, at least on the surface. Nye made another speech about foreign affairs and at the end was given an ovation – music to her ears. But better than that, in the election for the Shadow Cabinet he topped the poll. Once more he seemed poised to take over the leadership, even though Gaitskell was still in control, and Nye had remained loyal to him. But Jennie knew how hard he found it to be so, believing as he did that Gaitskell was not a true socialist, but also hating factions within the party. Gaitskell needed him, but if Labour lost the next election there would come the time when it would be right to challenge him and then Nye would win. Always, Jennie took the long view. It was a question, by 1958, of Nye biding his time. He couldn't afford to resign once more. Where once she had encouraged him to be a rebel and stand on his own on matters of principle, if necessary, sure he would effortlessly attract support the moment he did so, now she wanted him to hang in and play the power game. He was sixty-one years old and done with a young man's strategy – he didn't have the time for risky moves. No one, now, could accuse Jennie of being a 'dark angel', breathing daring revolt into her husband's ears. She had not helped so magnificently to bring him through the worst political time of his life only to urge him to gamble his recovery away – she wanted him to stay where he was and consolidate his position.

The 1959 election was called for 8 October, but before it Jennie was expected to go with Nye to the Soviet Union on an official visit with Gaitskell and Denis Healey and their wives. Jennie refused to go. The company could not have been less congenial for her – she did not get on very well with other wives and certainly had little in common with either Dora Gaitskell or Edna Healey. She and Nye had been to the Soviet Union the year before, to meet Krushchev, and Jennie undoubtedly thought of herself as superior because of this previous visit – she and Madame Khrushchev had got on very well indeed and Nye had been a great hit with Khrushchev himself. It was going to be irritating for Nye to have to revert to the dull, formal rules and atmosphere of an official delegation, to have to defer to Gaitskell as leader, and for her it would have been intolerable. Gaitskell himself didn't seem to realise how bored Nye was and thought him full of enthusiasm and in great form, but Jennie knew better. It was a relief to her when she had him home. She thought he seemed in reasonably good shape and ready to prepare for fighting the election which he was desperate for Labour to win. Another defeat was unthinkable. Jennie, of course, wanted Labour to win just as much as he did, but not so far at the back of her mind was the thought that if they did, Nye, as Foreign Secretary, would be pushed harder than ever. As a politician herself, she wanted that position (which might in due course lead on to becoming Prime Minister at last) for him, but as a wife she feared it. He needed rest, and that was precisely what he was not going to get in a Labour government.

V

The October 1959 election was a disaster for Labour, with the Tories increasing their majority to 100 seats. Nye had worked tirelessly throughout the election campaign, so it was to be expected he would be exhausted after it, but Jennie had begun to fear even before it was over that there was something more wrong with him than extreme tiredness. His appearance during one television performance, which she watched in her own constituency, had, she said, 'panicked her'. The minute the election was over (and herself as well as Nye safely re-elected) she rushed back home, knowing that Nye had been too ill to go to Devonport to speak for Michael Foot (who lost his seat) and worried his illness was not just flu or something equally unthreatening. Once he had rested, he seemed to rally, but Jennie's fears continued.

In fact, she had always worried about her husband's health. He looked so big and strong that people assumed there was nothing fragile about him, but Jennie had always known there was. Her main concern had been for his chest. When he was wheezing and struggling for breath, as sometimes when he had a cold, Jennie would become convinced he had the miner's disease pneumoconiosis, of which his own father had died, and she would call the doctor, who would reassure her and diagnose bronchitis or, on one occasion, pleurisy. It had been partly for the sake of Nye's chest that she agreed to move out of London to the farm at Asheridge where it was believed his lungs would benefit.

When Nye suffered these chest complaints it was noted by his family that Jennie did little of the actual nursing he needed.

Arianwen went so far as to state (with contempt) that Jennie was frightened of illness. She was right, Jennie was (as most people are). She was hardly ever ill herself, possessing a constitution far tougher than Nye's, as well as one never put under the strain his had been. So long as she saw to it that Nye *was* properly nursed, she felt no shame in keeping her distance till he was better. This, of course, was not how a good wife was meant to react – she was (and is) expected to minister to the sick husband herself and at the same time not *want* to carry on with her own life. Selfless devotion was the watchword at such times and Jennie was incapable of that.

She demanded it of others, though, when *she* was ill. Back in 1932, when she was still with Frank Wise, she had needed her tonsils out and made a great fuss about who was going to look after her. She inspected the King's Cross Nose and Throat Hospital, which was free, and finding herself 'profoundly depressed by the violation of privacy in that kind of place' she had booked herself into a private nursing-home in Bentinck Street (off Harley Street) where she would get the personal attention she wanted. But once the minor operation was over and she went home to her flat, her mother came down from Scotland at once *on the bus* to look after her, much to Jennie's gratification – her mother, at least, knew how to behave in times of need.

But, though Jennie did not follow the received opinion of how wives should behave when husbands were ill, it was not because she didn't care. She cared greatly. Her papers and letters are littered with expressions of concern about Nye's health right from the moment they married and she never tried to minimise his symptoms however much they scared her. Whenever he had been standing for any length of time, giving speeches or addressing conferences, his back would be agony, and she would urge the service of a physiotherapist. It was the same with his neck muscles, and his shoulders – if he tensed them, as he did when he was rousing himself into a passion during some argument, he would suffer acute, debilitating pain afterwards. Jennie knew this, and was forever preaching rest, rest and rest again as a cure.

She did nothing, though, to make Nye cut down on his

drinking, probably because she knew it would do no good trying to persuade him, but also because she didn't really believe alcohol was damaging him. He was never incapably drunk, or ill after drinking a lot (whereas she was), and his mind was always sharp, so the effect on his liver was hidden. Wine, his preferred drink, helped Nye relax and she was all for that. They ate well too, but again it was good food, cooked by her mother, or eaten in excellent restaurants, and not rubbish. Nye gained weight as he aged but not so much that he looked grossly fat. So Jennie had never worried about his more general health, obsessed as she was with the state of his chest and back. These were specific areas of concern and she could cope with them.

What she found difficult to cope with in 1959 was a dreadful underlying conviction that something she could not put her finger on was wrong with Nye. She would get sudden little rushes of terror at odd moments, as she did in the spring of that year, when she saw him sitting on a window-sill at Asheridge talking to a guest. He was talking animatedly, his face alive with interest in what he was saying, and yet she thought she saw something ominous in how he looked. She said nothing to him about it. At other times he had begun to say things she was afraid to interpret. There was a wistfulness, even a sadness, about him which had nothing to do with his political fortunes. An apparently innocent remark, such as 'Not many more springs' as he looked out on a particularly beautiful scene at Asheridge, could make her heart turn over. Then she'd bought a new double bed for his bedroom at Asheridge; he said why didn't she add a second bedside lamp, then they could both read and sleep there. They had had their own bedrooms for so long by then that it was a shock to her that he wanted her with him and, again, she wondered if there was some deeper significance in this.

Still she never suspected there was anything seriously wrong with his stomach. His eyes were troubling him more then. He started to complain he couldn't see, so she made him have his eyes examined and only then learned that he suffered from nystagmus, an eye condition left over from his days as a miner. Then she had noticed a swelling in his neck and was terrified he had a tumour, but it disappeared once he rested his voice. But even though she was alert to his physical condition, she did not notice any stomach problem until after the election, when he lost interest in food and started losing weight. This was unusual enough in itself to be alarming, and she was alarmed, but not anything like as worried as she had been over other ailments. He was sixty-two, and she knew that men of that age regularly suffered from ulcers. His own doctor suspected he had an ulcer, and wanted to have him examined in hospital and treated for it. Reluctantly, Nye agreed to go into the Royal Free, Hampstead, but not until after Christmas. He always grumbled about Christmas, saying it was just a festival of commercial exploitation, but Jennie's tradition-loving mother was used to ignoring him and went ahead with the usual celebrations which Nye, in the end, loved. That Christmas, two Yugoslavian friends, with their three children, were staying at Asheridge, and Jennie was glad of their company. Their presence meant a front had to be kept up, a pretence that Nye was not about to have an operation soon.

On 27 December, Nye went into hospital and Jennie stayed with friends in London so that she could be nearby and visit every day even though she hated hospitals and illness. The operation was a long one, and as the hours passed Jennie concluded correctly that this must be a bad sign. She even imagined the length of the operation must mean Nye's life was in danger, so when she was told it was safely over her first reaction was one of relief – he had survived, he had not died on the operating table. But seeing him was a great shock. He looked so dreadful, as anyone does after a major operation, and hardly had the strength to turn his head. She was very frightened and emotional, and could only bring herself to say, 'Darling, be on my side.' He couldn't speak, still dazed from the anaesthetic, but she interpreted the look he gave her as proof that he intended to fight to get well. She learned that most of his stomach had been removed, a horrifying piece of information in itself, but neither Mr George Quist, the surgeon who carried out the complicated operation, nor Nye's doctor and friend, Dan Davies, mentioned the malignant tumour that had been found.

For six weeks Nye lay in the Royal Free recovering without knowing what he was vainly trying to recover from. Naturally, he wanted to know what had been done to him and what the prognosis was and since he had acquired quite a bit of medical knowledge there was not much chance of hiding everything from him. He knew there would be a laboratory report, which he was quite capable of understanding, and requested to see it. Dan Davies had the laboratory findings typed out and asked Jennie to give it to Nye. She read it first. There was no mention of cancer. Nye studied it and appeared satisfied. But the day before Jennie was due to take him home to Asheridge, Dan Davies invited her to lunch at his house and gently broke the truth to her. Nye not only had cancer but it was terminal. Nobody could say how long he had left, but the informed guess was six months to a year, though since cancer was so unpredictable there was always the hope he would have longer. But the point was, there was no treatment possible. What could be done had been done. All that was left was palliative care.

When the news of her mother's inoperable cancer had been broken to her, Jennie had had Nye to cling on to and help her cope, and even then on her own admission she had become hysterical. Now, she could not afford hysterics. The very reason Dan Davies had waited six weeks to tell her the truth was because he had realised that if he told her as soon as the operation was over, Nye would see it in her eyes and would not fight to survive. The six weeks had given him the chance to stabilise and believe he was getting better, so that the implicit lie he had been fed had been worth it. But for Jennie the long delay had made everything harder – she, too, had believed Nye was getting better and now she was bound to begin acting a part much harder to do convincingly than it had been in front of her mother. Yet, at the same time, she agreed that Nye should not be told. She wanted the cancer to be kept secret from him, fearing that to know he was certainly dying would make his last months far more agonising than they need be. So she proposed to tell no one whatsoever, not his family, not his closest friends. Only his doctors and herself would know and they would conspire together to protect him from the awful truth.

Whatever the moral dilemma in this decision, Jennie was taking upon herself a task of Herculean proportion. Unlike her mother, Nye was not easily content with whatever was told him. He was far more astute and his relationship with his wife was far closer. Jennie was presupposing that he would not be able to sense her own distress and fear and come to the correct conclusion. She was sentencing herself to pretending for twenty-four hours in every single day and never having the relief of seeking comfort from anyone, because no one had to know. The strain was naturally colossal and it quickly told on her. She needed alcohol to help her cope and began drinking heavily. Her temper, never serene, became worse and she snapped at everyone except Nye. But what made everything even more terrible than it already was, was her growing conviction that Nye's cancer had been caused by those who had subjected him to such abuse during the H-bomb quarrel. Without knowing anything about the causes of cancer, she instinctively felt they were psychological. She began to torment herself with this theory. Those who had opposed Nye were 'murderers' and she wanted some sort of revenge. This took the form of keeping away people she accused of having put Nye through hell and it created great resentment. Jennie was in charge, Jennie had the power, Jennie was the wife whose permission was needed to see Nye.

At first, it seemed she was succeeding in protecting him. The weather was good that spring, and Nye seemed to be recovering not just some strength but his spirits. Every little improvement – the first walk he took, the first interview she allowed him to give – was greeted by her with the words, 'Going in the right direction,' which amused him. A journalist from the *Guardian*, interviewing him at the end of March, wrote that he was smiling and cheerful and seemed eager to get back to work, but that his wife was determined he should not rush things – 'He ought to have the fullest time in order to get back into fighting form.' She had almost been taken in by her own pretence and fantasised that this was indeed what Nye would do, get back to fighting form, defy the cancer, triumph over it and confound the doctors. Her mother, after all, had already survived five years since they'd been told her cancer was hopelessly advanced, so why should Nye not do the same?

In May, he seemed so much better that they went on holiday, only to Brighton, but still it was a start. Jennie was sure the sea air would be a tonic, and looked forward to Nye's benefiting from it. At first, it seemed the change of venue and air were working but it was all an illusion. Within a few days he was in terrible pain and it was obvious they must go home. On the way back to Asheridge, in a chauffeur-driven car, loaned to them by friends, they stopped briefly in Windsor Great Park. The chauffeur was a man Nye knew, like him a Welshman, and getting out of the car to stretch his legs, Nye said to him that he must go back to Wales to see the mountains 'before I go'. It was one of several indications that Nye did, in fact, know all along that he was dying and that just as Jennie was pretending so was he. It was a dreadfully sad, complicated game: she pretended to protect him, he pretended he didn't know she was pretending, to protect her. How long this cruel charade could go on neither of them knew. Nye's doctors wanted him to go back into the Royal Free, but he refused. He couldn't say he wanted to die at home, because he wasn't supposed to know he was dying, but clearly he had little faith in the reality of any kind of treatment, and Jennie did not carry pretence as far as urging hospital attention on him. But, as she put it, 'the bad time began'. If Nye was going to die at home, he would need round-the-clock nursing. He developed thrombosis in his right leg soon after the return from Brighton, and that inaugurated the new régime. Their Austrian friend, Trude, and Jack Buchan, a physiotherapist friend trained to give the pain-relieving injections Nye was becoming dependent on, became his daytime nurses. Jennie described herself as his night nurse. Every other day Dan Davies or George Quist came to visit, though there was little they could do. According to Jennie, Nye 'quizzed' them sharply about his state of health but they gave nothing away – 'they kept their promise to me.'

There was no one in those awful last weeks who was not wary, if not downright afraid, of Jennie. She was hardly sane, struggling as she was to give Nye confidence and yet confronted daily with the evidence that pretending he was going to get better was a sham. The sham didn't make her relent. On the contrary, it seemed more important than ever to encourage Nye to look forward, to plan ahead. She liked to see him sitting by the window, looking out and talking about what he was going to do when he was better and instead of the pathos of this tearing her apart, knowing as she did that he never would get better, it helped her hold herself together – 'going in the right direction' had in effect been their slogan long before Nye was convalescing. Her great terror was that the morphine administered by Jack Buchan would not continue to subdue the pain and that when it failed, Nye would guess he was dying. She couldn't bear the thought of a sudden last-minute confrontation during which Nye would realise she had lied to him.

But that moment never came. The morphine levels were increased and Nye slipped more and more into a drug-induced sleep. When, at the beginning of July, it was obvious the end was near, Jennie took the surprising decision to ask one of the Bevan family to be there, writing later: 'We thought it prudent.' Who she meant by that 'we' is not clear, nor why such a decision was 'prudent'. Perhaps she feared it might look bad afterwards (and she was very concerned about afterwards) if the press represented her as keeping Nye's relations away from him. At any rate, Arianwen's husband (not one of his blood family) came to help Jack Buchan and her with their vigil, and it was he and Jack who were sitting with Nye when he died early on the morning of 6 July 1960. They woke Jennie, told her, and took her to his bedside. She said her first emotion was one of thankfulness that 'There had been no last-minute awareness that we had deceived him.' Again, that 'we', that inability to accept the responsibility she knew was hers. The doctors and Jack had kept the secret because she had made them do so, and the weight of knowing it was her decision burdened her ever after. On the whole, she convinced herself that she had been right, but doubts kept on surfacing, and stifling these exhausted her almost as much as her grief.

This, when it broke over her, engulfed her completely. She had been with Nye for thirty years, and loved him as he loved her; and she had come to acknowledge that marriage was an institution which had worked to protect her. Now, she had no protection. She was a strong-minded, independent woman, but the utter loneliness of her new situation plunged her into overwhelming depression from which not only did she think she could not recover, but also did not want to. She wanted to die. It would have been easy, or as easy as such an agonising step ever can be. She had plenty of sleeping pills, supplied in abundance for Nye, and a bottle of whisky readily available to wash them down with. It was so tempting finally to obliterate herself. But what stopped her was the thought of her poor mother, so frail now, so near death herself and needing Jennie to help her through her own last days. Selfish though she may have been throughout her life, Jennie was not so selfish as to deny her mother that comfort. But another thing holding her back from suicide had nothing to do with her mother. She wanted to see justice done to Nye's memory – she had been his wife, she was the only possible keeper of the flame. The moment he was dead the misrepresentations (in her opinion) had begun, and she seethed with rage. They must be corrected. She would have to rebut all the lies, keep constantly vigilant to safeguard his reputation. Michael Foot could be trusted to write Nye's biography, but he could not be expected to scrutinise every word said and written about him. She would have to do that. Her sense of duty, and the bitterness which underlay it, kept her alive.

There were certain ordeals which, out of that same sense of duty, she had to go through. On 26 July, there was an official memorial service in Westminster Abbey, organised by the Labour Party. It would have been unthinkable for Nye's wife not to be present. The presence of so many ordinary people there among the famous mourners helped her through, but this very ordinariness of the assembled throng at the service a week earlier in Wales, when Nye's ashes were taken to be scattered on a hillside above Tredegar, had almost proved her undoing. Jennie, facing the crowd which had gathered, had the greatest struggle not to break down completely. 'In all the great battles of his life,' she managed to say, 'Nye came home to you. He never left you. He never will.' His spirit, she knew, had remained in Wales and, though neither she nor Nye had any religious faith, she felt profoundly moved to know this place, where his ashes lay, somehow also contained his essential self.

The two services over, Jennie found she could not go on without some sort of rest. At Asheridge, Nye was everywhere and in the first weeks after his death there was more pain than comfort in this. In spite of her mother's needs, she had to escape, and so she booked herself into a clinic in Edinburgh, leaving Ma Lee in good hands. Coming back from the clinic was hard – at least there she could sleep and be protected from the everyday reminders of Nye. As the months went by, her anguish increased, made worse as it was by her mother forgetting (her memory was severely affected by her illness) that Nye was dead and constantly going from room to room searching for him. Jennie felt she was going mad herself. She couldn't sleep, even taking sleeping pills and when she did succeed in knocking herself out for brief periods, she had terrifying nightmares. She scrawled on a piece of paper, one of the many upon which she made not always coherent jottings, 'Don't know if I can go on here. But if not, where else?' Where indeed? Her mother could not be moved, and in any case she hadn't the energy to uproot herself. There was no one who could take control and do it for her. Her only sibling was Tommy, who was useless, and she had no children. Her in-laws had little time for her, and she had never had any for them. The family could not close ranks and sustain her because to all intents and purposes she had no family. She was on her own.

Soon, she began to wonder if she had entirely lost sight of who she was in so willingly becoming part of Nye's life. She had, for ten years at least, sacrificed her own ambitions because she believed in Nye and saw him as being both more able and better placed to achieve what they both wanted to achieve. She felt she had had no real life of her own for so long that she had forgotten what it consisted of. 'I wander in and out of people's lives,' she wrote, '. . . but what else is there to do when there is next to nothing left of what could be called a life of your own?' Nye, when Frank died, had roused her from her misery by reminding her of the work she had to do. It had been the antidote to grief, the means of pulling herself out of it. But now she couldn't identify either what this 'work' was, or its value.

Yes, she was still Cannock's MP, but so what? She had never much liked constituency work and, since her majority there was large, she had never had to learn to like it. Sometimes she opened fairs or appeared at some of the other events that an attentive MP found it wise to agree to, but mostly she confined her efforts on Cannock's behalf to speaking on matters of importance to the constituency (any debate on coal, for example, found her participating vociferously). But once Nye was dead her duties as an MP did not inspire her. Nothing did. She began to drink as much as a bottle of gin a day, just to be able to carry on.

Even then, she would never have managed it without the help of her cousin, Bettina Stafford. Family did, after all, exist and rallied round. Bettina, alerted to Jennie's plight by her mother, Ma Lee's sister, came down to help nurse her aunt, bringing her husband Bill and her ten-year-old son Vincent. She meant to stay just a week, but stayed longer (in fact, stayed for the next thirty years). This stabilised Jennie at a crucial time, and then, after her mother had died (in 1962, not quite two years after Nye), Bettina's presence, or rather Vincent's, did more than that. Vincent became the son she had never had and truly gave her something to live for. It was a boy, and not work, which began to make her see there was a life still worth living without Nye – 'the child kept me from indulging my mood of total despair and desolation.' But, though Vincent did indeed rescue Jennie, he didn't send her back into the public life she had once relished, the life she had had with Nye. Some people wondered if she would give up her seat at the next election and it seems to have occurred to Jennie herself to consider doing so. But she didn't. The 1964 election came, and Labour won. The new Prime Minister, Harold Wilson, offered Jennie a job: she was to be the first ever Minister for the Arts.

Wilson had been impressed once by what Nye had said to him about Jennie's ability. Talking of Barbara Castle, Nye had told him, 'Jennie is just as good as Barbara, but because she's married to me she doesn't get any publicity.' He had remembered that, and now he made it possible for Jennie to achieve something of her own, the chance to prove to everyone that if she had never been Nye's wife she could have fulfilled other ambitions, including ministerial office, and put into practice what she believed in. Now she had her chance, and she seized it eagerly.

During the next decade, from 1964 when she became the first Minister of the Arts until 1970 when she lost her Cannock seat and was created Baroness Lee of Asheridge, Jennie relished the power she had been given. She was, in fact, a junior minister only, with the title of parliamentary under-secretary, but that was of no concern to her. She was sixty and had no illusions about subsequent preferment – it wasn't as though 1964 was 1929, when she had hoped for a great political future. It suited her fine not to have to care about party politics but instead to be able to concentrate on what *she* wanted to achieve: to make the arts more accessible to everyone without in any way cheapening them. She wanted to see theatres and concert halls and art galleries in every town and city, not just clustered in London, and at the same time she wanted to establish permanent centres of excellence in the capital itself.

Fine ideals, but all ultimately dependent, of course, on money. A National Theatre could not be built without money, nor could the arts be more widely disseminated without financial backing. Jennie's way of securing the support which would produce the money was to enlist the Prime Minister, Harold Wilson, in her cause and to use the invaluable help of the powerful man who had been her own and her husband's solicitor, Arnold Goodman. Her job she saw as primarily one of managing the right publicity, of making the arts high-profile, and this she achieved triumphantly, rising above attempts to patronise her (from those museum directors and suchlike who considered her ignorant). Just as Nye had overcome supposedly insuperable obstacles in establishing the NHS through his own passionate commitment to it, so Jennie did the same for the arts. The comparison is not ludicrous either even if in scale it seems so – there was just as much hostility around in the arts world as there had been in the medical, together with the additional contempt of those who thought anything to do with the arts was essentially trivial.

But Jennie didn't think her job or her aims trivial. She

believed in what she was trying to do. She was freed from all the constraints of being a famous man's wife and it showed – she was back to her old energetic, bossy self, glorying in *real work*. Her delight in her role showed all too clearly how held back she had been for years and underlined how much she had sacrificed by being (whatever others thought) a good wife, putting her husband's career first. Both in her achievements as Minister for the Arts and then by her part in the founding of the Open University she demonstrated how able she was, and always had been, and how she could rise to the challenge presented to her. She was, in those years, a success in a way she had never quite been since her marriage.

She also enjoyed herself. Pleasure came back into her life, and with it another lover, a man younger than herself with whom she had a tremendously physical and satisfying relationship. The question of marriage never arose (like Frank, this man was already married) but there would have been little chance of her becoming a wife again. She loved this new man, but was content with a long-running affair, and when she felt it had run its course she was happy to let it change into a comfortable friendship. Losing her Cannock seat in 1970 she was not quite so content to stop being a minister, but once in the Lords she found ample scope for harrying the Tories. There were plenty of people who were glad, of course, that she had been removed from the Commons and from her post, including the senior civil servants. Their dealings with Jennie as a minister perhaps suggest that she would never have been a success earlier in her life after all – they found her rude, not very clever, not prepared to tolerate the meetings they thought necessary, and quite unable to grasp how the system worked.

But whatever their opinion, Jennie ended her career on a high and was comforted by what she managed to achieve. Her life, unfortunately, did not end so well. In her seventies, she developed breast cancer, was troubled with arthritis, lost the ability to read clearly and was lonely. Her beloved nephew Vincent left to go to America after his second marriage and she missed him terribly. Only Bettina and Bill endured until her death, aged eighty-four, in 1988. She was cremated, and her ashes scattered where Nye's had been, on the same Welsh hillside. In death, she was, finally, a wife.

Reflections

I see myself reflected so clearly, at last, in Jennie Lee's resistance to being a wife at all and even, though to a lesser extent (because of the different circumstances of our lives) in how she interpreted the role once she had succumbed. Almost everything she wrote about marriage I feel I could have written myself and her general outrage at how women allowed themselves to be trapped into various kinds of servitude, once they became wives, was mine. But, of course, Jennie had dedicated her life to politics, she had a reason to refuse to marry. I didn't. I had no reason other than a dislike of what I saw as being a wife's fate. When she did marry Nye, it was for practical reasons, to protect both their careers, and not for personal ones. She apparently felt no need to protect her parents from any stigma associated then with 'living in sin', but then perhaps her parents needed no protection. They were not religious and, though Ma Lee was in most respects conventional enough, their own political convictions made them well able to accept unorthodox relationships. How much Jennie told them about her lovers is not recorded – they may never have known she was actually living with Nye or, before that, sleeping with Frank, though since she was in such close contact with them that is unlikely. But they were pleased when she did become what she had said she never would, a wife.

What she then made of the role, I approve of. I didn't make the same of it, but I like the way she hardly gave in at all to conventional ideas of wifely behaviour. She tried to stay true to her own ideas, and for the most part she succeeded, not caring in the least that in doing so she turned prevailing judgements on what made a good wife inside out. She delegated all domestic tasks to her mother, who, whatever the rights and wrongs of this, relished them, and she resisted absolutely becoming the little housewife. She was married to Nye, not to a house. If her career suffered because she was his wife, and there is no real proof that it did, she still pursued it with, for a long period at least, no lessening of her ambition. She was one of the women who, towards the middle of the last century, put new meaning into the word 'wife'.

But the influence of extraordinary women like Jennie Lee had not yet begun truly to permeate society. Very few wives had access to her knowledge about birth control, even fewer knew how to procure a safe abortion. Women of her own class still relied on hopelessly primitive methods to prevent pregnancy and even more drastically crude and dangerous methods to abort unwanted babies. The first birth control clinic did not open until 1921, and it was in London, making it useless for all except a tiny minority of women. My own maternal grandmother could have done with the information it supplied but instead gave birth to an illegitimate baby she was unable to keep. Illegitimate herself, with her mother dying when she was two, she was one of the thousands of women to whom Jennie Lee's liberated ideas would have seemed not only shocking but almost beyond their comprehension. What my grandmother wanted to be was a wife. Marriage to her still symbolised security, and when she married my grandfather, six years after her illegitimate baby was born, she felt safe for the first time in her life. She was rescued from the kind of disgrace and shame Jennie Lee never had to suffer.

'Wife', then, was still a seductive word to the majority of women at the beginning of the twentieth century, however much Jennie Lee held it in contempt, yet remaining single was not quite the miserable fate it had been seen as. The period following the end of the 1914–18 war saw a dramatic change in the morals of the young unmarried woman – it was not thought quite so terrible to 'go all the way', so long as one was discreet about it. Many women had slept with men going off to fight in the war without feeling this made them into sluts, and by the 1920s the term 'fast' carried overtones of admirable daring with it rather than disgust. Women even looked different, with their shape no longer what was thought 'womanly', and this had an effect on the way they behaved. Skirts remained long until the mid-1920s but then by 1927 they had shot up to knee level. Corsets all but disappeared, and so did waists, and hair was cropped. Women not only looked more like boys but some considered they had the licence to behave like them if they wished. They wanted to have fun before they married and carried into marriage – still the goal – new notions of their own needs.

Jennie and Nye shared the same social background which gave them automatically a comfortable, easy feeling about each other when they met at Westminster in an atmosphere and surroundings alien to both of them. They had so little explaining to do about where they came from, how they had grown up and how their political beliefs had been forged. It is a great binding force in a marriage, this shared inheritance, and I felt it myself. To some people, it would be dull – what about the excitement of discovering each other's roots? – but such effortless knowledge of each other's formative influences is a huge advantage. It may even make it easier to be a good wife. But I was misled at first. Carlisle is a compact city, and in the 1950s, so far as social class was concerned its demarcation lines were strictly drawn. The posh area was on the north bank of the River Eden, called Stanwix, sometimes Stanwix Bank; the most deprived was west of the castle, a council estate called Raffles. The name of your primary school gave everything away, without any need to know an exact address, even if you were at the girls' High School or the boys' Grammar School. I'd gone to Ashley Street where the catchment area was mainly Raffles, and he told me he'd gone to Stanwix School. He never actually said he lived in Stanwix, but I assumed he did. Then there were definite signs of social as well as cultural superiority in casual talk of his violin lessons and his sister's piano-playing of an evening. In my Raffles experience, no council house had room to accommodate a piano, so his house must be a private one, probably one of those detached jobs I envied so much, situated on the Bank itself above the river. The name of the sister who played the piano was significant too: Annabel. It was a name entirely unknown to me, belonging, I thought, to models in glossy magazines like *Vogue*. His father, though now an invalid, had been a civil servant, whereas mine was a fitter in a factory. His mother, I was told, read all the time, mostly Dickens novels. She apparently never had a book out of her hand. Immediately, I conjured up the image of an elegant woman lying, book on her lap, on a chaise-longue while in the background her daughter Annabel tinkled delightfully on the pianoforte . . .

He was out of my class and I was pleased because I wanted to be out of it too. It was therefore a shock to learn that he lived on the St Ann's council estate, bordering the affluent private sector of Stanwix, and he went to Stanwix School because one to serve St Ann's had not yet been built. This information changed everything. St Ann's estate was certainly superior in the pecking order to Raffles, but we had just moved to another estate, Longsowerby, which in turn was infinitely superior to St Ann's. There was a piano in their house, true, and he did own and play a violin (excruciatingly badly), but these were not after all indications of a leisurely life-style any more than his mother's reading of Dickens. Far from lolling on any chaise-longue, his mother never sat down. Her reading was done while stirring pans on the stove. She was always exhausted, a Scottish working-class woman so worn down by her circumstances that she made my own mother's way of life look almost genteel. The Davies household was chaotic and far shabbier than my own, and the struggle to make ends meet much, much harder.

So he wasn't out of my class at all. He was bang in the midst of it (though if his father hadn't become ill he might not have been). On the whole, once I'd realised this, it was a relief. I had ideas well above my station in life but then so did he. Each of us hankered after what we did not have, both in material and in general terms. Neither of us had to explain to the other why we wanted to have an existence quite different from that of our hard-up families, why we wanted money, why we wanted the life it could buy. These weren't trivial goods either – to have a spacious house to live in, and a car, and money in a bank to support us were deadly serious aims not for one moment to be despised as merely mercenary. We didn't have to waste time discussing it. Like Jennie and Nye, we knew the power of money, knew it could change our lives. Neither of us had been grindingly poor, we'd never gone hungry (though, like Jennie, I had been luckier than he had – I'd had the packed Christmas stocking, the new clothes). But all the same our experience was close enough to form a bond which mattered. If I'd been a wife with a privileged background I can see I might have run into trouble trying to understand a husband whose impoverished upbringing made him guard every penny closely. And the other way round, if I'd been the wife of a man indulged from birth, it would have been equally difficult – I'd have slipped into accusations of 'you-don't-know-what-it's-like-to-be-poor'.

So it is convenient, and maybe more than that, to share the same background. To share the same location was another bonus, one Jennie and Nye didn't have. I'd been born and brought up in Carlisle, where my family had lived for generations, whereas he had been born in Scotland, coming to the city aged four, leaving it again at seven, and finally settling there aged eleven. It didn't make him a Cumbrian, but nevertheless it made Carlisle his home too. He didn't know it the way I did, though. I knew every village for miles around the city, not to mention having a detailed knowledge of the Solway coast and the northern Lake District. He knew his own area and the centre of Carlisle and that was about it. With his father being an invalid, and his mother a stranger to the place, he'd never been introduced to the surrounding countryside as I had. I introduced him. We took buses to their respective termini, or little local trains which would drop us off at outlying villages, and then walked for miles. We cycled, too, and had picnics in hidden places he'd never have found on his own. Jennie showed Nye her part of Scotland, he showed her his part of Wales, but we absorbed together the beauty of our county and when we left home this gave us a shared geographical memory.

Coming from the same place as well as the same social background seems rarer today. Background matters more than place, but in my case both were significant when I became a wife. Having the same points of reference from which to develop cut out so many explanations and united us in common goals. Together we wanted to escape the limits of our social background and gain what our city couldn't give us. We wanted go to in the same direction, as did Jennie and Nye. The urge to succeed on a materialistic level was identical. It was desperately important to become householders, coming as we did from families who had only ever been able to rent council houses (and what they rented hardly worth the money). My passion to own my own house was greater than Jennie's. When I was young, the game I played more than any other was imagining having my own house. I'd draw it, and draw the furniture, over and over again. I'd eye other people's houses too, systematically invading those I liked until in my head I'd made them my own. I'd concentrate hard on the bathroom, loathing as I did our outside lavatory, and I always found space for a room which didn't exist in any house I knew, the *Library*. But buying a house was hard, if nothing like as hard as it is today in London, and it took us three years until, in 1963, we managed it.

It bore no resemblance to the house I'd yearned for, which was a romantic cottage a little like Jennie and Nye's first home. This house, the house we still live in, was late Victorian, flat-fronted with a balcony on the first floor, and semi-detached. It was in an appalling state of repair and, though it had an indoor lavatory, that was the only sign of modernisation. The woodwork and walls had remained untouched for nearly a hundred years and the place was falling to bits, dangerously so. It cost £5,250, and we bought it on a twenty-year mortgage. Once the deposit had been paid, we had no money to do more than put in a proper kitchen and bathroom, and have it rewired, and then the builders moved out, leaving us to do all the rest. It took a year of coming home from work each day (I was still teaching) to rip off filthy wallpapers and burn off the dark brown paint, before we could start decorating. We lived in two rooms, the kitchen and the bedroom. Our families, when they came to visit, were horrified – it seemed to them that their council houses were infinitely preferable to our ancient, decrepit, cold, mostly empty big house. But my joy in the house grew all the time. Like Jennie, that aspect of being a wife satisfied me – I loved sanding the floors (very daring for 1963) with a machine we hired and laying the black-and-white tiles in the kitchen so that it would look like a Dutch interior, and choosing paints and wallpapers. Gradually, the two floors of the house that were ours were cleaned and decorated even if only two of the five rooms had furniture in them.

There was another floor, the top floor, occupied by Mrs Hall, our sitting tenant, without whose presence the price of the house would have been much greater, making it impossible for us to buy. The estate agent had described her as an old woman who visited her daughter in America often and might soon move there for good. She was away during the negotiations, which naturally gave credence to the suggestion that she might never come back. She had two rooms and a kitchen on the top floor – we noted the thirty-eight steps up to it and hoped they would soon get too much for her – but no bathroom. She shared ours. For the first three months we lived in ignorance of what this would mean, but then she returned. We were startled to see that she wasn't old and feeble at all. She was only in her late sixties, and clearly good for another twenty years, and had a very forceful personality. Every day began with her thundering down to the lavatory where, after she'd finished, she used a vile Fresh Breeze spray. The bathroom was on a half-landing five steps down from our bedroom but the fumes were so heavy they drifted into it and we woke to their disgusting stench. What was almost worse than that was how noisy she was – just one thin, small woman, but she was endlessly rattling around, radio and television played at full volume and sometimes simultaneously. But there was nothing to be done. We had to remind ourselves that without her, we'd have no house, and we must just learn to enjoy the part of it we did have. It wasn't difficult. I loved it when we got to the stage of being able to furnish it. Like Jennie, I spent days, we both did, searching for the right desk, the prettiest mirror, the most comfortable chairs. This home-making was of incredible importance to me.

But to him, I think, it was more important to *own* the house. It was the significance of possession which made the greater impact. It was he, the husband, who'd done the buying, the vital organising of the finance, and I, as the wife, had fallen readily into the traditional role of doing the beautifying. Inside the house felt my territory more than his. I chose the colour schemes, I decided where things should go. Consultations with him were over the big things, usually because they involved expense, but the trivial decisions were all mine – he hadn't much interest in what kind of bread bin to buy, or where the cutlery drawer should be. Those were wives' concerns. And I relished every mundane purchase, feeling as they accumulated that I was gathering around me more than a lot of unimportant belongings. I was, in the most literal sense, making a home. I'd have made one even if I had never been a wife – it is no prerogative of the married woman after all – but doing it *as* a wife meant in that respect the home belonged to me more than to him. It is one way in which even wives like Mary Livingstone, never mind Jennie Lee, triumph. Being the wife is, in that respect, no disadvantage.

Money matters in a marriage. It always has done. First, it was wives not having any of their own, or, if they had, not having the right to keep it; then, once Acts like the Married Woman's Property Act had been passed (1882) and wives had the right to keep anything they earned or inherited, it was the sharing of the money, the managing of it, which was significant. Mary Livingstone suffered, first because she had no money and then because she didn't know how to handle what she was given; Fanny Stevenson yearned to have a job which would mean she would feel independent within her marriage but couldn't try to obtain one because this would reflect badly on her husband's ability to keep her. But Jennie Lee had her own money, gained through employment of a sort she enjoyed, and she knew how to manage it. In her marriage, most unusually, she was the one who looked after finance. In that respect, she was a good wife.

I know that, unlike Jennie, I have been a bad wife. It is not only that I do not share the managing of it, but that I have nothing whatsoever to do with it. I am a disgrace to my own feminist aspirations. To be obliged to admit, as I am obliged to admit, that I do not know how much money we have is disgraceful. I don't even know how much we have in our bank account. It is joint, and always has been. I don't have a separate account in my own name. If we have shares in anything, I don't know about them, and as for pension arrangements, they are a mystery. I have never once gone to the annual meeting with our accountant. I know nothing about any investments. If asked, I would not be able to tell you, either, how much we need to live on each year. In short, he handles every single thing to do with money and that is something of which I am ashamed.

Quite how this state of affairs came about, I'm not entirely sure. As a child, an adolescent and a student, I was brilliant with money. I have sweet little account books going back to when I was eleven in which every item of expenditure, and every incoming bit of pocket money, and amounts earned from doing jobs, are all solemnly listed. I saved, I spent wisely, and I was certainly interested in earning more money as soon as possible. But then, when I got married, I seemed perfectly happy to leave everything to do with managing our money to him. Since we didn't have much, it wasn't too complicated. His first wage packet contained £14. I remember spreading the notes out on the kitchen table and dividing them up: £1 for his mother, to be sent each week, and the rest going on rent and food. My wage, as a teacher, went into the bank. All of it. I was in charge of spending on food and household goods and I budgeted carefully, so my lack of interest in our money doesn't date from then. I'm sure I knew in 1960 how much we had and what our bills were. It was later, when we began to hit lucky, that any financial awareness gradually faded out of me, and now it is my nightmare that I might ever again have to take over handling our financial affairs. I tell myself that, of course, I could do it, that I am perfectly capable, just as capable as Jennie and much more so than Mary and Fanny, but I would hate to have to do so. I've become one of those simpering creatures who bleat that their husbands look after the money, implying that their pretty little heads can't cope with it.

I think myself lucky to have a husband who keeps an eagle eye on our money, and yet at the same time I am not proud of my own lack of involvement. I feel I should at least have my own bank account, as well as a joint account, with some modest sum in it which only I would know about. So why don't I? Because the only reason I would quite like it, apart from my feminist guilt, is that then he would never have to know how much I spend on presents, especially presents for him. I bought him a beautiful garden bench to celebrate our ruby wedding anniversary and knew that his pleasure in it would be marred when, a month later, the Barclaycard bill came in and he saw what it had cost.

If this gives the impression that I am a wife who is a spendthrift, then it is wrong, but I am constantly glad that, since I earn my own money, I do not really have to justify what I spend. I enjoy the fantastic freedom of not having to worry about how much a theatre ticket or a book costs, of buying clothes I don't really need, of doing the weekly shopping without regard for price. And yet within all this apparent disregard for money I am very far from extravagant and he knows it. I have never in my life bought designer clothes, or expensive jewellery, nor spent a fortune on having my hair cut. None of those allegedly 'feminine' things attracts me, he's never had to tut-tut and say, oh dear me, the amount my wife spends on herself. Sometimes, when I say that yes, it is a new coat, it was £160, he says he cannot believe the price, all that money for a new coat, especially when there was nothing wrong so far as he could see with the old one. One of my daughters laughs at him – to her, he is like a caricature of the controlling husband. And I have let myself become a caricature of the defensive wife.

It is a game played in countless marriages, but it shouldn't be played in mine. I would rather be a wife like Jennie, alert to making money work and capable of making sure it did to the advantage of the marriage in general. When I was poor, or passing-poor, I was, and if I were to be poor again I certainly would, but a sense of affluence has made me too relaxed about where my money goes and I am happy and relieved to let him attend to its welfare. I don't want to be a wife in charge of the money, even if much of it is my own.

Money comes into it again when I try to think of whether I am a brake on him in the way Jennie was not on Nye. A 'good wife' is somehow supposed to curb her husband's more reckless impulses but, of course, she never did. Instead, she urged him on, which many thought proved her a very bad wife indeed. It isn't a very attractive image, the thought of being some kind of restraining force, but I think I've tried to be, believing it is one of the functions of a wife. And I have failed, particularly when it comes to buying property.

With his famous financial acumen, he decided in the 1970s that, as self-employed people, we should prepare for a time when our books and his freelance journalism fell out of favour and we needed an income. What made sense to him was the purchase of another house which he would then convert into flats and let to tenants (one of whom would be his sister, who wanted to move to London). The whole idea made me feel ill. I could see immediately where this scheme would lead. Simply being a landlord to Mrs Hall, in his own house, which he could hardly cope with looking after anyway, had already proved a trial to him. The moans and groans when the roof leaked, or the plumbing went wrong, were dire. Please, I said, do not buy another house. It will give you nothing but headaches. Theoretically, I should have had the right of veto, but I didn't. He went ahead and bought this other house, in the same street as ours. It was in the same terrible state ours had originally been in, and it had not one but two sitting tenants, so there was only one floor to let. For the next ten years, he, as the landlord, was driven mad by having to cope with its leaking pipes, its collapsing ceilings, and the aggravation of tenants who naturally complained all the time. In the end, it was sold and as an investment justified its purchasing. But in terms of the stress owning it had given him, it was a disaster.

Fortunately, the other ways in which I have failed to act as a brake have never been important in the grand scheme of things. Far more significant has been my influence, as a wife, in providing a support system at crucial times, ready with sympathy and encouragement when things go wrong, but harder than that is *critical* support, the sort needed when I saw he had been at fault but he didn't recognise this. Dangerous ground, only to be trodden on very carefully, but if a wife can't be depended on to do this, who can? For the ordinary wife, it is hard enough, but for the wife of a public man it is as difficult as it is necessary. Public wives are supposed to 'stand by their man' whatever happens. Nobody knows if Hillary Clinton, say, or Mary Archer, lashed out unrelentingly in private at their respective husbands, but in public they stood by them. Big mistake, surely, in both those cases. Such visible loyalty only appeared to condone their husbands' behaviour, though it is quite possible each of these wives thought she was being noble and doing what she did for the sake of higher ideals.

In Hillary Clinton's case, it may well have been that during the Monica Lewinsky scandal the demands of being a public wife seemed greater than those of being a good one. Keeping quiet, in the sense of not openly criticising her husband and condemning his behaviour, may not have been seen by her as condoning it. Earlier in their marriage, when an affair of his had been exposed during an election campaign, she had appeared at his side on television asking voters to judge him on his political beliefs and not be influenced by what she admitted was a regrettable transgression. She was not, she emphatically stated, 'standing by her man' regardless. Presumably, she felt the same once he was President and accused of immoral acts – the important thing to her was not to provide ammunition for those who wished him to be impeached. She believed in him as a good President and that was more important than denouncing him as a bad husband.

But whatever stand Mrs Clinton had taken she would have been blamed. There were even those who blamed her for her husband's 'need' to resort to extra-marital sex of the variety he chose. If he had been happily married, this argument ran, he would never have thought of looking for satisfaction outside his marriage. The same kind of monstrous reasoning was used by the judge in the Jeffrey Archer case. 'Is she not fragrant?' he famously asked the jury to consider of Mary Archer, and if she was, how then could anyone believe her husband would go to a prostitute? A good wife, and in Mrs Archer's case a highly attractive one, was therefore the best alibi a husband could have.

All one can hope is that *in private* these public wives speak their minds. If they don't, then they are failing their husbands as much as their husbands have failed them. No one else is in a position to make them see themselves as they really are. No wife should, within her own home, suffer in silence and be all-forgiving to the point of cowardice. Such a wife is not worth much, such a marriage is a sham.

Jennie and Nye, when they became wife and husband, were rivals. If a married couple share the same career, they are automatically considered to be rivals. People watch married couples in the same profession with beady eyes, ever ready to spot jealousy and a subsequent souring of their relationship because one is succeeding and the other is not. Wife is measured against husband, husband against wife, and if the balance is not perfect, rivalry is suspected. I don't know where it comes from, this assumption that husband and wife must be in competition, but I know it is based on a misunderstanding of how a successful marriage operates. The truth is, the success of one *feels* like the success of both – if you're not succeeding yourself it is a comfort, not an irritant, that the other is. Success of one benefits both. Two failures are what make for trouble, not one. That, anyway, is the ideal, and it is realised far more often than the cynical allow.

But it is still far more acceptable for a husband to be more successful than a wife and not the other way round, and many a wife teaches herself to be self-deprecating to protect her husband. Crazy for a successful wife to abandon what she's successful at simply because she is sorry for a husband stuck in a rut and hating it, but how she handles her own success needs great skill. Successful wives are frequently judged almost to emasculate husbands – it's a sophisticated version of the 'henpecked' jibe – unless the husbands are successful too. Jennie, in spite of being an MP, knew that once Nye had become a Cabinet Minister, she could not match his success. She coped with this realisation by becoming a part of it – his success was truly also hers, they were both part of a plan, their joint plan to bring to fruition so many of their ideals. She was never jealous of what others saw as his success at the expense of her own ambition. They were not the rivals some people liked to see them as.

The great advantage of being in the same line of work is, of course, understanding each other's efforts. Jennie and Nye were supremely fortunate not just in sharing the same aims in their work but in being intimately acquainted with the minutiae of Labour Party politics within which they had to operate. Writing is a little different. Hunter and I write different kinds of things and have very different styles and ways of working. The interest we take in each other's work, and the use we are to each other, is entirely different. I don't want him to do for me what he wants me to do for him. He wants me, as his wife, to be his critic. I am delighted to oblige. Unlike Fanny Stevenson and much more like Jennie Lee, I have the credentials for it, used as I am to reviewing and commenting on all kinds of writing. I read everything he writes when it is still in manuscript. Usually, I'm called upon to speak my mind and I love doing it. He listens, but doesn't necessarily act on what I say – 'I thought that bit was really good,' he is inclined to reply, rather huffily, when I tear into some passage I think poorly written. But he likes having my opinion. I won't read his work in front of him, though – it is too tiring because if I smile he pounces and wants to know why – and I won't give a verdict until the very end (he'd like one after every page). It works well, being the wife-as-critic, being a good wife in that respect.

I like to think that whatever job he did I'd be useful as a critic. Difficult if his work was technical, if he were a rocket scientist or something, but I'd struggle to understand what he did so that I could hold a reasonable conversation about it. Wives who know nothing whatsoever about their husband's work and want to know less puzzle me. Their explanation, or defence, is that the husband wants to leave his work *at* work, home and work completely separate compartments. How peculiar. How can a wife understand a husband's problem, or a husband a wife's, if they don't know anything about what occupies the major part of each other's life? And if she doesn't want to understand his problem, or he hers, how can they be a unit at all? It sounds to me like a recipe for disaster, but maybe that's because work to me, his work as well as my own, is so vital to our happiness.

Yet at the same time I myself don't want what he wants, his involvement in what I'm doing. I don't want him to read what I've written (which is quite lucky because he hates reading books). If I'm working on non-fiction, then I'll sometimes talk a great deal about it when I'm at the researching stage; if I'm writing fiction, I've nothing at all to say. It's private, secret, until it goes to my publisher.

It is fairly unusual today for couples *not* to have lived together before they marry. Fanny and Jennie were of course daring in having done so, and even in the late 1950s so was I, and yet today it seems incredible that this was true. Without the experience of living together, how I wonder can people be sure they can do it at all? It's in the detail that all will be revealed, all those minor irritations which may soon loom so large and end up becoming intolerable. Sharing a house or flat or especially one room exposes all the unexpected clashes of temperament and taste and has nothing to do with sex. The phrase 'living together' is always used to denote sexual intimacy, which naturally it does, but it is the rest that matters more. Jennie knew, before she married Nye, that what she called 'the chemistry' was right between them but, though she meant the sexual chemistry, she also meant much more. They'd shared her flat and knew they could get along. The banality of everyday living needs to be tested, not just the grand passion – it's perfectly possible to love a man and yet find you can't stand living with him. In which case, surely it's obvious, don't become his wife.

Living together before we were married was by its very nature exciting, partly because it was furtive, a delicious secret from our families, just as it was for Fanny and Louis, and to a certain extent Jennie and Nye. The longest spells we had were three months, twice, those two long summer vacations while I was up at Oxford. It felt like playing at house and yet at the same time the feeling that this was how it was going to be, these details of how we managed the ordinary were what would matter.

By then, he was in London, the Daisy Bank Road flat in Manchester hastily vacated. Finding another in the great metropolis was even worse than finding that first bed-sitting-room in Manchester, but finally, just in time for me to join him, he installed himself on the top floor of a semi-detached house in Kingscroft Road, Kilburn. I hated it. He was deeply offended at

my reaction to what he thought a perfectly decent, if tiny, flat
which he'd had to struggle so hard to find, and wanted to know
not just what was wrong with it but why it mattered – we were
together, wasn't that enough? It mattered to me. The flat was
poky and dark and it depressed me. The rooms were claustrophobic and the furnishings garish and hideous. The windows
were festooned with netting and even after I'd ripped this down
they didn't let in much light. I prowled around desperately
trying to make more space and remove some of the uglier items
of furniture but it was hopeless. I felt as Jennie had felt about
the infamous Gosfield Street flat, without having the means she
had to do something about it.

But he loved coming home to this dreary flat merely because I
was there waiting for him and he couldn't understand why I
didn't feel the same, why I was so upset about my surroundings
– good grief, it wasn't as though I'd lived all my life in some
beautiful, spacious house surrounded by uplifting scenery. I
wasn't slumming it. Why, compared to Raffles estate, or even
Longsowerby, in Carlisle, this was urban chic. I knew he was
right. I struggled to rise above the meanness of the flat and
concentrate on what was good about having it at all.

I played the little wife far more seriously than I had ever done
before (or since) and discovered scores of things about the
reality of living together (as did he) which were a test of
devotion. For a start, I'd never realised he began each day in a
coma. I'd noticed, of course, that he was slow to wake up, but
I'd never realised this wasn't because he'd had a particularly
exhausting night but that it was a fact of his life – every single
day it was agony for him to emerge from sleep. At first, it was
funny watching him struggle to get one eye open, but then it
became less amusing as I saw it was going to be my job for ever
to ease him into every day.

How had he managed up to then? Why, by depending on his
mother to shake him awake, and then on a whole battery of
very loud alarm clocks. So I was to be his new alarm clock. One
that brought him tea to help revive him, and opened the
curtains, and turned on the radio. It was all easy enough to do,
there was no hardship involved since I bound up in the
mornings, with early morning my best time. But there was

something about this routine, so quickly established, which I didn't like. Often, that first long vacation, I had a great desire to pour the tea over his head. How on earth could we exist together if our habits were so different? I wanted him to be up bright and early with me, and not find myself doomed to waiting for at least an hour before he could even say good-morning.

And then there was the eating. I'd known he liked his food but I'd never appreciated quite how important meals were to him, though I ought to have done. Once, when we were youth-hostelling in the Yorkshire Dales, I worked out that with the money we had left (see, once *I* was in charge of the money) we could either have a meal that evening or extend our holiday by another day. He chose the meal. Going without food for even four hours never mind a whole day was impossible for him, whereas I quite liked doing this. Living together, the need to eat what he called 'proper' meals with what I thought of as absurd regularity became an issue. I maintained he never stopped to question whether he was actually hungry and he said he didn't have to, he was always hungry. I found myself giving into this, making meals for him when I didn't want anything myself. Wives did that, didn't they? I sheered away from thinking I was behaving like the sort of wife I despised and never would become, and assured myself I was indulging him out of love, not any imagined duty.

There were plenty of other examples, all of them trivial, of habits which grated and had to be adapted to. I liked silence, he liked the radio on as a kind of background at various times of the day; he liked to sleep in a room with curtains tightly closed, I liked them open. There were so many ridiculous, minor clashes, all of which had to be resolved before we were really living, as well as loving, together harmoniously. Many a woman only discovers the things that irritate after she's become a wife and is dismayed to find she must endure them or she won't be considered a good wife – she'll be labelled a shrew, endlessly nagging her husband to change his ways. The smaller the aggravation, the more maddening it can become and the harder to accept or escape. Mostly, it is unreasonable for a wife to want to change how her husband does things, because, by the very nature of the kind of habits which are annoying, they are harmless, but it is surely best to know about them before marriage. A whole new lot will emerge over the years, and a pattern of merely putting up with them is a bad one. These minuscule bits of grit can jam the works and bring the whole machine of marriage to a halt far more insidiously than the grand betrayal of an affair. The wise wife, never mind the good one, knows what she is getting into.

Jennie Lee didn't share a bedroom with her husband for many years of their marriage and never for one moment seemed to think (as Nye's family thought) that this called into question what kind of wife she was. She said she was a lark and he was an owl and they needed separate rooms so as not to disturb each other. Fanny Stevenson's rationale for having her own bedroom was that she liked different colours from her husband. Whatever the true reasons, and neither of these explanations strikes me as telling the whole story, both women eventually claimed their own territory at night. I don't think either of the men liked it. Louis wrote that he never slept well without Fanny at his side (though that was early in their marriage) and Jennie reported Nye as trying to induce her to come back and share his room (though that was when he was very ill).

Does a good wife have a duty to share her husband's bed and bedroom? Of course not. Whether she has the choice or not has always been to do with space, and that in turn has to do with wealth. From the Queen downwards, those who inhabit homes with a vast number of rooms invariably have their own bedrooms, sometimes adjoining their husbands', sometimes not. It is lower down the social scale, particularly today when few new houses have a great many bedrooms, that it is the norm for wife and husband to share both room and bed. The Bevans were bound to be shocked that Nye and Jennie did not, coming as they did from homes where there was no choice. They saw something significant in the sleeping arrangements and perhaps they were right. For married couples to choose to have separate bedrooms may indeed signal a break in intimacy, though not necessarily of the sexual sort – perfectly possible to argue that this kind of distancing could theoretically enhance that side of married life. It is a different kind of intimacy which is surely being rejected or grown tired of. The rituals of preparing to go to bed together, the lying side-by-side in the dark before sleep, the awareness of each other's presence wakening in the night, all breed a sort of closeness which cannot be precisely explained. It is not just the obvious physical proximity but the harder-to-prove emotional, maybe even psychic, togetherness it induces. If each is alone in a separate room, that kind of familiarity recedes. Maybe that is the object of each choosing to be in their own room for the majority of nights, maybe familiarity is the very enemy of the marriage, which a couple wishes to cast out, and it is beneficial to separate in that respect.

I can't imagine doing it, though. I like to have a room of my own to write in, I like being on my own for stretches of every day, but choosing to have my own bedroom has never appealed because of what I would lose, that very atmosphere I've tried to indicate. Sometimes, it hasn't been sensible to stay in the same bed, the same bedroom. If one of us is ill, it would be better to separate temporarily, but we never seem to have done. Perhaps if we were coping with the kind of ongoing illness Louis and Fanny had to put up with we would have been forced into it. There are no rules.

Jennie believed in protecting Nye. At one time in her marriage, she saw it as her prime function as a wife. She did this quite openly, even flamboyantly, almost glorying in her own power. Few wives are as confident in their right to do this, but a lot of less brazen protecting goes on.

The role of protector has never appealed to me. I don't want to be the-wife-as-guard-dog. The only kind of protecting I do is of the mild variety, obligingly saying he is not available when he is. Sometimes I won't even do that. He tries to get me to ask who is calling, if the phone rings and he doesn't want to answer it, before revealing his presence or not – if it's X, Y or Z, he *is* in, if it's anyone else, he isn't. But I won't. I'll agree to say an absolute no, but not to sifting the callers. But if, like Nye, he had been an important man, I suppose I would have been driven to screening calls, knowing how harassed he was and how many callers were sheer time-wasters. I've no doubt I could be as fearsome as Jenny if necessary.

He would like a protector. He is a friendly person who likes to be popular and finds it hard to say no. He'd love it if I were prepared to say no for him. The only time I can recall leaping to his defence was over an encounter with that redoubtable sitting tenant of ours. She spotted straight away that she could get round him, and used her age, her infirmities and her gender as a means of doing so. He dreaded her appearance in our part of the house, and for a while tried to get her to communicate by note. Our own landlord in Hampstead had always asked us to do this – he was shy and timid and hated personal confrontation, and we were only too willing to agree to write notes. Sometimes, ludicrously, we'd pass each other on the stairs, each leaving a note about something or other on the hall table.

Mrs Hall was having none of that. She believed in eye-to-eye contact and her eye was daunting. He quailed before her, groaning the moment he heard the creak of the stairs which heralded her approach. In spite of her diminutive size and frail look, she was formidable, with a hectoring quality to her voice which belied her appearance. She had a way of stumping into our kitchen which was curiously threatening – fragile body slightly stooped, legs moving strongly in spite of her arthritis, and feet, encased in heavy black shoes, looking as if they could aim a kick if provoked. She would rap on the kitchen door and shout, 'Mr Davies! It is your tenant. I wish to speak to you, now!' He'd invite her to sit down and then ask if she would like a cup of tea. She'd snort at the idea of tea when she'd come to complain – he was the enemy, trying to soften her up, and she was much too smart to fall for that. The force of her indignation was extraordinary, rousing herself as she did over a leaking pipe or an ill-fitting window, and always ended with 'You'll have to see to it, you're the landlord, I pay my rent to you.' He always did see to it. He would calm her down, resisting the temptation to point out that since he'd become her landlord the state of her flat had been immeasurably improved. He was so kind and nice to her, but she only complained more and more.

One day, she went too far. He'd just got home, at nearly ten o'clock one summer's evening, as she undoubtedly knew. She'd probably been watching from her window and had seen him put his car in the garage because she came thumping down the stairs a mere five minutes later before he'd had time to have anything to eat or drink. He'd had a particularly trying day, driving back from a frustrating time with John Lennon (he was writing the Beatles' biography then) who had swum up and down his pool without speaking for hours on end. The last thing he was up to was being harangued by Mrs Hall; but there she was, hammering on the door as usual and shouting his name. I was furious, so this time I opened the door myself, and before she could start said I was sorry but my husband was tired and not able to listen to her at the moment. She could either tell me what she wanted or else wait until the morning. She glared at me through her enormous spectacles and said, 'He's there. I know he's there. Mr Davies, I know you're there!' I told her I hadn't denied that he was there, that on the contrary I'd said he'd just come home and was exhausted, far too exhausted to attend to her needs. I repeated that she could tell me what the problem was or else wait until the morning. I knew it couldn't be a real emergency or she'd have made a great drama out of it, so it must be something trivial. But she wouldn't reveal what it was. For a moment, I thought she was going to push the door further open and barge into the kitchen but she obviously thought better of it – I was bigger and fitter than she and just as good at bullying if need be – and muttering to herself she went back up to her own quarters.

The next morning, he went up as promised and mended the washer on a tap. He said she was quite polite and even grateful, going so far as to hope he'd had a good night's sleep. But later that week a friend of hers came to visit and I heard what Mrs Hall said to her, as they toiled up the stairs. '*He*'s a nice young man, Maudie,' she confided, 'but her, the wife, she's a tough one, she wears the trousers and no mistake. I feel sorry for the poor fellow, I do really.' The fate of every wife-as-protector is to be portrayed as a battle-axe, as a harridan, with her husband to be pitied. It amused me to capitalise on Mrs Hall's image of me thereafter, but the little incident nicely pointed up the dangers of being that kind of 'good wife'.

The wife who protects must never be seen to do so.

It was held against Jennie, and not just by her husband's own family, that she gave Nye no children. It was her duty, wasn't it? Her decision not to have children however much Nye wanted them (and it is probably true he wanted them very much indeed) was seen as selfish, yet another example of her putting her own wishes first, another instance of her repudiating her wifely duty.

But I would defend Jennie absolutely – it was not her duty. She was not married in church and never agreed that marriage was for the procreation of children. Before ever she agreed to become Nye's wife, she made it clear that she didn't intend to become pregnant. He fully understood why, and didn't consider he had any right to overrule Jennie's wishes. She had been honest, and he accepted what this meant. To her, it all seemed quite simple and straightforward, but in general it is neither. It is one of the trickiest problems a wife who does not want children faces if her husband does want them, and can remain a running issue, never quite resolved till she is past child-bearing age.

I certainly worried about it because, like Jennie, though with nothing like her conviction, I thought I didn't want children. I had no great career they would get in the way of, but I couldn't see how I could make myself into a good mother. And apart from that, I had no maternal urge. Looking at my contemporaries, it seemed to me that most women had babies either because they had been careless or because it was the next stage in life and followed on automatically from getting married, or else because they simply longed for children. But I wasn't careless, and I didn't follow any course automatically. Since I didn't feel any real longing for children, I would have to have actual reasons for having them. I couldn't think of any. It was pure self-indulgence. I imagined a child of mine asking me, as I'd asked my mother, 'Why did you have me?' and not being able to give a reason except the one she gave ('Because I wanted children'), which I'd found so unsatisfactory.

But my husband, like Nye, wanted them. He'd always wanted them. Told I didn't, he had an irritating confidence that

I would change my mind. Maybe Nye secretly had the same confidence – Jennie would come round to the idea and he needn't fret about it. But on the other hand, he knew her very well and knew how dedicated she was to her work, so he can't have counted on such a change of heart. The vital thing was, it didn't matter. He loved her, and never saw her as a mere vehicle to carry and bear his offspring.

Three years after we were married, we stood outside the house we'd bought, looking up at it, and Hunter talked in a sentimental fashion about its being a real family house. He said, 'I'd like a little face at every window.' I counted the windows. Five. No chance. But by that time it was true that I had indeed begun to have second thoughts. It was very strange, the discovery that I could experience this odd physical sensation of suddenly craving a baby. I resisted it. I still had no reasons, other than the body's demands and the pleading of emotions. There was the awful temptation to give into them. Instead of 'why?' it became 'why not?' Duty didn't come into it. It had always worried me that in not having children I would be thwarting his great desire to father them, which would be unfair and wrong, and I'd imagined I would have to struggle with my conscience, and maybe I'd lose the struggle. I watched him, as Jennie watched Nye, playing with other people's children, and saw how he loved them and how they loved him and what a wonderful father he would make. If I hadn't then felt that famous maternal urge myself, I might have given in to his need. Otherwise, however much my mind stoutly defended my own right to remain childless, I would have felt guilty, unlike Jennie who never felt guilty about anything.

Not so very long ago, when all women were married in church, they promised, in effect, to breed. It was the very fear of becoming pregnant that led so many of them into becoming wives when what they really wanted, in the short term at least, was to be lovers. But once women acquired the means of avoiding pregnancy, as Jennie did, they didn't need to become wives for that reason alone. They were enlightened. Outside the Church, marriage need not be primarily for the procreation of children. And yet there lingers on the attitude the Bevan family had towards Nye's childless wife – people do still think it *is* a wife's duty to bear a husband's children. They think less of her as a wife, less of her as a woman, if she refuses to. The rising numbers of women who do refuse mystify people; even today they are seen as denying their own natures. Fifty years ago, Jennie Lee chose what *she* wanted. She wanted to be his wife, not some kind of battery hen.

Jennie shocked herself in that letter she wrote but never sent, in which she came to the reluctant conclusion that in the event of a crisis it was the wife's place, the woman's place not the man's, to give up her work to relieve the stress of the marriage. To suggest this went against everything she had always believed, it turned upside-down her personal creed. She was depressed when she wrote the letter, and she certainly never acted upon it by giving up her own work, but nevertheless the fact that she could think the unthinkable was heresy. It showed that even she had encountered the same problems as other, more conventional wives and had found no way round them. If a wife knows her husband's job is more 'important' than her own, should she give up her work in order to make both their lives easier and their marriage more serene?

Jennie knew the answer in theory: a resounding no. But in practice she had been compelled for a while to contemplate the inevitable. In her case it never happened, but it was a close-run thing. Sacrifice was very nearly called for, and she was obliged in her darkest moments to think of casting herself in the role of wife-as-martyr, one for which she could not have been less suited. Nothing must get in the way of Nye's leading the Labour Party one day and by giving up her work in order that her energy might further this, she felt she would be doing a far, far better thing than she had ever done. It was horribly tempting, just for a short time, to see self-fulfilment in the suppression of her own ambitions to secure his. She didn't succumb to the temptation, but if she had done, doubtless she would have been thought a very good wife indeed.

Translated into the language of the average marriage, this kind of thinking still goes on. As ever, there are good old economic reasons for it (though they are beginning to change): the husband's work is more important because he earns the money to support the family. In thousands of marriages, where the wife is said not to *work* because she stays at home and looks after children and house, it is as simple as that. It was in mine. He was the one for years and years with the 'real' job, the one bringing in a regular salary. My work, writing, brought in very little for almost twenty years, not even enough to buy our food never mind pay bills. It seemed entirely proper that when things were tough my work should go on hold and that he should be protected from whatever circumstances were making them tough. Babies screaming all night, mostly. He never once got up to attend to them and I never once expected him to. He had to go to work. If he was to do his job, he had to have a good night's sleep. There was no argument about it, and I felt no resentment. But I often wished I was the one whose work mattered enough for me to get that night's sleep.

Things changed when the children were older and he himself had become a freelance journalist and was also at home writing books, but they didn't change enough. He used his work as a shield to protect him against any disruption or crisis. 'I have to go and work now,' he was given to announcing loudly, at crucial moments. Somehow I never said it. Partly this was because writing had never seemed as important to me as the children, but also – and this was irrational – it was because I couldn't rid myself of the belief that what he was doing was more serious. He was still, to me, the breadwinner, even though I was by then winning a good share of the bread. It was stupid, but I felt my real job was bringing up the children and writing was an extra. He never felt that. Wives dealt with everything domestic, including managing the children.

The children have long since gone, and we both have as much time as we want to work, to write. Has that made us equal? Unfortunately not. His work still *seems* more important than mine, simply because it is a more important part of his life. He can't set it aside the way I can, and do. I know perfectly well that if we had been in a situation where we both had jobs outside the house and there had been the need for one of us to give up work in order to be at home when, say, a child was ill, it would have been me. But it wouldn't have been because I was the wife, or because it was the woman's role, but because I wouldn't have been able to choose work over family. My head would have said this attitude was ridiculous, and that I should do it, but I wouldn't have listened. If I couldn't organise my work so that it could run side by side with looking after my family, without exhausting myself, there would be no contest. I am not proud of this. It is not right or rational. But in this respect, I am feeble. I would have given in at the first clash between the needs of the family and my own need to work. As it is, I haven't had to. I am profoundly grateful that my sort of work has never demanded a straight choice from me. The strain on wives from whom it has been demanded fills me with alarm. Jennie's opinion (if never put to the real test) that the woman should give up her work to keep the marriage running smoothly, in the event of unbearable pressure of work for both husband and wife, is not one that, rationally, I share.

It is just that for me it has been easier.

Jennie hated to be called Mrs Bevan. I dislike being called Mrs Davies. She kept her own name because she had a separate and well-established public identity before she married. I didn't have any such thing, but I never for one moment thought of calling myself Margaret Davies when I had a book published. Who was she? Not anyone I recognised. Davies seems to me a dull name anyway, whereas Forster is Cumbrian, with a strong, regional pull to it. I like having two names, reflecting two distinct roles. Forster is the writer, Davies is the wife and mother, and I can choose which to be.

I don't like being referred to as 'my wife' and I don't like saying 'my husband'. Even after forty years, these terms sound awkward and quaint to me, somehow pompous. He likes saying 'my wife' – possessiveness, again? I try hard never to refer to him as 'my husband', even when it is absurd and confusing not to do so. 'This is Hunter' says very little. It is silly of me to avoid using the correct and useful term. On the other hand, the term 'partner' seems to me equally confusing. Partner in what? Business, crime? Whenever I hear it, I think of American westerns – 'How do, pardner' – and it sounds hilarious. 'Friend' is coy, 'lover' flash. And yet some accurate, descriptive word is needed.

'Wife' is accurate, 'wife' is descriptive, though not descriptive enough. But recast the mould of 'wife' and it would be perfect. A wife is no longer what she once was. She is a much stronger creature, not at all submissive, able to match her husband right for right.

Epilogue

To study the form of Solemnisation of Matrimony in the original Anglican prayer-book, according to which Mary Livingstone was married (and many women still are), is to be startled by the emphatic way in which it expects a woman to agree to such sweeping subjection to the will of a man. It is a truly terrifying step to become a wife. Even leaving aside the promise to 'obey and serve', the language of the other promises, of the psalms and of the prayers, makes it painfully clear that this is no partnership being legitimised but an act of domination sanctified by the Church. It appears designed not just to impress but to alarm and create an atmosphere of tension. Even if the banns have gone unchallenged, there is still that last ringing inquiry at the beginning of the service itself – 'Therefore if any man can shew any just cause, why they may not be lawfully joined together, let him now speak, or else hereafter for ever hold his peace.' Followed by that awful pause, lasting no more than a minute, a minute of rustling and discreet coughing, but a minute of rising panic – what if someone did shout 'Stop this marriage!'? The imagination could run away with itself, aided and abetted by such dramatic pauses.

Then there are the ponderous, introductory words of the priest to consider. Holy matrimony, it is alleged, is not a simple matter of a man and a woman coming together but 'instituted of God in the time of man's innocence, signifying unto us the mystical union that is betwixt Christ and his Church'. The man, this implies, is the Christ figure, the woman the Church, a confusing and difficult metaphor. Progressing, as the priest is instructed to, to the 'causes for which matrimony was ordained', is to find most of them tough on the woman. First, the procreation of children, 'to be brought up in the fear and nurture of the Lord'; second, as 'a remedy against sin, and to avoid fornication'; third, 'for mutual society, help and comfort'. Marriage is for those 'as have not the gift of continency', a wife is merely to be a handy way of making incontinency respectable. The suggested prayers hold little comfort. Once more, the woman is told to be 'loving and amiable, faithful and obedient to her husband; and in all quietness, sobriety and peace to be a follower of holy and godly matrons.'

As a contract, it is binding until death with absolutely no room for manoeuvre. Of course, women like Mary Livingstone did not and do not see marriage as a social contract, but as a union blessed by God, subject to God's law. But regarded as a contract the Anglican Solemnisation of Matrimony is vague in the extreme, enough to keep lawyers arguing for centuries about its implications if they wished (or dared). It was a clever but legally shoddy piece of work.

Contrast it with the civil ceremony, first instituted in this country in 1837. No banns had to be called, though notice of a marriage had to be given well in advance to a superintendent registrar. The room in which the short ceremony took place was invariably office-like, the atmosphere formal and quite unlike that of a church. The superintendent, however hard he tried to introduce a note of solemnity and dignity, could not hope to match the magnificence of the priest in his vestments. There was no music, no prayers, no hymns, no psalms. Someone might put a bunch of flowers on a table but otherwise there was no adornment of the premises. Numbers of guests allowed in were restricted. There was no attempt made to overawe with procedure, though the registrar was required to preface the ceremony with a reminder of the binding nature of marriage. But the words of the simple declaration both man and woman had to make were not intimidating – no mention of death, fornication or subjection. All that had to be said was 'I do solemnly declare that I know not of any lawful impediment why I [name] may not be joined in matrimony to [name]', followed by 'I call upon these persons here present to witness that I do take thee to be my lawful wedded [wife/husband]'. The words are identical for man and woman. Rings could then be exchanged but they were not obligatory, and there was no blessing of them if they were. An entry was made in the register, signed, and a certificate made out.

That was it, over in ten minutes. As a contract, it was even vaguer than the religious version, with nothing specific promised, no mention of duties, and nothing to scare the most nervous of wives-to-be. And so it stands today, with only (since 1997) a marginally different wording to the declaration, a matter of substituting 'no legal reason' for 'just impediment', making the wording even simpler and clearer than it already was. Meanwhile the Solemnisation of Matrimony in church has also moved with the times. *Common Worship: Pastoral Services*, published in 2000, follows the example of the 1980 *Alternative Prayer Book* in that it emphasises that marriage is meant to be full of 'joy', 'tenderness' and 'delight'. The vows to be made by bride and bridegroom are now exactly the same, and they may, if they wish, enter the church together, dispensing with any 'giving away' of the bride. Marriage, in the pastoral introduction to be read before the service begins, is described as a 'creative relationship', bringing husband and wife together 'in the delight and tenderness of sexual union'. It is also claimed marriage 'enriches society and strengthens the community' – bold and unsubstantiated claims indeed, but preferable to the language of intimidation used in the old, traditional service.

But the pomp goes on, and the church is still the place for it, with that long walk down the aisle and the sonorous organ music and the priest in his vestments, making the whole affair into a kind of theatre. The Church encourages it because the dressing up, the parading, the grand staging of the event emphasises the seriousness of what is taking place – getting married is a Big Thing, especially for the woman, who remains the centre of attention. When the ceremony is conducted elsewhere, in all the many other locations now possible (since 1995 'Approved Premises' are allowed), there is not quite the same reverent atmosphere (though mostly because 'reverence' is precisely what is no longer wanted by some couples). The

Church still has the advantage, and uses it. Couples who have never darkened a church door in their lives and have no religious faith whatsoever, regularly get married in church with the vicar quite happy to let them (and a contribution to church funds would be welcome).

But others scorn the glitter. The register office wedding will do for them. My son and daughter-in-law chose to be married in a register office. The ceremony itself was short – ten minutes – but certainly not lacking in atmosphere, the woman registrar conducting it with dignity and surprising warmth. But what happened afterwards was an indication of how, in modern times, couples not wishing to marry in church have nevertheless felt the need to capture in other ways the sense of occasion the church service gives and which the register office ceremony cannot emulate. Family and friends went from Islington Town Hall to a warehouse in Docklands, lately converted into the film studios where Rosa (my daughter-in-law) worked. There, there was another little ceremony, involving poetry recitations and singing, in a magnificently decorated hall. The banquet that followed echoed the traditional wedding breakfast and yet was much more informal and party-like. This huge, lavish celebration was what my son and his wife had wanted – they were eager to commit themselves to each other in front of all the people they cared about and who cared about them. No sneaking off as we had done. It seemed to be important to them, as it still is to so many couples, to make a public declaration of their intent.

But the question remains for me: why do women get married today? Why do they still go through these rituals, however basic they have become, which turn a woman into a wife? I know why Mary Livingstone did, I know why Fanny Stevenson did, I know why Jennie Lee grudgingly did, and I know why I myself did. We all had our very different reasons, but the reasons why women today are still prepared, even eager, to become wives are much harder for me to identify and understand. Some of the old reasons still obtain. For those who have a religious faith, of whatever kind, marriage is essential and remains a blessing. There are undoubtedly still those who marry for economic reasons, to achieve what they think of as security; there may well be those who feel marriage bestows upon them a respectability otherwise lacking, ensuring a status they see as valuable whatever the evidence to the contrary; and there are almost certainly many more who become wives without much pondering over what the role means, who regard it as a rite of passage. But that still must surely leave many of the 131,757 women who married in 1999 subscribing to none of these reasons, those who don't need security (they have their own, thank you) or respectability (an old-fashioned notion) and who will have thought about it deeply, refusing to marry just because it seems the thing to do. So why do these independent, intelligent, strong-minded women agree to become wives? What do they still see in the role that attracts them when for decades now feminist theory has depicted it as very nearly a fate worse than death?

Once, the feminists were right. To marry was indeed a trap for women, one in which they would suffer and lose their independence in a life of unremitting subjection to their husbands. In 1869, seven years after that most submissive of wives, Mary Livingstone, died, Louisa May Alcott published *Good Wives*, making it very plain what a 'good' wife still was. Meg, first of the 'Little Women' to marry 'began her married life with the determination to be a model housekeeper.' Well, of course she did, it was a major requirement in a good wife. A model housekeeper, a devoted mother, a perfect hostess – that was Meg, and millions of others. Then she has twins and – oh, wicked Meg! – begins to neglect her husband. She is no longer a good wife at all and her own mother severely reprimands her, telling her 'You have . . . made the mistake . . . forgotten your duty to your husband in your love for your children.' Duty to husband must always come first. And for Meg it does, harmony is restored, husband is happy (he even helps with the twins). All this from an author who never herself married, declaring 'I'd rather be a free spinster and paddle my own canoe.'

Can a woman today be a free wife and still paddle her own canoe? Is it not safer, for her independence, to be a partner, however inadequate and confusing the title? The woman who prefers to be a partner rather than a wife simply sees no point whatsoever in marriage. Her view is that not only is it unnecessary but that it is still a trap, one in which she does not wish to be caught. Her understanding, then, seems to be that partnership equals freedom, marriage restriction of one sort or another. But what does this freedom consist of? What does a partner make of it that, as a wife, she could not? The freedom to leave the partnership without the trouble and expense of a divorce? True, that is a freedom, if a rather negative one. But more important than wanting to believe herself free is the partner's pride and confidence that she does not *need* to become a wife in order to signify her commitment to the partnership she has entered into. The implication is that only the feeble, the insecure, those who want to be seen as having 'caught' their man, need to marry. Partners are above such ploys. If they want legal safeguards, to protect their independence which they rightly value so highly, they make their own contracts. They make sure their name is on mortgage agreements and that they share equally in all that is possessed by the partnership. Marriage would do this but it would also enclose them and, by being such a vague contract, commit them in a general way which might prove disadvantageous. So the sensible female partner keeps her freedom and by being very particular in her contracts ensures her standing is absolutely equal to the male partner's.

But many female partners are not so sensible. They are not sensible at all. They make no contracts, agree to no legally binding arrangements. Trust is all, and when trust turns out to have been misplaced, they are the ones who suffer most. But on the other hand, they can break the trust themselves without being held to any obligations, as they would if married. Perhaps this is what is attractive, the very fluidity of a partnership in which no contracts have been agreed to. There are no figures for the break-up of partnerships of this sort whereas there are plenty for the break-up of marriages, giving it a bad press: just under 145,000 in 1999. Would some of those wives going through divorces have preferred to be partners? No stigma, no public admission of failure, in leaving a partnership. Yet still in 1999, 131,757 women chose to become wives, and this after forty-odd years of modern feminism during which it has been pointed out again and again that to become a wife is to doom oneself to become the extension of a man's ego. Marriage has been represented as a form of financial feudalism, with self-sacrifice as its leitmotif, in which the wife is forced into a tough, twenty-four-hour a day job still often endured within the loneliness of the domestic environment. Nothing has been said recently about either the pleasures or the advantages of becoming a wife.

The solid, practical advantages of marriage are in any case difficult to identify. A couple about to marry, whether in a church or a register office, are not informed of their rights in law once they are married. This seems surprising – wouldn't a pamphlet, listing such rights, be a good idea? – until it is realised that it is only when a marriage *breaks down* that laws come into operation. The only real advantage of marrying is that it keeps things simple. Everything is automatically assumed to be shared. But even that is no great advantage when today a woman can be considered a common law wife within such a remarkably short time (anything over a year of having been seen to live in a partnership) and enjoy the same benefits.

But marriage is no longer so important for economic and financial reasons. It seems instead to be more about emotional commitment than it ever was and within that framework a woman can make the role of wife what she wishes.

So, what does she wish? That will vary from wife to wife, but high up on any list of hopes will be those for mutual love, mutual respect, mutual caring for each other, all within the framework of a public commitment. 'Public' is perhaps the key word. Why should a woman care about going public? Why does she still want to stand in front of family and friends and vow loyalty to another person before a priest or registrar? Is it simply a form of showing off, or of giving way to the demands of society? Why doesn't a woman commit herself quietly and privately, as a partner presumably does? The private commitment comes before the public one. The public bit is an extra, yet it is this extra which still attracts – the desire to be *seen* to have committed oneself, and to have this union registered legally, emerges as surprisingly strong. Women who would never have considered becoming a wife a hundred years ago, because of what it meant sacrificing, are now at liberty to cast the role into whatever shape they like. And they do. Like Jennie Lee, they reject the old forms of servitude and express themselves entirely differently with the full approval of their partners. Becoming a wife isn't a humiliating business but a way of wanting the world to know with whom you are happy to be associated and to whom you have committed yourself for the future.

Nevertheless, I am bound to admit, in spite of believing this to be true, and in spite of being a happy wife for more than forty years, that in today's climate I would have chosen to be a partner (assuming that I had no parents whom it would hurt). I would have been one of the 'why get married?' young women rather than the 'why not?' I would probably have laughed at those who wanted to do something as conventional as getting married – far smarter, far more adventurous, far more *independent* to be a partner and not give a damn about pieces of paper like marriage certificates. I can just see myself, glorying in my own imagined daring. But once I'd felt that longing for children, I think I would have weakened – 'why get married?' would have been answered with several persuasive reasons. I would have felt – and do feel – that marriage safeguards their interests better. Logically, I can see that this need not necessarily be so but logic would have been laid aside. It would have been instinctive for me to want to provide what at least looked like a more solid social framework in which to bring up children. It would have been the children, not the man, who would have persuaded me to become a wife.

But I did become one, of course, before ever children were thought of. My head was still full of misguided notions of what being a wife might mean but I found myself not at all in the Mary Livingstone mould. Even forty years ago there was nothing subservient about the role. Any submission on my part was voluntary, even willing, and it did not make a martyr of me. The cut and thrust of married life has seen me having to learn when to give way but never at any time have I had a sense of defeat. I feel I've retained absolutely my own individuality. What may have looked to others like allowing myself to put my husband's interests before my own, to my own detriment, hasn't looked like that to me – I've always seen what I was doing and chosen to do it. And unlike Fanny Stevenson, I have been able to earn my own living for a large proportion of that time. I am a wife in the Jennie Lee mould, if with significant variations. There has been no stigma about the word 'wife' for me, as there was at first for her. It has lost the taint it came to have in the last quarter of the nineteenth century, when it was associated with overwhelming self-sacrifice by the early feminists, and again in the third quarter of the last century, when it was equated with a loss of independence. Then, it came near to becoming a term of abuse, signifying a woman who relied for her identity on a man, but it has been rescued from that fate by a new breed of wives who have not only triumphantly related their own identity but gone on to give marriage a new identity too.

The marriage and partnership research organisation One Plus One estimates that, if present trends continue, by 2021 married people will be in the minority – 45 per cent of the total population, the lowest figure since 1851. The number of co-habitants, they estimate, will have doubled. But even if it comes to appeal only to a minority, marriage, in its new and freer form, will endure. I think many women will still be happy to be wives after an apprenticeship as partners.

Recently, the American feminist Gloria Steinem (founder of the magazine *MS* and of the National Women's Political Caucus), who once declared that marriage made a woman half a person, got married. She was sixty-six. Quite an apprentice-ship, then. She issued a statement saying: 'Though I have worked many years to make marriage more equal, I never expected to take advantage of it myself.' So where, for her, lay this advantage? She didn't need a husband for status, having plenty of her own already, and she didn't need one for income. Children, because of her age, didn't need to be considered. It makes it very difficult, but also very interesting, to identify any 'advantage' to her in marrying. She went on to say: 'I hope this proves what feminists have always said – that feminism is about the ability to choose what's right at each time in our lives.'

Suddenly, marriage was 'right' for her, and no longer, it seems, capable of making her into half a person. Was it she herself who had changed, or the institutions she once felt threatened by? Marriage was surely now 'right' because so many elements within it that had been wrong were corrected. A wife is no longer a chattel, no longer expected to be submissive. The role of wife goes on being redefined and in time, as marriage is constantly redesigned to meet new demands, it may even come to be seen as being as attractive as it once was, though for entirely different reasons.

Source Notes and Bibliography

SOURCE NOTES

Prologue

p. 7, l. 20 – Statistics have been supplied by the Office for National Statistics. They are for 1999 because those for 2000, at the time of writing, are as yet only estimates. Even the fixed figures cannot be absolutely accurate because so many couples now get married abroad and are not obliged to register their marriages when they return to the United Kingdom.

Mary Livingstone

Few of Mary Livingstone's letters have survived but I have consulted all those held by the National Library of Scotland, the National Archives of Zimbabwe, and the School of Oriental and African Studies (University of London). David Livingstone's own letters naturally contain much information about his wife and I have used those relevant to her. The source of any direct quotation is listed. Particularly useful for details of Mary's background and domestic life have been two books: Mora Dickson, *Beloved Partner: Mary Moffat of Kuruman* and Janet Wagner Parsons, *The Livingstones at Kolobeng 1847–1852*. Information on Mary's schooling was supplied by Howard Kilby (Department of Archives, Methodist Church of Southern Africa).

I

p. 16, l. 18 – 'a missionary ... an oar': Robert Moffat (RM) to his father, April 1819, John Smith Moffat, *The Lives of Robert and Mary Moffat.*

l. 28 – 'you know . . . solitude': Mary Moffat (MM) to RM, 28 July 1824, Moffat, *Lives.*

p. 18, l. 11 – 'keeping . . . improper': MM to Miss Lees, 15 September 1830, Moffat, *Lives.*

p. 20, ll. 16, 17 – 'she bore . . . dangerous passage': MM to RM, 2 May 1836, Moffat, *Lives.*

p. 21, l. 4 – 'everywhere . . . plant': MM to R. Hamilton, 25 November 1840, Moffat, *Lives.*

p. 22, l. 18 – 'foolish . . . conundrums': David Livingstone (DL) to Mrs Sewell, 7 April 1842, National Library of Scotland, MS 10775.

l. 30 – 'for the happiness . . . roof': DL to Mrs Sewell, 3 August 1840, National Library of Scotland, MS 10780.

p. 23, l. 17 – 'a good stock . . . philosophy': DL to Benjamin Pyne, 22 June 1843, London Missionary Society (LMS), Africa Odds, Box 14 (School of African and Oriental Studies [SOAS], University of London).

l. 26 – 'with respect . . . in Africa': DL to D. G. Watt, 7 July 1841, LMS, Africa Odds, Box 3 (SOAS).

l. 34 – 'My friends . . . experiment': DL to B. Pyne, 22 June 1843, LMS, Africa Odds, Box 1 (SOAS).

p. 24, l. 2 – 'miserably . . . ladies': DL to D. G. Watt, 23 September 1841, LMS, Africa Odds, Box 3 (SOAS).

l. 6 – 'not the thing . . . saucy': DL to B. Pyne, 22 December 1841, LMS, Africa Odds, Box 1 (SOAS).

p. 25, l. 2 – 'criminal . . . congress': I. Schapera (ed.), *Livingstone's Private Journals 1851–53.*

p. 26, l. 7 – 'a matter of fact . . . I want': DL to D. G. Watt, 2 April 1845, LMS, Africa Odds, Box 3 (SOAS).

p. 27, l. 5 – 'Mr Livingstone's . . . event': RM to Dr Philip, January 1845, LMS Archives.

II

p. 28, l. 7 – 'The woman . . . connection': DL to D. G. Watt, 23 May 1845, LMS, Africa Odds, Box 2 (SOAS).

l. 11 – 'abundantly . . . bachelor': DL to Mrs Sewell, 19 April 1851, National Library of Scotland.

p. 33, l. 11 – 'Our visit . . . there, too': DL to Mrs Sewell, 20 September 1847, National Library of Scotland.

l. 21 – 'Chonwane . . . beginning': DL to Mrs Sewell, 20 September 1847, National Library of Scotland.

p. 37, l. 5 – 'respectable . . . will do': DL to H. Drummond, 19 June 1848, LMS, Africa Odds, Box 2 (SOAS).

p. 39, l. 19 – 'My poor . . . again': DL to his brother Charles Livingstone, 16 May 1849, I. Schapera (ed.), *David Livingstone: Family Letters 1841–56*, vol. ii.

p. 44, l. 24 – 'I must . . . field': quoted by MM to DL, Schapera (ed.), *Livingstone's Private Journals* [the letter itself did not survive].

p. 45, l. 1 – 'My dear Livingstone . . . perturbation': MM to DL, Schapera (ed.), *Livingstone's Private Journals*; DL quotes her letter, September 1851.

p. 47, l. 22 – 'Mary . . . illness': DL to parents, February 1851, Schapera (ed.), *Family Letters*, vol. ii.

III

p. 50, l. 23 – 'A very good . . . ladies': DL to RM, 22 January 1852, Schapera (ed.), *Family Letters*, vol. ii.
l. 29 – 'How I miss . . . you better': DL to ML, 5 May 1852, Schapera (ed.), *Family Letters*, vol. ii.
l. 35 – 'I should feel . . . disease': DL to Tidman (T), April 1852, LMS, Africa Odds, Box 14 (SOAS).

p. 52, l. 1 – 'after our . . . changed person': Neil Livingstone (NL) to T, 24 June 1853.
l. 14 – 'we feel anxious . . . much': NL to T, 25 June 1853, LMS, Africa Odds, Box 2 (SOAS).

p. 54, l. 1 – 'as you so kindly . . . expenses': ML to T, November 1853, LMS, Wooden Box [the same reference applies to all ML letters to T].

p. 55, l. 7 – 'each has . . . hand': DL to ML, 20 March 1855, Schapera (ed.), *Family Letters*, vol. ii.
l. 38 – 'I have asked . . . country': ML to T, 12 January 1854, LMS, Wooden Box.

p. 57, poem – quoted by W. G. Blaikie in *The Personal Life of David Livingstone* (1880).

IV

p. 66, l. 8 – 'she and the young 'un . . . expedition': R. Foskett (ed.), *The Zambesi Journal and Letters of Dr John Kirk 1858–63*, 2 vols. [The same source applies in all quotes of Kirk's.]
l. 30 – 'this is a great trial . . . hindrance': J. P. R. Wallis (ed.), *The Zambesi Expedition of David Livingstone, 1858–1863*.

p. 67, l. 26 – 'It was a bitter . . . out of one': DL to James Young, 1 May 1858, G. Seaver, *David Livingstone: His Life and Letters*.

p. 67, l. 39 – 'surely we shall be drowned': Emily Moffat to her father, J. P. R. Wallis (ed.), *The Matabele Mission: A Selection from the*

Correspondence of John and Emily Moffat, David Livingstone and others 1858–1878. [All Emily Moffat quotes come from this source.]

p. 73, l. 13 – 'only with . . . so much': ML to Mrs Fitch, 20 August 1831, National Library of Scotland.

l. 21 – 'I received . . . orders have come': ML to Mrs Fitch, 13 July 1861, National Archives of Zimbabwe.

p. 74, l. 24 – 'some of them . . . worse': O. Chadwick, *Mackenzie's Grave.*

p. 77, l. 4 – 'a motherly . . . déshabille': W. C. Devereux, *A Cruise in the Gorgon.* [All Devereux quotes come from this source.]

V

p. 85, l. 16 – 'proving to be . . . child': Chadwick, *Mackenzie's Grave.*

p. 87, l. 27 – 'My dearie . . . Jesus?': Schapera (ed.), *Livingstone's Journal.*

p. 88, l. 36 – 'With a sore . . . so and so': DL to MM, 29 April 1862, National Library of Scotland.

p. 89, l. 14 – 'At Kolobeng . . . was she': DL to Lady Murchison, Schapera (ed.), *Family Letters*, vol. ii.

l. 34 – 'It is the first . . . the more': Blaikie, *Personal Life of David Livingstone.*

p. 91, l. 12 – 'as much pleasure . . . wife' – DL to Mrs Robinson, 24 October 1862, LMS, Africa Odds, Box 2 (SOAS).

Fanny Stevenson

Fanny's daughter Belle wrote a memoir of her mother (Isobel Osbourne Strong, *This Life I Have Loved*) and so did her sister Nellie (Nellie Van de Grift Sanchez, *The Life of Mrs Robert Louis Stevenson*). These two volumes provide much material, particularly on Fanny's early life, and so do two biographies of her: Margaret MacKay, *The Violent Friend: The Story of Mrs Robert Louis Stevenson*; and Alexandra Lapierre, *Fanny Stevenson: A Romance of Destiny* [though this one is heavily fictionalised]. But by far the most important source for knowledge of Fanny after she married Robert Louis Stevenson (RLS), apart from her own diary (*The Cruise of the 'Janet Nichol' among the South Sea Islands*) and the account she wrote with RLS of 'Our Samoan Adventure', is Bradford A. Booth and Ernest Mehew (eds), *The Letters of Robert Louis Stevenson*, 8 vols. Many letters written by Fanny herself are included, mostly as part of letters written by RLS himself, but also as footnotes to the main text. These often show her in a new and sympathetic light.

I

p. 119, l. 37 – 'When in . . . assistance': Belle, quoted in Margaret Mackay, *The Violent Friend*.

p. 123, l. 9 – 'only . . . of you': RLS to Mrs Sitwell, Booth and Mehew (eds), *Letters*, vol. 1, 26 January 1873.

l. 14 – 'a good . . . move': RLS to Mrs Sitwell, *Letters*, vol. 1, 7 January 1876.

l. 20 – 'I was greatly . . . ladies': RLS to Mrs Sitwell, *Letters*, vol. 2, 7 December 1873.

p. 124, l. 28 – 'Life is . . . heart': RLS to Mrs Sitwell, *Letters*, vol. 2, November 1876.

l. 31 – 'I am . . . love': RLS to Chas Baxter (CB), *Letters*, vol. 2, November 1876.

l. 36 – 'love . . . marriage': RLS to CB, *Letters*, vol. 2, April 1877.

p. 126, l. 6 – 'the solemn . . . kitten': Fanny Stevenson (FS) to T. Rearden, *Letters*, vol. 2, 27 November 1877.

l. 16 – 'I want . . . badly': RLS to S. Colvin, *Letters*, vol. 2, 1 January 1878.

l. 19 – 'We have . . . month': RLS to Mrs Sitwell, *Letters*, February 1878.

II

p. 129, l. 8 – 'true cause . . . come': RLS to Colvin, *Letters*, vol. 2, April 1879.

p. 130, l. 24 – 'perhaps . . . delicate': RLS to Colvin, *Letters*, vol. 2, March 1879.

p. 131, l. 22 – 'the impersonation . . .': RLS to Gosse, *Letters*, vol. 2, July 1879.

l. 25 – 'Hold tight . . .': quoted in Lapierre, *Romance of Destiny*.

l. 28 – 'Fanny seems . . .': RLS to Bob Stevenson, *Letters*, vol. 3, August 1879.

l. 34 – 'I hoped . . . up': Henley to Baxter, *Letters*, vol. 3, 16 August 1879.

p. 132, l. 35 – 'The effect . . . out': RLS to Baxter, *Letters*, vol. 3, October 1879.

p. 133, l. 15 – 'I won't . . .': RLS to Henley, *Letters*, vol. 3, November 1879.

p. 134, l. 20 – 'few people . . . mine will be': RLS to Gosse, *Letters*, vol. 3, January 1880.

p. 136, l. 20 – 'I do try . . .': FS to Margaret Stevenson (MS) [joint letter with RLS], *Letters*, vol. 3, July 1880.

l. 34 – 'I don't care . . .': MS to FS [footnote, p. 89], *Letters*, vol. 3.

p. 137, l. 4 – 'They are . . . otherwise' – RLS to Jacob Van de Grift, *Letters*, vol. 3, July 1880.

p. 138, l. 11 – 'his mother . . . dolls': FS to Dora Williams [joint letter with RLS], *Letters*, vol. 3, October 1880.

p. 140, l. 16 – 'A couple of Babes . . .': Henley to Baxter, *Letters*, vol. 3, May 1881.

p. 141, l. 17 – 'this fat . . .': RLS to Belle, *Letters*, vol. 3, November 1880.

l. 26 – 'The word OBESITY . . .': RLS to parents, *Letters*, vol. 3, November 1880.

III

p. 144, l. 16 – 'be brought . . . foolish': FS to Henley [joint letter with RLS], *Letters*, vol. 3, July 1881.

l. 36 – 'the pert . . . rewritten': RLS to Henley, *Letters*, vol. 3, February 1881.

p. 145, l. 35 – 'I am not fit . . .': RLS to MS, *Letters*, vol. 3, December 1881.

p. 146, l. 7 – 'I am eaten . . .': RLS to Henley, *Letters*, vol. 3, April 1882.

p. 148, l. 27 – 'And I *don't want* . . . for you': FS to Dora Williams [footnote, p. 153], *Letters*, vol. 3, February 1887.

p. 151, l. 15 – 'so beautiful . . . world': RLS to MS, *Letters*, vol. 5, October 1885.

l. 32 – 'We have had . . . bad one': RLS to Thomas Stevenson, *Letters*, vol. 5, October 1885.

p. 152, l. 12 – 'It is the mark . . .': RLS to Henley, *Letters*, vol. 5, 1885/86).

p. 153, l. 32 – 'Do for God's . . .': RLS to FS, *Letters*, vol. 5, October 1885.

p. 155, l. 17 – 'being pinched . . .': RLS to Anne Jenkin, *Letters*, vol. 5, September 1886.

l. 24 – 'I have remorse . . .': RLS to FS, *Letters*, vol. 5, September 1886.

p. 156, l. 15 – 'I do not love . . .': RLS to Anne Jenkin, *Letters*, vol. 5, April 1887.

p. 157, l. 13 – 'if you won't . . .': RLS to MS, *Letters*, vol. 5, June 1887.
l. 17 – 'I could not . . .': FS to MS, *Letters*, vol. 5, June 1887.

IV

p. 158, l. 14 – 'a hardy mariner . . .': MS to her sister. [All quotes from MS's letters are taken from MS, *From Saranac to the Marquesas: being letters written to her sister Jane, 1887–8* unless otherwise cited.]

p. 166, l. 33 – 'In fact . . . it would be': RLS and FS, *Our Samoan Adventure*.

p. 171, l. 23 – 'But this money . . .': RLS and FS, *Our Samoan Adventure*.

V

p. 174, l. 7 – 'rain or shine': RLS to Colvin, *Letters*, vol. 6.

l. 29 – 'My vanity . . .': RLS and FS, *Our Samoan Adventure*.

p. 178, l. 3 – 'Fanny has not been . . .': MS, *Letters from Samoa 1891–95*, August 1891.

l. 20 – 'robbing . . .': RLS and FS, *Our Samoan Adventure*.

p. 179, l. 1 – 'something wrong . . .': (and all following quotes): *Letters*, vol. 8, April 1893.

p. 180, l. 23 – 'pale, penetratin' . . .': RLS to Henry James, *Letters*, vol. 8, June 1893.

p. 181, l. 3 – 'I am honest . . .': Mackay, *The Violent Friend*.

l. 19 – 'in despair . . . ': RLS to MS, *Letters*, vol. 8, August 1893.

l. 30 – 'You should have seen . . .': RLS to MS, *Letters*, vol. 8, February 1894.

p. 182, l. 12 – 'salad . . . tin': RLS to Colvin, *Letters*, vol. 8, August 1893.

p. 184, l. 13 – 'I sometimes feel . . .': RLS to Bob, *Letters*, vol. 8, June 1894.

l. 33 – 'I intend . . .': RLS and FS, *Our Samoan Adventure*.

p. 185, l. 21 – 'What sort of . . .': RLS and FS, *Our Samoan Adventure*.

p. 187, l. 21 – 'Go with each . . .': Mackay, *The Violent Friend*.

l. 33 – 'What's that?': Mackay, *The Violent Friend*.

Jennie Lee

Jennie Lee's papers are collected together in the library of the Open University where they were deposited by Patricia Hollis after she had completed the official biography, *Jennie Lee: A Life* (1997). I have used these papers extensively and relied on the biography greatly since it contains masses of information gleaned from people close to Jennie who are now dead. There are also two volumes of autobiography: *Tomorrow is a New Day* (1939) and *My Life With Nye* (1980).

I

p. 211, l. 20 – 'marriage . . .': Norman and Jeanne MacKenzie (eds), *The Diary of Beatrice Webb*.

p. 213, l. 1 – 'a being . . . unacquisitive': Benn Levy, quoted in Jennie Lee (JL), *My Life With Nye*.

p. 214, l. 6 – 'She had . . . stern': JL, *Tomorrow is a New Day*.

l. 34 – 'I was not . . . stubborn': JL, *Tomorrow is a New Day*.

p. 216, l. 10 – 'mother was . . . could': JL, *Tomorrow is a New Day*.

l. 25 – 'why try . . . size 4 shoes': 'J.L. Diaries 1936–8', Open University (OU) Papers.

l. 29 – 'How is it . . . differently': exercise book, OU Papers.

p. 217, l. 25 – 'bad . . . temptation': JL to Suse Saemann (SS), 4 August 1926, OU Papers.

l. 34 – 'I intended . . .' – JL to SS (no date [n.d.] – Hollis estimates May 1926).

p. 218, l. 7 – 'exceedingly handsome . . .': JL to SS (n.d.), OU Papers.

l. 25 – 'Thank goodness . . . occurred': JL to SS, 21 July 1926, OU Papers.

l. 29 – 'I have been told . . .': JL to SS (n.d.), OU Papers.

l. 35 – 'a deep crimson . . . satin': JL to SS, 18 January 1926, OU Papers.

p. 220, l. 9 – 'until I . . . Westminster': JL to SS, 29 December 1926, OU Papers.

l. 21 – 'infinitely . . .' (and following quotes): JL to SS, 17 June 1927, OU Papers.

p. 223, l. 7 – 'very clear-headed . . .': Frank Wise (FW) to Chas Trevelyan, 13 November 1931, OU Papers.

l. 32 – 'Darling . . . flirt with': JL to FW, 10 February 1931, OU Papers.

p. 224, l. 22 – 'a kind of . . . rang' (and following quotes): JL to FW, 8 December 1931, OU Papers.

p. 226, l. 15 – Dorothy Wise, letter to JL, 12 November 1933, OU Papers.

II

p. 231, l. 28 – 'dressed . . . mood': JL, *My Life With Nye*.

p. 241, l. 12 – 'dragged . . . powers': JL, *My Life With Nye*.

l. 19 – 'He was . . . no me': JL, Notes for her biography, 3 February 1967, OU Papers.

III

p. 243, l. 9 – 'his old chauvinist . . .': JL, *My Life With Nye*.

l. 20 – 'shielded . . .': JL, Notes for her biography, 3 February 1967, OU Papers.

p. 246, l. 24 – 'with her black . . .': Hollis, *Jennie Lee*, p. 115.

p. 247, l. 2 – 'dragging round . . .': JL, Notes for her biography, OU Papers.

l. 38 – 'So much . . . nature': JL, Notes for her biography, OU Papers.

p. 249, l. 34 – 'I look like . . .': Thomas Lee (TL) to Rose Lee, Box 10 (n.d.), OU Papers.

p. 250, l. 11 – 'at least . . . behaviour': JL to TL, Box 10 (n.d.), OU Papers.

p. 253, l. 1 – 'the most . . .': JL, Notes for her biography, OU Papers.

l. 8 – 'the days . . .': JL, *My Life With Nye*.

p. 256, l. 2 – 'You yellow-livered ...': quoted by John Campbell, *Nye Bevan*.

IV

p. 258, l. 21 – 'it is ... strain': JL, Diary Notes, 1945–50 (n.d.), OU Papers.
p. 259, l. 12 – 'a few ... storms': JL, *My Life With Nye*.
p. 261, l. 27 – 'an appallingly ...': JL, *My Life With Nye*.
p. 265, l. 16 – 'is it your real ...': JL, unsent letter, dated 3 June 1957 [partly quoted in JL, *My Life With Nye* and fully quoted in Hollis, *Jennie Lee*].
p. 266, l. 37 – 'He did not have ...' JL, *My Life With Nye*.

V

p. 273, l. 16 – 'profoundly ... place': JL to FW, 3 October 1932, OUP.
p. 280, l. 35 – 'In all the great ...': Hollis, *Jennie Lee*, p. 233.
p. 281, l. 19 – 'Don't know ...': Hollis, *Jennie Lee*, p. 235.
l. 33 – 'I wander ...': Hollis, *Jennie Lee*, p. 235.
p. 282, l. 35 – 'Jennie is ... publicity': Harold Wilson, quoted in Hollis, *Jennie Lee*, p. 255.

BIBLIOGRAPHY

Mary Livingstone

Manuscript Material

1. School of Oriental and African Studies [London Missionary Society Collection, Special Series: Africa Odds and Personals, Boxes 2, 3, 5, 11 and Wooden Box].
2. Methodist Archives, Rhodes University, Grahamstown, South Africa.
3. National Library of Scotland – MS 656/10780/10777/10775.
4. National Archives of Zimbabwe – Folios L1: 33–40/41–4.
5. Royal Geographical Society – Livingstone Letters.

Printed Sources

Blaikie, W. G., *The Personal Life of David Livingstone* (1880).
Chadwick, O., *Mackenzie's Grave* (1959).
Chamberlin, D. (ed.), *Some Letters from Livingstone 1840–72* (1940).
Devereux, W. C., *A Cruise in the Gorgon* (1869).
Dickson, M., *Beloved Partner: Mary Moffat of Kuruman* (1974).
Foskett, R. (ed.), *The Zambesi Journal and Letters of Dr John Kirk 1858–63*, 2 vols (1965).
Healey, E., *Wives of Fame* (1986).
Jeal, T., *Livingstone* (1973).
Moffat, J. S., *The Lives of Robert and Mary Moffat* (1885).
Northcott, C., *Robert Moffat: Pioneer in Africa* (1961).
Oswell, W. E., *William Cotton Oswell*, 2 vols (1900).
Parsons, J. W., *The Livingstones at Kolobeng 1847–1852* (1997).
Schapera, I. (ed.), *Apprenticeship at Kuruman: being the journal and letters of Robert and Mary Moffat 1821–8* (1951); *David Livingstone: Family Letters 1841–56*, 2 vols (1959); *Livingstone's Private Journals 1851–3* (1960); *Livingstone's African Journal 1853–6*, 2 vols (1963).
Seaver, G., *David Livingstone: His Life and Letters* (1957).
Wallis, J. P. R. (ed.), *The Matabele Mission: A Selection from the Correspondence of John and Emily Moffat, David Livingstone and others 1858–1878* (1945); *The Zambesi Journal of James Stewart 1862–1863* (1952); *The Zambesi Expedition of David Livingstone, 1858–1863* (1956).

Source Notes and Bibliography

Fanny Stevenson

Printed Sources

Boodle, A., *Robert Louis Stevenson and his Sine Qua Non* (1926).

Booth, Bradford A. and Mehew, Ernest (eds), *The Letters of Robert Louis Stevenson*, 8 vols (1994).

Field, I., *This Life I Have Loved* (1937).

Furnas, J. C., *Voyage to Windward* (1952).

Lapierre, A., *Fanny Stevenson: A Romance of Destiny* (1995).

Lockett, W. G., *Robert Louis Stevenson at Davos* (1940).

Mackay, M., *The Violent Friend: The Story of Mrs Robert Louis Stevenson* (1968).

McLynn, F., *Robert Louis Stevenson* (1993).

Sanchez, N. Van de Grift, *Life of Mrs R. L. Stevenson* (1920).

Stevenson, F., *The Cruise of the 'Janet Nichol' Among the South Sea Islands – A Diary* (1915).

Stevenson, Margaret, *From Saranac to the Marquesas: being letters written to her sister Jane 1887–8*; *Letters from Samoa 1891–95*.

Stevenson, R. L. and Stevenson, F., *Our Samoan Adventure* (1956).

Jennie Lee

Manuscript Material

1. Jennie Lee Papers (60 boxes) – Open University Library.

Printed Sources

Campbell, J., *Nye Bevan* (1997).

Castle, B., *Fighting All the Way* (1993).

Foot, M., *Aneurin Bevan*, 2 vols (1975).

Hollis, P., *Jennie Lee: A Life* (1997).

Lee, J., *Tomorrow is a New Day* (1939); *My Life With Nye* (1980).

MacKenzie, Norman and Jeanne (eds), *The Diary of Beatrice Webb*, 4 vols (1982–5).

Vallance, E., *Women in the House* (1979).

Index

'AB' indicates Aneurin Bevan, 'DL' David Livingstone, 'JL' Jennie Lee, 'ML' Mary Livingstone, 'FS' Fanny Stevenson, 'RLS' Robert Louis Stevenson.

Index